I0015341

Visual Studio 2010 Best Practices

Learn and implement recommended practices for the complete software development life cycle with Visual Studio 2010

Peter Ritchie

[PACKT] PUBLISHING enterprise professional expertise distilled

BIRMINGHAM - MUMBAI

Visual Studio 2010 Best Practices

First published: August 2012

Production Reference: 1170812

Published by Packt Publishing Ltd.
Livery Place
35 Livery Street
Birmingham B3 2PB, UK.

ISBN 978-1-84968-716-4

www.packtpub.com

Cover Image by Sandeep Babu (sandyjb@gmail.com)

Credits

Author
Peter Ritchie

Reviewers
Ognjen Bajic
Carlos Hulot
Ahmed Ilyas
Ken Tucker

Acquisition Editor
Rashmi Phadnis

Lead Technical Editor
Dayan Hyames

Technical Editors
Manmeet Singh Vasir
Merin Jose
Manasi Poonthottam

Project Coordinator
Joel Goveya

Proofreader
Joel T. Johnson

Indexer
Rekha Nair

Graphics
Valentina D,silva
Manu Joseph

Production Coordinators
Aparna Bhagat
Nitesh Thakur

Cover Work
Aparna Bhagat
Nitesh Thakur

About the Author

Peter Ritchie is a software development consultant. He is the president of Peter Ritchie Inc. Software Consulting Co., a software consulting company in Canada,s National Capital Region, which specializes in Windows-based software development management, process, and implementation consulting.

Peter has worked with clients such as Mitel, Nortel, Passport Canada, and Innvapost, from mentoring, to architecture, to implementation. He has considerable experience in building software development teams and working with startups towards agile software development. Peter,s experience ranges from designing and implementing simple stand-alone applications, to architecting n-tier applications spanning dozens of computers, and from C++ to C#.

Peter is active in the software development community, attending and speaking at various events, as well as authoring various works including *Refactoring with Microsoft Visual Studio 2010, Packt Publishing*.

There are countless number of people that have contributed to my knowledge and motivation to contribute to the community with projects like this book. In particular, I would like to thank Joe Miller for his sharp eyes and having clearly better editing abilities than mine.

I would also like to thank my wife Sherry for the continued love and support despite all the extra time I had to put into projects like book writing.

I would also like to thank my parents, Helen and Bruce; I still miss you.

About the Reviewers

Carlos Hulot has been working in the IT area for more than 20 years in different capabilities, from software development, project management, to IT marketing, product development, and management. He has worked for multinational companies such as Royal Philips Electronics, Pricewaterhouse Coopers, and Microsoft.

Carlos currently works as an independent IT consultant. He is also a Computer Science lecturer at two Brazilian universities. Carlos holds a Ph.D. in Computer Science and Electronics from the University of Southampton, UK and a B.Sc. in Physics from University of São Paulo, Brazil.

Ahmed Ilyas has a BEng degree from Napier University in Edinburgh, Scotland, having majored in Software development. He has 15 years of professional experience in software development.

After leaving Microsoft, Ahmed ventured into setting up his consultancy company Sandler Ltd. (UK), offering the best possible solutions for a magnitude of industries, and providing real-world answers to those problems. The company uses the Microsoft stack to build these technologies. Being able to bring in the best practices, patterns, and software to its client base for enabling long term stability and compliance in the ever changing software industry, pushing the limits in technology, as well as improving software developers around the globe.

Ahmed has been awarded the MVP in C# by Microsoft three times, for providing excellence and independent real-world solutions to problems that developers face.

Ahmed,s breadth and depth of knowledge has been obtained from his research and from the valuable wealth of information and research at Microsoft. By knowing the fact that 90 percent of the world uses at least one form of Microsoft technology, motivates and inspires him.

Ahmed has worked for a number of clients and employers. With the great reputation that he has, it has resulted in having a large client base for his consultancy company, which includes clients from different industries. From media to medical and beyond. Some clients have included him on their "approved contractors/consultants" list. The list includes ICS Solution Ltd. (placed on their DreamTeam portal) and also EPS Software Corp. (based in the USA).

I would like to thank the author and the publisher for giving me the opportunity to review this book. I would also like to thank my client base and especially my colleagues at Microsoft for enabling me to become a reputable leader as a software developer in the industry, which is my passion.

Ken Tucker is a Microsoft MVP (2003–present) in Visual Basic and currently works at Amovius LLC in Melbourne, Florida (FL). He is also the President of the Space Coast .Net User Group and a frequent speaker at Florida Code Camps. Ken be reached at `Ken@VB-Tips.com`.

I'd like to thank my wife Alice-Marie.

---

www.PacktPub.com

Support files, eBooks, discount offers and more

You might want to visit `www.PacktPub.com` for support files and downloads related to your book.

Did you know that Packt offers eBook versions of every book published, with PDF and ePub files available? You can upgrade to the eBook version at `www.PacktPub.com` and as a print book customer, you are entitled to a discount on the eBook copy. Get in touch with us at `service@packtpub.com` for more details.

At `www.PacktPub.com`, you can also read a collection of free technical articles, sign up for a range of free newsletters and receive exclusive discounts and offers on Packt books and eBooks.

PACKTLIB®

`http://PacktLib.PacktPub.com`

Do you need instant solutions to your IT questions? PacktLib is Packt,s online digital book library. Here, you can access, read and search across Packt,s entire library of books.

Why Subscribe?

- Fully searchable across every book published by Packt
- Copy and paste, print and bookmark content
- On demand and accessible via web browser

Free Access for Packt account holders

If you have an account with Packt at `www.PacktPub.com`, you can use this to access PacktLib today and view nine entirely free books. Simply use your login credentials for immediate access.

Instant Updates on New Packt Books

Get notified! Find out when new books are published by following `@PacktEnterprise` on Twitter, or the *Packt Enterprise* Facebook page.

Table of Contents

Preface

When you are developing on the Microsoft platform, Visual Studio 2010 offers you a range of powerful tools and makes the entire process easier and faster. After learning it, if you think that you can sit back and relax, you cannot be further away from truth. To beat the crowd, you need to be better than others, learn tips and tricks that other don't know yet. This book is a compilation of the best practices of programming with Visual Studio.

Visual Studio 2010 Best Practices will take you through the practices you need to master programming with the .NET Framework. The book goes on to detail several practices involving many aspects of software development with Visual Studio. These practices include debugging, exception handling, and design. It details building and maintaining a recommended practices library and the criteria by which to document recommended practices.

The book begins with practices on source code control (SCC). It includes different types of SCC and discusses how to choose them based on different scenarios. Advanced syntax in C# is then covered with practices covering generics, iterator methods, lambdas, and closures.

The next set of practices focus on deployment, as well as creating MSI deployments with Windows Installer XML (WiX), including Windows applications and services. The book then takes you through practices for developing with WCF and Web Service.

The software development lifecycle is completed with practices on testing, such as project structure, naming, and the different types of automated tests. Topics such as test coverage, continuous testing and deployment, and mocking are included. Although this book uses Visual Studio as an example, you can use these practices with any IDE.

What this book covers

Chapter 1, Working with Best Practices, discusses several motivating factors about why we might want to use "recommended practices" and why we're sometimes forced to resort to "recommended practices" rather than *figure it out.*

Chapter 2, Source Code Control Practices, looks at source code control terminology, architectures, and usage practices.

Chapter 3, Low-level C# Practices, looks at some low-level, language-specific practices. Topics like generics, lambdas, iterator members, extension methods, and exception handling will be detailed.

Chapter 4, Architectural Practices, looks at some architecture-specific practices. These practices will include things such as decoupling, data-centric applications, and a brief look at some recommendations for distributed architectures.

Chapter 5, Recommended Practices for Deployment, discusses installation technologies and covers some of the more common features required by the majority application installations. The chapter focuses mainly on deployment of applications through Windows Installer

Chapter 6, Automated Testing Practices, covers automated testing practices. Practices regarding test naming and structure, coverage, mocking, and types of tests will be covered.

Chapter 7, Optimizing Visual Studio, discusses ways of making Visual Studio operate more efficiently, work to our advantage, and ways to make working with Visual Studio friendlier.

Chapter 8, Parallelization Practices, discusses techniques such as threading, distributed architecture, and thread synchronization. Technologies such as Task Parallel Library, Asynchronous CTP, and asynchronous additions to C# 5.0 and Visual Basic 10 are also covered.

Chapter 9, Distributed Applications, discusses ways of architecting distributed applications, as well as specific technologies that help communication of nodes within a distributed application. In addition, it covers ways of debugging, monitoring, and maintaining distributed applications.

Chapter 10, Web Service Recommended Practices, discusses web services. It covers practices with WCF services, ASMX services, implementing services, consuming services, and authentication and authorization.

What you need for this book

- Visual Studio 2010 Express (Professional recommended) or better
- Windows XP SP3 or better
- Optional: NUnit or XUnit

Who this book is for

.NET developers using Visual Studio for programming will find this book useful. If you are developing your application with C#, you will find better ways to do things with Visual Studio.

You should know basics of development with the .NET Framework and will need working knowledge on Visual Studio.

Conventions

In this book, you will find a number of styles of text that distinguish between different kinds of information. Here are some examples of these styles, and an explanation of their meaning.

Code words in text are shown as follows: "The `Iterator` method returns `IEnumerable` that results in three `DateTime` values."

A block of code is set as follows:

```
public static IEnumerable<DateTime> Iterator()
{
  Thread.Sleep(1000);
  yield return DateTime.Now;
  Thread.Sleep(1000);
  yield return DateTime.Now;
  Thread.Sleep(1000);
  yield return DateTime.Now;
}
```

When we wish to draw your attention to a particular part of a code block, the relevant lines or items are set in bold:

```
namespace ConsoleApplication
{
  using Numerical;
  internal class Program
  {
```

```
    private static void Main(string[] args)
    {
      var values = new int[] {1, 2, 3};
      foreach (var v in values.Cubes())
      {
        Console.WriteLine(v);
      }
    }
  }
}
```

New terms and **important words** are shown in bold. Words that you see on the screen, in menus or dialog boxes for example, appear in the text like this: "right-click on a project in **Solution Explorer** and select **Unload Project**."

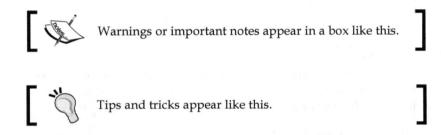

> Warnings or important notes appear in a box like this.

> Tips and tricks appear like this.

Reader feedback

Feedback from our readers is always welcome. Let us know what you think about this book—what you liked or may have disliked. Reader feedback is important for us to develop titles that you really get the most out of.

To send us general feedback, simply send an e-mail to `feedback@packtpub.com`, and mention the book title through the subject of your message.

If there is a topic that you have expertise in and you are interested in either writing or contributing to a book, see our author guide on `www.packtpub.com/authors`.

Customer support

Now that you are the proud owner of a Packt book, we have a number of things to help you to get the most from your purchase.

Downloading the example code

You can download the example code files for all Packt books you have purchased from your account at `http://www.packtpub.com`. If you purchased this book elsewhere, you can visit `http://www.packtpub.com/support` and register to have the files e-mailed directly to you.

Errata

Although we have taken every care to ensure the accuracy of our content, mistakes do happen. If you find a mistake in one of our books—maybe a mistake in the text or the code—we would be grateful if you would report this to us. By doing so, you can save other readers from frustration and help us improve subsequent versions of this book. If you find any errata, please report them by visiting `http://www.packtpub.com/support`, selecting your book, clicking on the **errata submission form** link, and entering the details of your errata. Once your errata are verified, your submission will be accepted and the errata will be uploaded to our website, or added to any list of existing errata, under the Errata section of that title.

Piracy

Piracy of copyright material on the Internet is an ongoing problem across all media. At Packt, we take the protection of our copyright and licenses very seriously. If you come across any illegal copies of our works, in any form, on the Internet, please provide us with the location address or website name immediately so that we can pursue a remedy.

Please contact us at `copyright@packtpub.com` with a link to the suspected pirated material.

We appreciate your help in protecting our authors, and our ability to bring you valuable content.

Questions

You can contact us at `questions@packtpub.com` if you are having a problem with any aspect of the book, and we will do our best to address it.

1
Working with Best Practices

In any given software developer's career, there are many different things they need to create. Of the software they need to create, given time constraints and resources, it's almost impossible for them to perform the research involved to produce everything correctly from scratch.

There are all sorts of barriers and roadblocks to researching how to correctly write this bit of code or that bit of code, use that technology, or this interface. Documentation may be lacking or missing, or documentation may be completely wrong. Documentation is the same as software, sometimes it has bugs. Sometimes the act of writing software is unit testing documentation. This, of course, provides no value to most software development projects. It's great when the documentation is correct, but when it's not, it can be devastating to a software project.

Even with correct documentation, sometimes we don't have the time to read all of the documentation and become total experts in some technology or API. We just need a subset of the API to do what we need done and that's all.

Recommended practices

I call them "recommended practices" instead of "best practices." The superlative "best" implies some degree of completeness. In almost all circumstances, the *completeness* of these practices has a shelf-life. Some best practices have a *very small* shelf-life due to the degree to which technology and our knowledge of it changes.

Recommended practices detail working with several different technologies with a finite set of knowledge. Knowledge of each technology will increase in the future, and each technology will evolve in the future. Thus, what may be a *best* practice today may be out of date, obsolete, and possibly even deprecated sometime in the future.

One of the problems I've encountered with "best practices" is the inferred gospel people assume from *best*. They see "best" and assume that means "best always and forever." In software, that's rarely the case. To a certain extent, the Internet hasn't helped matters either. Blogs, articles, answers to questions, and so on, are usually on the Internet forever. If someone blogs about a "best practice" in 2002 it may very well have been the recommended approach when it was posted, but may be the opposite now. Just because a practice *works* doesn't make it a best practice.

Sometimes the mere source of a process, procedure, or coding recipe has the reader inferring "best practice." This is probably one of the most disturbing trends in certain software communities. While a source can be deemed reliable, not everything that a source presents was ever intended to be a "best practice", documentation at best. Be wary of accepting code from reputable sources as "best practices." In fact, read on to get some ideas on how to either make that code one of your recommended practices, or refute it as not being a best practice at all.

Further, some industries or organizations define business practices. They're defined as the one and only practice and sometimes referred to as "best" because there is nothing to compare. I would question the use of "best" in such a way because it implies comparison with at least one other practice, and that other practice was deemed insufficient in some way. To that end, in software practices, just because there is only one known way to do something, that doesn't mean it should be coined a "best practice."

There have been many other people who have questioned "best" in "best practice." Take Scott Ambler for example. Scott is a leader in the agile software development community. He is espousing "contextual practices" as any given "best practice" is limited at least to one *context*. As we'll see shortly a "best practice" may be good in one context but bad in another context.

"Best" is a judgment. While the reader of the word "best" judges a practice as *best* through acceptance, in the general case, most "best practices" haven't really been judged. For a practice to be *best* the practice needs to be vetted, and the requisite work involved in proving *how* and *why* the practice is *best* is never done. It's this very caveat that make people like Eugene Bardach question "best practices" as a general concept. In his article *The Problem with "Best Practice"*, Bardach suggests terms like "good" or "smart." But that's really the same problem. Who vets "good" or "smart?" At best they could be described as "known practices."

Without vetting, it's often taken at face value by the reader based either solely on the fact that "best" was used, or based on the source of the practice. This is why people like Ambler and Bardach are beginning to openly question the safety of calling something a "best practice."

Most practices are simply a series of steps to perform a certain action. Most of the time, context is either implied or the practice is completely devoid of context. It leaves the reader with the sense that the context is *anywhere*, which is dangerous.

Intransitive "best" practices

Intransitive relationships in math can be denoted by *A = B, B = C Δ C may or may not equal A*. Moving from one framework to another, or one language to another, may mean some "best practices" are not transitive (that is, they can't be moved from one context to another and be expected to be true).

In the early days of C#, for example, it was assumed that the gospel of the double-checked locking pattern was transitive from C++ to C# (at least by a few people). The double-checked locking pattern is a pattern by which, in order to avoid slow locking operations, a variable is checked for null prior to locking as an optimization. This variable checking is done in order to implement lazy-initialization (for example, in a singleton). For example (as stolen from Jon Skeet, comments mine):

```
public sealed class Singleton
{
  static Singleton instance = null;
  static readonly object padlock = new object();
  Singleton()
  {
  }
  public static Singleton Instance
  {
    get
    {
      if (instance == null) // first check
      {
        lock (padlock)
        {
          if (instance == null) // double-checked
          {
            instance = new Singleton();
          }
        }
      }
      return instance;
    }
  }
}
```

Downloading the example code

You can download the example code files for all Packt books you have purchased from your account at `http://www.packtpub.com`. If you purchased this book elsewhere, you can visit `http://www.packtpub.com/support` and register to have the files e-mailed directly to you.

As you can see from the code, it's apparent where the name "double-checked" came from. The assumption with this code is that a `lock` is only needed if the one and only initialization of `instance` needs to be performed. It's assumed that once it's initialized (and thus, no longer null) there's no need to lock because it never changes again. All fairly logical assumptions, unless we take into account the memory model of .NET (1.x, at the time). Neither the compiler nor the processor were required to perform the previous instructions in the order they were written, and the processor wasn't guaranteed not to be using a cached value (more on the Itanium than the x86, but who knows what processor will be used when we run our code). I won't get into the nitty-gritty details, but suffice it to say, an established "best" practice in C++ was a "worst" practice in C#.

Incidentally, the double-checked locking pattern was never really a good idea in C++. It was proved flawed in 2004 by Scott Meyers and Andrei Alexandrescu for very similar reasons compared to C#. This goes to show how some practices are not only intransitive, but become "worst" practices with further research or knowledge.

In .NET 2.0 (as well as later versions of Java) the memory model was changed to actually make double-checked locking work (at least in a non-debug build in .NET). You could actually write it in such a way as to get it to work in both .NET 1.x and .NET 2.0+, but, by that point the damage was done and double-checked locking had become evil. It certainly wasn't the quickest code anyway, but I digress. If you are interested in more of the details, I'd recommend Jon Skeet's *C# In Depth*, where he details use of the static initialization feature of C# to implement singletons and avoid the need for double-check locking altogether.

Benefits of using practices

There is no point to using practices if they don't add any value. It's important to understand at least some of the benefits that can be obtained from using practices. Let's have a look at some of the common practices.

Avoiding pragmatic re-use

We can sometimes find good documentation. It describes the API or technology correctly and includes sample code. Sample code helps us understand the API as well as the concepts. I don't know about you, but I think in code; sample code is often easier for me to understand than prose, but , sample code is a double-edged sword.

One *drawback* of sample code is it may have the side-effects you're looking for, so you take it at face value and re-use it in your code. This is a form of **pragmatic re-use**.

Pragmatic re-use is when a developer re-uses code in a way which the original code was not intended to be re-used. This is quite common, and one of the most common forms of pragmatic re-use is copying and pasting code, such as copying and pasting the sample code as shown earlier.

In C#, classes are open for derivation unless they are modified with the `sealed` keyword to prevent inheritance. The lack of modification with `sealed` doesn't necessarily imply that the class is intended to be derived from. Deriving from a class like this is another form of pragmatic re-use because it's being re-used where re-use was not expected.

There are many motivators for pragmatic re-use. When a developer has neither the time nor the resources to learn code to perform a certain task, they often resort to a form of pragmatic re-use such as copy and paste.

Reducing technical debt

Technical debt is a fairly well understood concept, but, it bears repeating as one of the potential motivators of best practices. **Technical debt** refers to the negative consequences of code, design, or architecture. There are all sorts of negative consequences that can occur from code. One common consequence is from code with no test coverage. The negative consequence of this is the lack of stability introduced from any change to that code.

Pragmatic re-use has the side-effect of taking on technical debt. At the very least, the code is doing something in a way it was never intended. This means it was not designed to do that, and therefore could never have been tested to work correctly in that scenario. The most common impetus for pragmatic re-use is that the developer either didn't understand how to do it himself, or didn't understand the original code. This means there is code in the code base that potentially no one understands. This means they don't understand why it works, how to test it correctly, what to do if something goes wrong with the code, or how to correctly change in response to changing requirements.

To be clear, technical debt isn't always bad. A team can take on technical debt for a variety of reasons. The important part is that they know the consequences and are willing to live with those consequences, maybe for a short period of time, to get some sort of benefit. This benefit could be time-to-market, proof-of-concept (maybe directly related to funding) meeting a deadline, budget, and so on.

There are all sorts of great sources of information on managing technical debt, so we won't get into technical debt beyond its impetus behind using best practices. If you're not clear on technical debt, I recommend as an exercise for the reader to learn more about it. Perhaps Martin Fowler's bliki (`http://martinfowler.com/bliki/TechnicalDebt.html`) or Steve McConnell's blog (`http://blogs.construx.com/blogs/stevemcc/archive/2007/11/01/technical-debt-2.aspx`) would be a good start.

Not invented here syndrome

Not invented here (NIH) syndrome has become much more understood over the past decade or so. There was a time when there were a handful of developers in the world developing software. Most knew development teams needed to figure out how to write basic data structures such as linked lists, and basic sorting algorithms such as quick sort, or how to perform spell checking. This knowledge wasn't generally available and componentization of software had yet to occur. The *value* of their project was overshadowed by the sheer complexity of the infrastructure around producing effective software.

Shoot ahead in time slightly into an era of componentized software. Components, libraries, APIs, and frameworks began to appear, that took the *infrastructure-like* aspects of a software project, and made sharable components that anyone within reason could simply drop into their project and start using. Presumably, the time required to understand and learn the API would be less than having to write that component from scratch.

To a select few people this isn't the case. Their ability to write software is at such a high level that for them to understand and accept an API was a larger friction (they thought) than it was to write their own. Thus, the NIH syndrome began. Because a certain technology, library, API, or framework wasn't invented by a member of the developer team, and therefore under their entire control, it needed to be written from scratch.

In the early days, this wasn't so bad. Writing a linked list implementation was indeed quicker than trying to download, install, and understand someone else's linked list implementation (for most people). These libraries grew to millions of lines of code, and hundreds of person-hours worth of work, but NIH continued. Language frameworks and runtimes became more popular. C++'s STL, Java, .NET, and so on, included standard algorithms (framework) and abstractions to interface with underlying operating systems (runtimes), so it has become harder to ignore these libraries and write everything from scratch. But the sheer magnitude of the detail and complexity of these libraries was difficult to grasp given the detail of the documentation. In order to better utilize these libraries and frameworks, information on how to use them began to be shared. Things like best practices made it easier for teams to accept third-party libraries and frameworks. Lessons learned were being communicated within the community as best practices. "I spent 3 days reading documentation and tweaking code to perform operation Y, here's how I did it" became common.

Practices are a form of componentization. We don't actually get the component, but we get instructions on where, why, and how to make our own component. It can help us keep our software structured and componentized.

Beyond practices

Some methodologies from other disciplines have recently begun to be re-used in the software industry. Some of that has come from lean manufacturing, such as kaizen, and some from the martial arts, such as katas. Let's have a brief look at using these two methodologies.

Using katas

In the martial arts, students perform what are known as **katas**. These are essentially choreographed movements that the student is to master. Students master these katas through repetition or practice. Depending on the type of martial art, students move through *dan* grades through judgment of how well they can perform certain katas.

The principle behind kata is the muscle memory. As students become proficient in each kata the movements become second nature to them, and they can be performed without thought. The idea is that in battle the muscle memory gained from the katas would become reflexive and they would be more successful.

In the software development communities, kata-like sessions have become common. Developers take on specific tasks to be done in software. One way is to learn how to do that task, another is to repeat it as a way of remembering how to implement that specific algorithm or technique. The theory is that once you've done it at least once you've got "muscle memory" for that particular task. Worst-case is that you now have experience in that particular task.

"Kata" suffers slightly from the same syndrome as "best practice", in that "kata" isn't necessarily the most appropriate term for what is described previously. Getting better at a practice through repeated implementation results in working code. Kata is repeating movement not necessarily so the movement will be repeated in combat/competition, but so that your mind and body have experience with many moves that it will better react when needed. Software katas could be better viewed as *kumites* ("sparring" with code resulting in specific outcomes) or *kihons* (performing atomic movements like punches or kicks). But this is what coding katas have come to signify based on a rudimentary understanding of "kata" and the coding exercises being applied.

At one level, you can view practices as katas. You can implement them as is, repeating them to improve proficiency and experience, the more you practice. At another level, you could consider these practices as a part, or start, of your library of practices.

Reaching kaizen

In the past few years, there has been much in the way of process improvement in the software industry that has been taken from Japanese business and social practices. Much like kata, kaizen is another adopted word in some circles of software development. Originally borrowed from the lean manufacturing principles, lean manufacturing was originally attributed to Toyota. **Kaizen**, in Japanese means "improvement."

This book does not attempt to document a series of recipes, but rather a series of starting points for improvement. Each practice is simply one way of eliminating waste. At the most shallow-level, each practice illuminates the waste of trying to find a way to produce the same results as the detailed practice. In the spirit of kaizen, think of each practice as a starting point. A starting point not only to improve yourself and your knowledge, but to improve the practice as well.

Once you're comfortable with practices and have a few under your belt, you should be able to start recognizing practices in some of the libraries or frameworks you're using or developing. If you're on a development team that has its own framework or library, consider sharing what you've learned about the library in a series of recommended practices.

How would you start with something like this? Well, recommended practices are based on people's experience, so start with your experiences with a given framework or library. If you've got some experience with a given library, you've probably noticed certain things you've had to do repeatedly. As you've repeated doing certain tasks, you've probably built up certain ways of doing it that are more correct than others. It has evolved over time to get better. Start with documenting what you've learned, and how that has resulted in something that you'd be willing to recommend to someone else as a way of accomplishing a certain task.

It's one thing to accept practices to allow you to focus on the value-added of the project you're working on. It's another to build on that knowledge and build libraries of practices, improving, organizing, and potentially sharing practices.

Aspects of a practice

At one level, a practice can simply be a recipe. This is often acceptable, "Just Do It" this way. Sometimes it might not be obvious why a practice is implemented in a certain way. Including motivators or the impetus behind why the practice is the way it is can be helpful not only to people learning the practice, but also to people already skilled in that area of technology. People with skills can then open a dialog to provide feedback and begin collaborating on evolving practices.

Okay, but really, what is a "best practice?" Wikipedia defines it as:

> *"...a method or technique that has consistently shown results superior to those achieved with other means...".*

The only flaw in this definition is when there's only one way to achieve certain results, it can't still be "best" without being compared to some other means. "...method or technique" leaves it pretty open to interpretation on whether something could be construed as a best practice. If we take these basic truths, and expand on them, we can derive a way to communicate recommended practices.

The technique or method is pretty straightforward (although ambiguous to a certain degree). That really just distills down to a procedure or a list of steps. This is great if we want to perform or implement the practice, but, what do we need to communicate the procedure, intent, impetus, and context?

Evaluating practices

I could have easily jumped into *using* practices first, but, one of the points I'm trying to get across here is the contextual nature of practices whether they're referred to as "best practices" or not. I think it's important to put some sort of thought into the use of a practice before using it. So, let's look at evaluation first.

Once we define a practice we need a way for others to evaluate it. In order to evaluate practices, an ability to browse or discover them is needed.

In order for someone else to evaluate one of our practices, we need to provide the expected context. This will allow them to compare their context with the expected context to decide if the practice is even applicable.

In order for us to evaluate the applicability of another process, we need to know our context. This is an important point that almost everyone misses when accepting "best practices." The "best" implies there's no need for evaluation, it's "best", right? Once you can define what your context means you can better evaluate whether the practice is right for you, whether it can still be used but with a little evolution, or simply isn't right for you.

Documenting practices

Documenting a practice is an attempt at communicating that practice. To a certain degree, written or diagrammatic documentation suffers from an *impedance mismatch.* We simply don't have the same flexibility in those types of communication that we do in face-to-face or spoken communication. The practice isn't just about the steps involved or the required result, it's about the context in which it should be used.

I have yet to find a "standard" way to documenting practices. We can pull some of what we've learned from patterns and devise a more acceptable way of communicating practices. We must first start out with the context in which the practice is intended to be used, or the context in which the required outcome applies.

Scott Ambler provides some criteria for providing context about teams that can help a team evaluate or define their context. These factors are part of what Ambler calls **Agile Scaling Model** (**ASM**). The model is clearly agile-slanted, but many of the factors apply to any team. These factors are discussed next.

Geographic distribution

This involves the distribution of the team. Is the team co-located or are they distributed over some geographic location? This distribution could be as small as cubes separated by other teams, team members separated by floors, team members in different buildings, cities, or countries and time zones. A practice that assumes the context is a co-located team might be more difficult to implement with a globally-distributed team. Scrum stand-ups is an example. **Scrum stand-ups** are very short meetings, held usually once a day, where everyone on the team participates to communicate what they have worked on, what they are working on, and any roadblocks. Clearly, it would be hard to do a "stand up" with a team geographically distributed across ten time zones.

Team size

Team size is fairly obvious and can be related to geographic distribution (smaller teams are less likely to be very geographically distributed). Although different from geographic distribution, similar contextual issues arise.

Regulatory compliance

Many companies are burdened with complying with regulatory mandates. Public companies in the United States, for example, need to abide by Sarbanes-Oxley. This basically defines reporting, auditing, and responsibilities an organization must implement. Applicability of practices involving audit or reporting of data, transactions, customer information, and so on, may be impacted by such regulations.

Domain complexity

Domain complexity involves the complexity of a problem the software is trying to solve. If the problem domain is simple, certain best practices might not be applicable. A calculator application, for example, may not need to employ **domain-driven design** (**DDD**) because the extra overhead to manage domain complexity may be more complex than the domain itself. Whereas a domain to manage an insurance domain may be so complex that using DDD will have partitioned the domain complexity and would make it easier to manage and understand.

Organizational distribution

Similar to team distribution, organizational distribution relates to the geographic distribution of the entire organization. Your team may be co-located but the actual organization may be global. An example of where a globally-distributed company may impact the viability of a practice could be the location of the IT department. If a particular practice involves drastically changing or adding to IT infrastructure, the friction or push back to implementing this practice may outweigh the benefit.

Technical complexity

Technical complexity can be related to domain complexity, but really involves the actual technical implementation of the system. Simple domain complexity could be implemented in a distributed environment using multiple subsystems and systems, some of which could be legacy systems. While the domain may be simple, the technical complexity is high. For example, practices involving managing a legacy system or code would not be applicable in a greenfield project where there are yet to be any legacy systems or code.

Organizational complexity

Organizational complexity can be related to organizational distribution but is generally independent. It's independent for our purposes of evaluating a practice. For example, in a complex organization with double-digit management levels, it may be easier to re-use hardware than it is to purchase new hardware. Practices that involve partitioning work amongst multiple systems (scaling out) may be more applicable than best practices that involve scaling up.

Enterprise discipline

Some enterprises have teams that drive their own discipline, and some enterprises have consistent discipline across the enterprise, not just the software development effort. Practices that are grounded in engineering disciplines may be easier to implement in enterprises that are already very disciplined.

Life-cycle scope

Some projects span a larger life cycle than others. Enterprise applications, for example, often span from conception to IT delivery and maintenance. Practices that are geared towards an off-the-shelf model of delivery (where deployment and maintenance is done by the customer) and ignore the enterprise-specific aspects of the project, may be counterproductive in a full life-cycle scope.

Paradigm

Finally, when attempting to evaluate practices, the development paradigm involved should be taken into account. For example, on an agile project, best practices around "waterfall" paradigms may not be applicable.

Regardless of the team factor, it's important to not discount practices just because factors may be different or opposite. Just because the context is different doesn't mean that the practice is completely incompatible.

One way of viewing a context is as a *requirement*. There are various practices for eliciting, documenting, and engineering requirements that we can inspire our method of documenting the context. Practices are a behavior, or an action. **Behavior-driven design** (**BDD**), although completely orthogonal to documenting the context of a practice, builds on the fact that users of software use the software's behavior. In order to better describe their requirements so that the correct behavior can be discovered, the concept of "specifications" is used.

Specifications in BDD are a more flexible way of specifying requirements. One form of documenting these specifications is using the Gherkin syntax. This syntax is basically `Given X [and X2] When Y [and Y2] Then Z [and Z2]`. Building on that type of syntax, we can simply re-use `Given` to document our context.

For example, with the canonical source code control example, we could document our context as follows:

```
Given a multi-person, collaborative, software project
  And the software evolves over time
  And may change concurrently for different reasons
When making changes to source code
Then use an off-the-shelf source code control system
```

But, there's no reason why you should limit yourself to re-using existing documentation semantics. If something is clearer to read and easier to follow, use that method.

Categorization

There is not much documented on categorizing practices. For the most part, this can be fairly obvious. We could have procedural practices (using source code control), design practices (employing authentication to ensure correct access to private data), and so on.

Starting out, building a practices library may not need much, if any, of categorization. As you build on your skill set, and increase your knowledge and experience with more practices, you may find that certain degrees of categorization for you and your team may be necessary. It's one thing to have your own knowledge and experience with practices, but if you're trying to mentor a team and help the team improve as a whole, then categorization can begin to prove its worth.

This is another area which we can draw upon how structured patterns have become in their proliferation and dissemination. Patterns too have somewhat ambiguous recommendations for categorization, but to build on something already in place requires less reinvention, learning, and a broader audience.

Although categorization is useful for organizing practices, you might also want to consider aggregating certain practices into one practice, and detailing the different steps involved in the different contexts. Performing lengthy operations on a background thread, for example, has many different contexts, and each context may have a specific way of implementing the practice (WPF, WinForm, WCF, and so on).

Just because we use the term "category" doesn't mean membership in this category is mutually exclusive.

Patterns are generally pre-categorized as "design," but some categories are often used to group patterns. These categories are discussed next.

Creational

Patterns that apply to the creation of objects. Probably not something you'd normally classify a practice under.

Structural

Structural patterns are patterns involving specific ways to design or manage relationships between classes, objects, or components in a code. Could be used as a subcategory of architecture practices.

Behavioral

Technically, this category involves patterns that relate to designing how classes, objects, or components communicate between one another, but it depends on your interpretation of "behavioral." Stands well enough alone.

Integration

Practices involving integration of systems or subsystems.

Procedural

These are generally business procedures. While most of what this book discusses is not business procedures, there are some really good business practices in the software development industry that I'd recommend, for example, agile practices.

Anti-patterns

There's much written on ways not to write software. We could go out on a limb and do the same thing with practices. But, for the most part, there aren't anti-practices. Almost all practices should be considered useful. It's mere context that defines where the practices are useful. I wouldn't suggest building a category of anti-practices as much as spending time improving how contexts are described in practices. However, would include *invalid contexts* (contexts where the practice is not recommended) when documenting the context of a given practice.

Practices are generally less focused than patterns so their categories can include various other categories, such as:

- **Security**: Practices involving improving or retaining security of data could be grouped here. This can be topics like authentication, authorization, encryption, and so on.
- **Architectural**: This always ends up being a broad and subjective category, and can end up being a catch-all for practices that just don't fit anywhere else. However, we can use this category to subcategorize other categories. For example, a practice may be tagged as security and architectural, for example, a practice to keep private data within its own database and on a separate server.
- **Quality**: To a certain extent all practices have something to do with quality. The mere use of a practice implies that someone else has implemented and worked out all of the kinks, just improving the quality of your software over having to invent the practice yourself. However, some practices are specifically geared towards improving the quality of your software. The practices of using unit tests or using **test-driven design** (**TDD**), for example, are practices specifically geared at helping improve quality.
- **User experience**: I'm sure on any given day you can find dozens and dozens of practices around **user interface** (**UI**) design, **user experience** (**UX**) design, and so on. There are lots of UX practices out there. An example of such a practice relating more about software design than UI design could be: perform lengthy operations on a background thread.
- **Application health**: This category deals with the dissemination and reporting of application or system health. In simple applications, this may deal with informing the user of errors, warnings, and so on. These are fairly simple practices that can often be covered under UX. In larger, more complex, distributed systems, or systems with components without a UI, it's vital that problems with the system, such as being able to perform its intended tasks (health), be communicated outside of the system. For example, given a Windows service when errors are encountered then log the error to Windows Event Log.
- **Performance**: Performance practices are a bit tricky because performance improvements are always something that need to be observed and evaluated, for example, premature optimizations. But there are some practices that programmers can use that are known to be faster than other types of implementations. Picking the fastest algorithm for a given situation (context) is never a premature optimization.

- **Scalability**: Practices involving the ability for a system to scale, either horizontally (out) or vertically (up) can be categorized as scalability practices. Examples of such practices may involve things like breaking work into individual tasks that can be executed concurrently, or employing the use of messaging.
- **Language**: Some practices can get down to a much lower-level, such as the language level. Practices about using language features in a specific way could be categorized here, for example, avoiding closures within loops. Many such practices in this category can be monitored and/or evaluated through static code analysis. Tools such as Visual Studio Code Analysis can be used to monitor compliance with such practices.
- **Deployment**: Deploying systems and applications in and of itself can have many practices. There are many tools that basically implement these practices for you, but some complex situations require their own practices relating to deployment, for example, preferring WiX over Visual Studio deployment projects.

In this book

For the purposes of this book, I'll keep it simple. Practices in this book will be documented as follows:

Context: In the context of X.

Practice: Consider/do Y.

Context details the situation in which *practice* should apply.

Evolving practices—a collaborative effort

We don't really want to reinvent the wheel, and neither do most other people. But, as we create, communicate, and evolve practices we often begin a dialog. We interact with people on practices involving frameworks and libraries that they also have had experience with. Their experiences may have been different than yours. Collaborate with team or community members to evolve and improve practices so that other, less-skilled people can write software concentrating on the value to be added quicker, and with higher quality.

Axiomatic practices

At some point you'll either encounter or create an axiomatic practice. Axiomatic means "self-evident truth." "Use source code control" is an axiomatic practice. No one can really argue against it, they may not be doing it, but they know they should.

Axiomatic practices are fine, but they should be avoided when possible. They could indicate that they are too vague and too hard to evolve. Part of the goal here is to improve over time.

Most "best practices" are presented as axiomatic practices. There's no expected context and the implication is that it applies in all circumstances. It's important to read-between-the-lines with these types of practices. Try to figure out what the context might be then compare it to yours. If that's difficult, make sure you evaluate every possible angle.

Patterns

It may seem like these types of practices are patterns. Indeed some of the practices actually detail certain patterns and how to implement them, but they're different from patterns in that they are not specific implementations of logic to produce a specific result or fulfill a specific need. Practices can detail implementation but they don't need to. They can detail higher-level tasks or process without providing specific detail of how to implement the practice.

"Use source code control," for example, is a very common recommended practice. Any given software project involves collaborating with other team members working on the same code base and sometimes the same files in the code base. The team also needs to deal with subsequent and concurrent versions of the code base in their work of creating and maintaining the code base.

Why practices?

There are various reasons why practices can help teams write software. Let's have a look at some common reasons why you'd want to use practices to help improve the process of writing a software.

An empirical and not a defined process

Software development is generally an empirical process. The empirical process control model is one that imposes control over process through inspection and adaptation. A defined process documents all of the steps to arrive at a known result. Through the use of a defined process to detail ways of developing a software and defining processes through practices, we can offload much of the burden of inspection and adaptation in software development. But any unknown or undiscovered areas of software development will require empirical process control. As we become more skilled in our understanding of many practices, much of the thought that goes into developing software can also be concentrated on the value of the solution we're trying to implement.

At lower-levels, we can't really define the process by which we will implement most software in its entirety. We try to impose a defined process on a software with things like the **software development life cycle** (**SDLC**), and define that there are several phases to writing software such as: inception, analysis, architecture, design, development, test, delivery, operations, maintenance, and so on. In fact there have been *processes* defined throughout the history of software development to try and turn what is generally an empirical process into a defined process, or at least taking what is known of the process and making it defined. Unfortunately, these defined processes hide the fact that much of the details of producing software are empirical.

The practices in this book do not try to distract from the fact that most software projects are empirical and try to impose processes. In a way, practices are a way of making more of the software development process defined rather than empirical. This book tries to define a way to reach commonly required goals of many software development projects. The goals shared amongst many software development projects cease to become value-added to that particular project, they become commodities. Commodities are important to the delivery and health of the software, but are neither unique to the project, nor require much, if any, research. Research, into areas of a project that don't add value obviously doesn't provide the same return on investment. If we can implement one of these commodities with little or no research then the project is better for it. Better because it can move on to spending time on the value that the project is intending to provide.

The quintessential example in so many contexts is logging. Microsoft Word is not an application, library, or framework that provides logging, but Word may perform its own logging in order to debug, gauge health, aid support, gather metrics, and so on. All of which help Word satisfy existing and future customers. But the software developers on the Word team do not need to discover any particular logging implementation because they are trying to produce a word processing product.

Cross-cutting concerns

Based on what you have just read, and if you look closely at practices, you'll notice that the goal of each practice is a goal shared by many software teams or products. This book obviously does not try to detail how to write a word processor or how to write a web browser. However, it does detail certain practices that would aid in the development of almost all software: cross-cutting concerns. A **cross-cutting concern** is a task that needs to be performed by more than one piece of software, more than one module in your software, or more than one class in your module. It is said that each class/module/software has concerns over and above what is deemed to be its responsibility.

An invoicing module has the responsibility of tracking line items, prices, discounts, customer, applying taxes, and so on. But in many aspects it needs to take on more than it is responsible for. An invoicing module may need to log the actions it performs, it may need to perform data caching, it may need to provide health monitoring, and so on. None of these things are really what the software does, but they help the software do what it does in a more efficient and effective way.

Focus on the value

In many of the earlier paragraphs one thing should shine through: practices are a means by which we can take what isn't truly our "value proposition" in the software solution we're trying to implement (such as infrastructure), and concentrate our efforts on the value we want to provide. This gets our value out sooner and theoretically lets us spend more time on ensuring quality of that value.

As software developers move from journeymen to craftsmen or masters, much of what we gain in skill is through learning practices that allow us to focus on a solution's value. Craftsmen and masters need to communicate practices as well as mentor journeymen in a better way if our industry is going to thrive and improve.

The power of mantras

"Best practices" is so commonly used that it has become a mantra. One definition of **mantra** is a word or phrase commonly repeated. I believe commonly used terms begin to take on a life of their own and begin to lose their meaning. People repeat them because they're so common, not because of their meaning. "Best practices" is one of those phrases. Many people use the term "best practice" simply because it's part of our technical vocabulary, not because they really think the practices are "best" in all places. They use the term as an idiom not to be taken literally, but to take as "recommended practices," "contextual practices," or even "generally accepted practices."

The unfortunate problem with "best practice" as a mantra is that some people take the phrase literally. They haven't learned that you need to take it with a grain of salt. I believe if we use terms more appropriate for our industry, the way it works, and the degree to which technology changes within it, the more we use these terms the greater adoption they will have. Eventually, we can relegate "best practices" to the niche to which it describes.

"Best Practices" is an inter-industry term that's been around for a long time and is well recognized. It will be a long time before we can move to a more accurate term. I, of course, can only speculate how it started being used in the software development industry. Other industries, like woodworking, don't suffer from the quick technology turnover, so their "best practices" can be recommended for a very long time, and are therefore more accurately be called "best practices".

Still other industries openly boast different terms. Accounting and other organizations have chosen "generally accepted" to refer to principles and practices.

Summary

I hope the information in this chapter has motivated you to help become part of the solution of thinking more about "recommended practices" or "contextual practices." I've tried to ensure that each practice is complete, correct, and up-to-date when it was written. But over time, each of these practices will become more and more out-of-date. I leave it as an exercise to the reader to improve each practice as time goes on.

So don't take this as a recipe book. You should try to understand each of the recommended practices, recognize the context for which it is intended, and try your hardest to either improve it or to tailor it to your project or your context. You're doing yourself a disservice if you simply take these practices and employ pragmatic re-use.

I hope this chapter has either re-enforced your thoughts on the term "best practices", or opened your eyes slightly. "Best practices" are far from a panacea, and far from "best" in every context. We've seen several motivating factors about why we might want to "use recommended practices" and why we're sometimes forced to resort to "recommended practices" rather than *figure it out*. I hope the information in this chapter has motivated you to help become part of the solution of thinking more about "recommended practices" or "contextual practices." Finding and using recommended practices is just the first part of the puzzle. In order to use a practice properly, we need to evaluate the practice: we need to know the context for which it's intended as well as the context in which we'd like to use it. This can be a complex endeavor, but several criteria can help us evaluate applicability of a practice. Once we know our own context, the context in which we would like to apply a particular pattern, it is only then we can truly evaluate a practice and use it properly. After all, we don't want to use a practice to save time and avoid technical debt if, in fact, it increases our technical debt and reduces quality.

In the next chapter we'll begin looking at source control practices. We'll look at some terminology, source code control architectures, and source code control usage practices.

2
Source Code Control Practices

At some point as a software developer you end up working with other developers in a team. It quickly becomes apparent that it's frequently necessary for multiple people to work on the same file without hindering productivity, and that it's vital to be able to return to past known states.

Source code control (**SCC**) systems help aid team dynamics of software developers. They provide the ability to track changes to source code and provide isolation between those changes.

SCC systems do not come for free. They are like any other tool in our tool belt, there's a wrong way to use them and a right way to use them.

This chapter serves to help provide the developer, team lead, or manager with a brief but hopefully *detailed enough* description of some common SCC practices.

This chapter will cover the following topics:

- Terminology
- Principles
- Evaluating SCC software
- SCC-friendly solution and directory structures
- Commit practices
- Branching practices
- Occasionally connected and distributed SCC

Terminology

The best practice is using a consistent vocabulary. So, let's talk about some SCC terms.

Repository

Repository is a bit of an overused term, but it refers to the location where the source code is ultimately stored. It's sometimes referred to as a **repo**. Some systems refer to this as a **depot**. Repository is more common in several circles, so I'll stick with that.

SCC

Source code control – the technology and/or management of, and changes to, source code. The acronym SCC seems to be used more often in Microsoft circles. It has more historically been referred to as **revision control** or **version control**, or even **source control**. There are other systems that deal with revisions to files in a broader sense. So, I prefer "source code control" when talking about managing changes to just source code.

Edit/merge/commit

There are two basic models for how SCC systems manage the concurrency of changes made to files under their control. One is the edit/merge/commit model. This model is quickly becoming the most popular amongst the more recent SCC systems. It basically works on the fact that the system knows what version of a file you started with, and putting edits to that file into the repository is the act of merging the changes into the current version before committing the change.

Lock/edit/check-in

The other model of managing concurrent changes to a file controlled by an SCC system is lock/edit/check-in. This model is based on the principle that someone makes an exclusive lock on a file before making edits to the file and "checking them in". A drawback of this model is that only one person can edit a file at a time. Some systems get around that by switching a *lock* with a *check-out*, and making you manually deal with merging changes between concurrent edits.

Trunk

Typically, the **trunk** is the baseline of the source code. It's the in-development version of the source that is generally considered *in development* or *most recent*. Sometimes it is called **mainline**, but mainline could mean the baseline of any existing branch, not just the trunk. Whether or not a project has a trunk largely depends on the branching strategy. The overwhelming recommendation is to retain a trunk and have independent branches based on need or strategy.

Branch

Just as with real-life trees, a *branch* is something that divides off from the trunk. In SCC, a **branch** is something that is independent from the trunk, with the expectation that changes to the branch will be merged back into the trunk (or the parent branch). In many SCC systems, *trunk* is a type of branch.

Fork

Fork is typically another name for a branch (that is "a fork in the road"). Recently, this has become known as taking a copy of a trunk or a project, with potentially no expectation to merge anything back into the source of the fork. This is typically seen in open source projects where someone publishes a source code and someone else who wants to use it for their own purposes *forks* it to get a copy for themselves.

Merge

The act of integrating changes from one branch to another. Depending on the branching strategy, one of the branches may typically be the trunk.

Check-out

With more recent advances in the SCC technology, this typically isn't needed. Checking-out code generally means registering with a SCC system that you want to modify a specific revision. It has come to mean simply getting the latest version of the source code in systems that are edit/merge/commit.

Check-in

In the broadest sense this simply means moving revised code into a repository. At a more pedantic level this terminology is from source control systems that mandate a *check-out* model, and *check-in* means you no longer have code checked-out.

Changeset

Considered one or more changes made to code/files that is committed. This can be changes to files, addition of files, or deletion of files. All of the files' modifications committed at once are considered a **changeset**.

Lock

Although more prevalent in the lock/edit/check-in model, this refers to *locking* a file down for concurrent changes, so that only one change can be made at a time. Some files don't merge well (like binary files) and require that merging be avoided. Locking a file before edit/commit or edit/check-in prevents merge corruption.

Commit

Similar to *check-in*, this means putting edits of one or more file into the source control system. Edits will not be tracked by the system until being committed.

Push

Typically *push* is the term used only with distributed SCC systems. **Push** means merging local commits into a remote repository or a master branch stored in a remote repository.

Pull

Typically a term used with regards to distributed SCC systems. It has come to mean a request to merge independent changes. A *pull* request is typically done from a *fork* of a project. Someone working on their own code could have someone else *fork* from that code (unbeknownst to them). That external party could find a bug and fix it or add a feature that they feel would be useful to the original author, at which time they request the original author to *pull* that change into the original source (which is likely to be modified by now).

Tag/label

Most SCC systems have an ability to tag some or all of the source code under control with a name. This is a good way to *pin* the source code at a specific time and date. This is often a good option instead of branching if you're not sure whether you're going to need to make any changes to that code once *tagged*. You should be aware of how the SCC you choose performs tagging. For example, **Subversion** (**SVN**) implements tagging as a branching. That is when you tag source code in SVN it does the same thing as a branch and copies the source code. Most SCC systems let you branch from a tag or label, so if you find you do need to make changes specific to that labeled source code, you can branch first.

Shelving/shelvesets

Most SCC systems have a feature called shelving. This is generally the ability to take existing changes and put them on the server without committing or checking-in. Some teams use this as a way of code review. One team member puts their changes in a shelveset and another member gets the changes off the shelf and reviews them. When approved, the original member can commit the code or the reviewer can commit the code.

The intention of shelving is for times when you're currently in the middle of some work and need to temporarily abandon the work, to work with source code prior to your changes. As shelvesets are stored in the SCC, they are controlled in their own right and are accessible by anyone who has access to the SCC. Due to this, shelvesets can be shared between users without affecting any branches. This is useful if you want to transfer work-in-progress from one person to another, or for senior developers to review work before it is committed.

Principles

To get an idea of what can be done, and thus what should be done with SCC, it's a good idea to briefly describe the principles of source code control:

- **Tracking**: First and foremost, source code control deals with tracking changes. SCC systems generally track the deltas (just the changes) made from one commit to the next.
- **History**: SCC keeps a history of what was done to each file for each commit. This includes date/time, user, changes, comments, and so on. This history allows users to see what has been done to the code in the past and thus supports the next principle.

- **Collaboration**: SCC systems aid in collaboration by providing means to isolate the changes of one team member from another. These systems also provide very powerful tools to merge isolated changes together.
- **Auditing**: SCC allows auditing of changes. Many systems have an *annotate* or *blame* feature that allows you to track the modification of a particular line in a particular file to a specific person. I don't generally think "blaming" someone for something is particularly productive, but it can come in handy.
- **Backup**: Of course, anything that maintains a history of changes that have been made over time is a form of backup. If you run into a problem with the source code at some point, you can return to the previous version(s) of the source code (backups). This allows you to find where a problem was first introduced or to simply start over from some past state.

Recommended SCC software evaluation criteria

Of course not all source code control software is made equal. Any choice of any tool is best done by first evaluating the alternatives.

There are a few tools or technologies to choose from when thinking of deploying your own source code system. A single chapter can't possibly detail all of the possible tools and technologies that are available, so I'll just give some examples of some popular Windows options.

If you have an MSDN license, the first thing that comes to mind is **Team Foundation Server** (**TFS**). TFS is much more than just source code control (about one-ninth of its features). TFS also has features such as work item tracking (including requirements, defects, tasks, and so on), reporting, collaboration (implemented with SharePoint), build automation, and project management. If your team needs more than source code control, you may want to look at TFS. The caveat is that the current licensing model requires **client access licenses** (**CALs**) in certain circumstances, and thus can get pretty pricy for relatively smaller teams. TFS roughly uses the lock/edit/check-in model (by default it *checks-out* rather than *locks*, but still prefers an available connection to the SCC server in order to perform a *check-out*). TFS usually requires separate installations of SharePoint and SQL Server in order to perform collaboration and store data.

Another popular choice on the Windows platform has been Subversion (often referred to as SVN). SVN is an open source SCC system. Technically free, some third parties such as VisualSVN offer redistributions of the system that includes support options. Generally, the SVN distributions only contain SCC, but many third-party tools integrate to offer things like collaboration, build, and work item management. SVN uses its own database schema to store data, so only one installation is required to get started. To integrate with other tools, of course, requires installation of those tools and potentially manual integration steps. Tools like TeamCity will integrate with SVN quickly and easily to perform automated builds.

Given the focus of the book, I'll focus on criteria that would apply only for developers working in Windows.

Workflow model

Each SCC tool uses a specific workflow model: lock/edit/check-in or edit/merge/commit. Each model has some caveats. Lock/edit/check-in assumes that you have a constant connection to the SCC server in order to lock files or check them out. Although some of these tools attempt to deal with being disconnected in certain circumstances; during periods of network disconnection (failure or off-site) these technologies can be troublesome. TFS is an example of one such technology.

Total cost of ownership

Total cost of ownership (**TCO**) is important. If you decide on a particular brand of SCC and deploying that SCC is too expensive, you will run into issues very quickly in the deployment. Consider the various aspects of cost when evaluating SCC options. Make sure you know the costs of the various options and requirements before you take the plunge. Be sure you account for CALs (if necessary), server costs, resources to deploy and maintain third-party tools, integration costs, and so on.

Integration options

SCC is its own beast, but, it can integrate well with other workflows or tools. Work items, for example, integrate well with SCC-type workflow because you're often working on a specific work item when you commit changes. You may want to associate those commits with a work item and close the work item when all of the changes have been made.

There are other tools that integrate with various SCC offerings. If you think your team needs tools that might integrate, be sure to include those needs when evaluating particular SCC offerings.

Team dynamics and location

Deciding whether you can use lock/edit/check-in or edit/merge/commit depends largely on the organization of your team. If your team is occasionally or mostly disconnected, a lock/edit/check-in model may be problematic for the team. If members cannot *lock* or *check-out* a file as they edit it, then checking-in becomes extremely time-consuming because every commit becomes a merge operation.

Self or third-party hosting

Over the past few years there have been many companies that have started to offer source code control server hosting. I'm not going to provide an exhaustive list, but some of these companies include: GitHub, Bitbucket, Unfuddle, TeamDevCentral, Phase2, and Assembla.

Getting up and running with a self-hosted SCC system could be cost prohibitive, require resources you don't have, or otherwise take time you can't make available, so consider using third-party SCC hosting.

Authentication

Each SCC has specific authentication needs. TFS uses Windows, built-in authentication which could be Active Directory, NTLM, and so on. Other tools may have their own authentication scheme or provide something that integrates into Windows authentication. If you need something that doesn't tie you to a specific authentication scheme, be sure the SCC system supports that option. For example, if you want to work with team members in and outside of your organization on different domains or workgroups, be sure the tool supports that.

Context: Given the choice of which SCC technology to use.

Practice: Thoroughly evaluate all alternatives based on needs.

Organizing for source code control

Despite having Visual Studio, working with an SCC system doesn't come without some planning and caveats. We will discuss them next.

Organizing directory structures

Generally, when you're working with SCC, the source code in the repository is in a state that builds (for example, a commit could "break the build"). This, of course, assumes that everything the build needs to run is actually in source code control, and referenced in the same structure that it is in source control. One of the biggest issues with users of SCC is that what the user has on their local system builds fine, but if someone else clones or fetches everything from SCC it doesn't build.

The biggest culprit for build errors like this has been that some dependencies, like libraries or frameworks, are missing. To a certain extent, there are dependencies we are not capable of storing in SCC. You can't store whether a development environment works in Windows, Linux, or some other operating system. For example, fetching code from a repository that works on Windows won't compile well at all on a Linux computer. Everything required to build should be included in SCC.

When working with a team, it's important for each computer to abide by the baseline in order to work effectively on the team. Things to consider when deciding what should be in the baseline rather than stored in SCC are as follows:

- OS type
- OS version
- Frameworks (Java, .NET, and so on)
- Framework versions
- Developer tools (Visual Studio, SVN, Git, and so on)

SCC systems basically just copy files. Anything that only needs to be copied from one place to another, is a dependency of the source code in some way, or can be modified and tracked over time is a good candidate for placing in SCC rather than the workstation baseline.

Context: When working with teams of developers with multiple computers.

Practice: Define a minimalistic baseline that every computer connecting to SCC must adhere to.

Once you define what the workstation baseline is, it's important to keep things, such as third-party libraries, in SCC so that anyone fetching from the repository is able to build on any workstation that adheres to the baseline. It's preferred to do this in a directory, within the source directory `src`. `lib` is a common directory for such dependencies. Having a `src\lib` relationship helps when building within Visual Studio. It's more common to have `lib` and `src` at the same level, especially when the build occurs outside of Visual Studio.

Context: When taking dependencies on third-party libraries or frameworks.

Practice: Keep dependencies within the source code directory of the project.

Generally, you also have other files you may want to keep in SCC that aren't really source code but do change over time and would be aided by tracking revisions and history. It's common to have a directory at the same level as the source code to contain such files. It's common for there to be a `doc` directory at the same level as `src`. For example, the directory structure may look like the following screenshot:

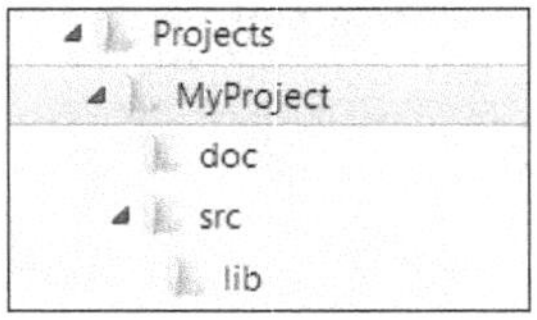

Or maybe like the following screenshot:

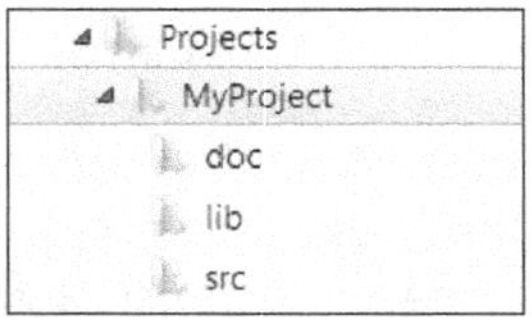

When creating projects and solutions with Visual Studio you, of course, are not given the option of naming the source directory. The name of the solution is used for the source code directory name. It's fine to accept that and rename the directory afterwards.

Context: When creating a solution in Visual Studio.

Practice: Do not name the solution `src` to get all of the source code within a `src` directory.

Some SCC systems actually require a little more work when it comes to directory structure. Systems like Subversion keep branches and tags within the directory structure. Without some preplanning it's easy to create a Subversion repository that is difficult to manage because these directories were not taken into account.

It sounds simpler to create a directory to hold a Visual Studio solution and its projects than to simply create a repository and start checking these files into the root. Unfortunately, when it comes time to tag or branch you'll be asked where you want to store that information. That information must be somewhere within the repository. If you haven't accounted for it and you've put your source in the root of the repository (that is the SLN file) you'll be forced to put the branches and the tags in the same directory.

"Yeah, so?" you're probably thinking. Well, let's say you work on this project for several years and you've created 20 or so branches and tagged about 50 times. This means you have 71 copies of your source code in the root of the repository (if using SVN). Whenever you ask the SCC to check-out or export you're going to get all 71 versions of that code, every time! Believe me when I say, that's only mildly better than sticking bamboo under your finger nails.

Fortunately, the creators of Subversion have defined a set of recommended directories to create when you create a Subversion repository. By creating a `branches`, `tags`, and `trunk` directory in the root, you can avoid these hassles. The source code would initially be placed in `trunk`, and branches and tags of that source would go in the `branches` and `tags` directories respectively. You can now check-out or export from `https://servername/svn/ProjectName/trunk`, and avoid having to fetch multiple copies of the source code every time you get the latest version of the source.

For example, in a popular Subversion server distribution *VisualSVN*, the project `ProjectName` may appear like the following screenshot in the repository hierarchy:

Solution structure

For the most part, the out of the box solution structure (or out of the wizard, in this case) is perfectly acceptable.

When working with SCC systems that integrate into Visual Studio, what is retrieved and updated in SCC is largely defined by what is in a solution. For example, by selecting **File** | **Source Control** | **Open from Source Control**, Visual Studio actually only retrieves the files that the solution knows about. This has been a problem with teams and build errors when getting the "new guy" up to speed.

Of course, this generally means that we need to also have all of the files that are required to build somewhere in the solution (despite Visual Studio being perfectly happy to find them only in the local filesystem). In much the same way as we did with our directory structure, we can accommodate that by having a similar folder structure in Visual Studio. You can use the same naming as we did with directories to make it easier to remember and correlate the files to directories that match the solution folders (since solution folders are not stored as a filesystem directory). You can add a solution folder to a solution by right-clicking the solution in **Solution Explorer** and selecting **Add** | **New Solution Folder**. For example, if we added a `lib` solution folder, and added a third-party library to it in our solution, our Solution Explorer may look the following screenshot:

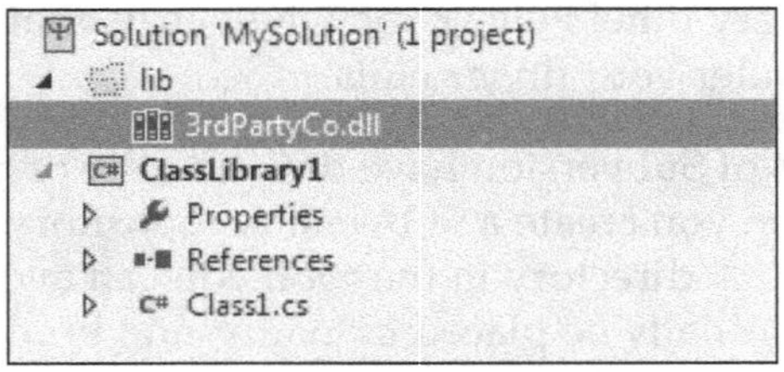

Context: When working with a SCC that is integrated into Visual Studio.

Practice: Ensure that all files that are in SCC are also in the Visual Studio solution or project.

Continuous integration

As we'll detail shortly, what you have locally on your computer, your ability to build, and what is in SCC may not be in sync. It is quite feasible that you may check something on your computer (forgetting a single file, for example) that will create something in SCC that will not build (should anyone else fetch that particular point in the repository's history). To minimize this, it's important to be able to automate the build early and make use of continuous integration tools. Continuous integration tools can be configured to point at your repository, check for new changesets, fetch all source code, and perform a build automatically. This allows detection of broken builds almost as quickly as they occur.

Context: When working on a team with SCC.

Practice: Ensure build failures are detected early by using continuous integration tools.

Continuous integration tools are much more powerful than simply fetching from SCC and performing an automated build. The process can include labeling/tagging, reporting, deployment, emailing success/failure, and so on.

Branching strategies

We've talked about branching briefly: what it is and what it's for. Let's now talk about how to use it. Branching provides isolation. A branch isolates changes to source code from other changes (not just "other's changes") to source code. Once branched code is worked on in isolation, changes are then merged back into the parent branch (or the trunk if that's the parent branch). This can be visualized with the following diagram:

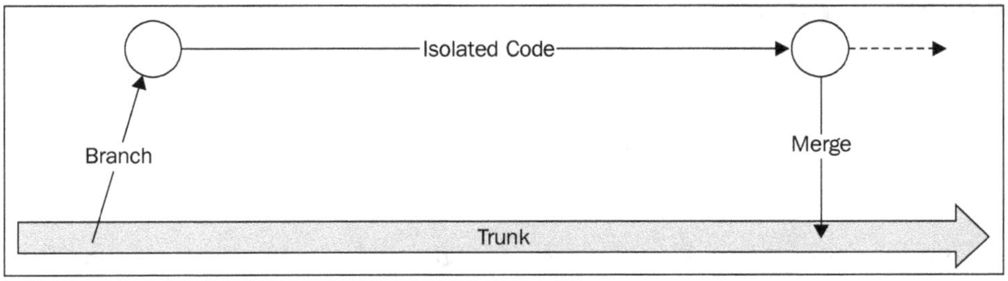

While the branch may have been merged back into the trunk, work could continue on that branch and, presumably, merged back into the trunk again at a later date. There are a few reasons why you'd want to have that isolation.

Isolation

In the most general sense, there are various reasons to isolate certain changes to source code from other changes to source code. Dependent code requires dependencies to have a certain degree of stability. When code is being modified or redesigned you can no longer guarantee that stability and risk breaking the dependent code. When there is a need to isolate these changes, branch the code in the SCC system.

Context: When a code change isolation is required.

Practice: Choose to branch the code.

However, branching is generally expensive. It entails making a copy of the code from one place to another and when work is done, it involves a merge. A merge could introduce conflicts that need to be resolved manually. Some merges take several days in teams that haven't been organized appropriately, or haven't picked an appropriate branching strategy.

Context: When a code change isolation is not required.

Practice: Do not use branching.

Ad hoc isolation

In the simplest of teams you may find that you may never need to branch. You simply have a trunk and do your work, committing to that trunk. You may decide that what is in the trunk is perfectly acceptable to simply tag or label for a particular release, rather than branch. In this scenario, you probably have little collaboration with other teams.

Testing isolation

In more complex teams you may be dependent on rigorous processes where you have specific QC, user acceptance, or release phases in addition to development. In these cases, you may find that having a Test or Release branch that branches from the trunk when the code is in a state deemed worthy of release (and thus worthy of test) is best.

This strategy isolates the code under test from the code under development. If testing results in no changes required, nothing needs to be merged back into trunk. If testing does result in fixes or changes, then those can be merged back into trunk when they are fully tested and vetted.

This is fairly common in environments with frequent or even concurrent releases. Websites are a good example of this. Testing and production may be in a separate branch in order to facilitate transient fixes only in those branches that would be merged back into the trunk.

This assumes that work in the trunk is simply merged into the production and test branches periodically (usually after *release*), to refresh the branch and the branches live on forever.

There is a distinct possibility that important fixes made in the trunk will need to make their way into the branch after the code has been isolated, that is, merging can occur in both directions. The following diagram visualizes this scenario:

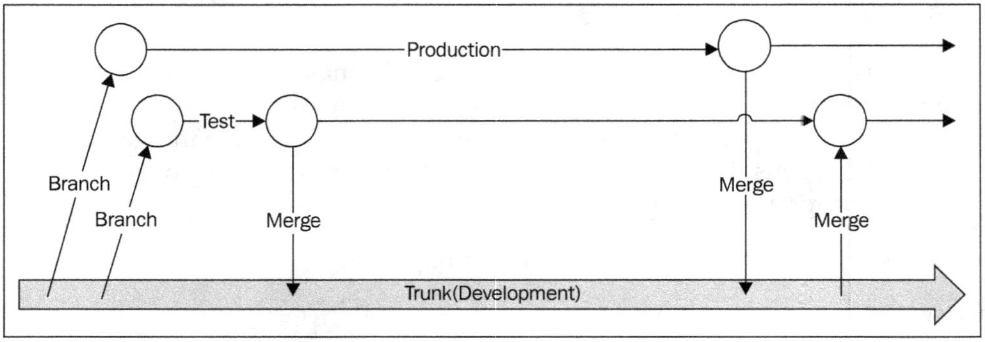

Context: When needed to isolate testing from development.

Practice: Isolate code under test by creating separate branches for separate testing phases.

Some teams have a one-way relationship from the trunk to the production and testing branches. In other words, they only merge to production or testing and only make changes in the trunk. The branches then become a read-only snapshot of the code. It is preferred to use tags or labels in this scenario because there are really no isolated changes.

Context: When needing read-only testing and production code bases.

Practice: Prefer tags or labels to branches when possible.

This, of course, assumes that there is some way to limit access to code restricted by a tag or label to people responsible for testing or deploying to production.

This type of branching requires bi-directional merges, maintaining three branches (two plus *trunk*), and is not for the faint of heart. It is borne of an organization with many independent teams (maybe Test, Dev, Deploy, QA, and so on). If you don't have this type of an organization, avoid this branching strategy.

Release isolation

In many cases, you'll get to a specific point in development where it is deemed necessary to release the software to the public. There may be several different types of impetuses that drive releasing the software, such as when a hotfix or service pack need to be released.

In cases like this, it is often useful to create a branch to isolate any changes that need to be made for that release without affecting the general development effort. If anything specific is needed to be changed for the release, those changes can then be merged back into the trunk as soon as the release has been made public.

Context: When code changes need to be isolated based on the need to release the code.

Practice: Create a branch to isolate the code changes related to that release.

The following diagram visualizes a couple of potential scenarios of release branching:

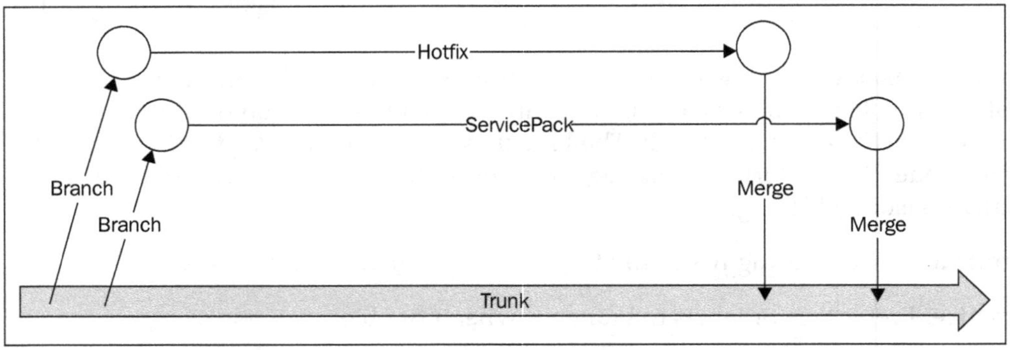

Feature isolation

Another form of isolation is based on features. This is sometimes called **feature branching**. If your team is focused on implementing *features*, then creating a branch-per-feature may make a lot of sense for your team. In agile circles, a *feature* is often delineated by a *user story*. If you're not sure if you are organized by feature, or aren't using *user stories*, then feature branching will often add confusion because what delineates a feature isn't clear. Therefore, lines between features are blurred and merge conflicts increase in frequency, as seen in the following diagram:

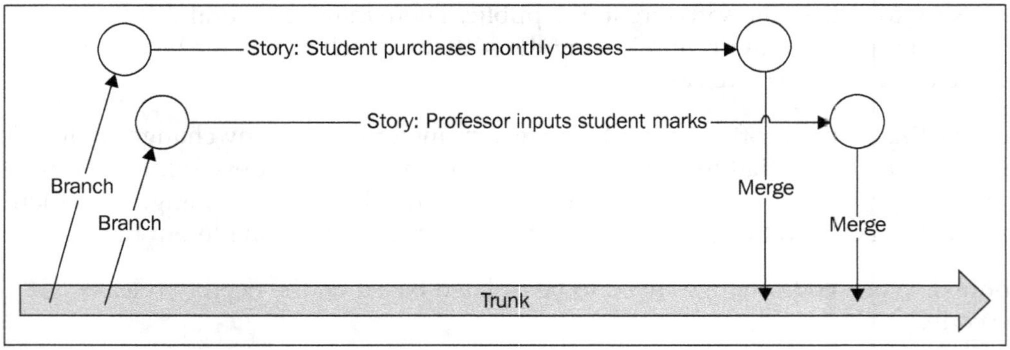

Context: If not partitioning work by feature.

Practice: Avoid feature branching.

Even though features may seem reasonably independent, one caveat with this branching strategy is that if the features are not actually independent, then frequent merge conflicts could occur. If this tends to happen, consider reviewing the granularity of your features or users stories as the goal of easier collaboration via SCC isn't being realized.

Context: When realizing frequent merge conflicts with feature branching.

Practice: Re-evaluate granularity of features.

Team isolation

Yet another form of isolation is team isolation. Team isolation occurs when members of the team are subdivided into groups. How the team is divided varies from team to team and can be categorized by component, by layer, and so on.

Teams of this type of organization generally have dependencies between them. Hopefully this dependency is one-way. Generally, this means one team needs to work with the stable work product of the other group or groups. In this case, the work of each group can be branched off from the trunk.

In teams of this organization, where presumably the work of one *team* depends on the work of another, each group can create their own branch where they do their day-to-day work, and occasionally coordinate with dependent teams on merging and integrating.

This type of structure assumes that all of the source code is in one place and each group compiles all of the code themselves. There are other structures that can take a much more independent stance, where packages are delivered to dependent groups for them to be installed by-hand. In structures like this, it doesn't make much sense to do branch-by-team since isolation already exists between the teams and is likely to be enforced by authorization in the SCC system. For example, a member from Team X doesn't have access to the source code in SCC for Team Y.

Context: When teams share source code but need to have changes isolated.

Practice: Consider branch-by-team.

Commit (check-in) practices

Committing changes in SCC is one of the tasks where you're guaranteed to have to cooperate with other team members. There are practices that can help make committing your changes much smoother. As the saying goes, "we can do this the hard way, or we can do this the easy way." The root cause of most commit pain is merge conflicts. The person at fault is always the person trying to commit and you'll usually not get much sympathy from the rest of the team, especially if they ascribe to the practices discussed in the following sections.

Merge remote changes before commit

When you commit your changes to the repository you run the risk of having a merge conflict. This conflict can be recognized by the SCC system (such as when two people modified the same file) and simply be rejected, or it may be more severe. You are certainly capable of committing a change that doesn't cause the SCC system to recognize a conflict, yet there could still be a conflict at the code or build level that causes build errors.

Simply committing changes will cause grief to the rest of the team (and could invoke the broke-the-build policy—which is sometimes harsh :). This can be avoided by merging the existing code into your local copy of the code before committing. It's as if you've committed your changes but that merge is only available locally.

Fortunately, some SCC systems, such as Git, simply don't let you commit anything, if there are any changes that you haven't fetched locally. Unfortunately, some SCC systems, such as TFS, don't mandate this and you run the risk of having to resolve build-time merge issues right in the trunk. Team members will not appreciate this.

Depending on the type of SCC this may be a matter of fetching the current code or performing a **Get Latest** command.

Context: When committing changes.

Practice: Fetch any changes that occurred while you were modifying the code.

To make life easier with regard to having many merges to deal with when you fetch the latest code, see the next section.

Commit frequently

Most of the principles around SCC help make working with source code over time easier. Tracking and backups are great features of SCC in that we can return to a specific state of the source code at any time.

Returning to this specific state is only possible if changes are committed to the repository. Anything that isn't committed to the repository cannot be returned to from within SCC.

Checking-in as frequently as possible is recommended. This generally means checking-in as soon as everything builds and all tests pass. If you don't commit that, continue working, and later realize that you had something that worked and now doesn't, you can't get SCC to help you find out where it stopped working the way you wanted it to. Had you committed your changes as soon as they *worked*, SCC would have had a record of that code.

If your changes *work* but can't be checked-in (that is, you need to work in isolation from the rest of the team), you should consider creating a branch. Practices such as feature branching might be a good fit for these particular scenarios because you'll likely be working on a *feature* that needs to be *feature complete*, before making its way into the trunk or into a parent branch.

Context: When making changes to code.

Practice: Check-in as soon as it is compiled and all tests pass.

Atomic commits

This may not seem intuitive without explanation. For any given group of code modifications, you may have several reasons to have modified the code, that is, I could have a set of code modifications that fixed a bug as well as added a feature.

Committing code changes such as this are not atomic changes—they include changes for many reasons. One of the benefits of SCC is that you can back out any given commit (or changeset). If there was a reason to back out a bug fix but the changeset included a new feature, backing out that changeset would require the feature to be re-implemented.

You could view this as another instance of the single responsibility principle. To paraphrase, every changeset should have only one reason to be backed out.

Context: When committing changesets.

Practice: Ensure that each changeset is atomic and has only one reason to be backed out.

This is best coupled with the commit frequently practice. The more often you commit, the more likely it will be that it is an atomic commit.

Occasionally connected source control

In this day and age, it's almost uncommon for a software development team to all be working in the same place at the same time. I see many teams with one or more remote developers that occasionally connect to the SCC. Even though you may have picked a SCC that doesn't play nice in this scenario, there are some tools you can get to help out with that. Tools such as SVNBridge and GoOffline make working offline with SCC systems, such as TFS, easier.

In most circumstances, SCC systems that don't support offline edits use the lock/edit/check-in model. In these cases you can simply perform a *check-out* before going offline. Adding new files to a project or solution can get a bit hairy, but with tools such as TFS and the TFPT `online` command, checking-in your changes will occur more smoothly when you're finally back online.

Context: When dealing with a SCC that doesn't fully support offline and you know you will be working offline.

Practice: Check-out all files as soon as you know you will be working offline.

Distributed source control

Distributed source control or **Distributed Version Control System** (**DVCS**), as the name might suggest, is neither source control for a distributed team, nor a source control system that operates on multiple computers. Distributed source control refers to how repositories can be interconnected and how commits can proliferate throughout the interconnected repositories.

For example, in a DVCS, the local computer acts as its own SCC. You can commit changes to your local SCC as often as you want and never be connected to the master source SCC. Only when you want to consolidate your changes back to the master do you need to actually connect to it, at which time you push your changes up the master.

A DVCS works slightly differently than a centralized SCC. For one thing, each local copy of the master is technically a branch, as you're committing to that branch in isolation from the master. If you view committing a change as one that gets committed to the master, then you have two commands to run, such as `commit` then `push`.

DVCSs work really well if all team members are offline from the master. Pushing changes back to the master is a manual process done whenever the user wishes changes to make their way into the master source code. This particular model is well suited for the open source community as members of a team are typically geographically distributed. However, any team that is geographically distributed can benefit from a DVCS.

There are a few DVCS implementations out there like Git and Mercurial (hg). Each of these tools performs the same basic tasks and has the same basic features. They both support local commits (both use the term *commit*) and both support pushing to a remote master (both use the term *push*).

Context: When dealing with a geographically distributed team.

Practice: Prefer a Distributed Version Control System or a distributed SCC.

As we're working in isolation with DVCS, whenever we commit we'll never *break the build* simply by committing. Pushing that commit up to the master without first checking to make sure it didn't break the build will, of course, introduce the possibility of breaking the build for the rest of the team.

Git, for whatever reason, allows direct manipulation of the history. You can rebase, reset, commit amend, and so on. This of course means that for any given copy of a repo it may contain code that never really existed because the history was modified after the clone or fetch. It's important to remember this when evaluating whether to use Git or Mercurial.

Context: In situations where repository immutability is important.

Practice: Choose Mercurial over Git.

Summary

As we've seen, source code control can be very complex indeed. We can manage the complexity of source code control systems that integrate into Visual Studio with some well-planned directory and solution structures. Working and collaborating with a team of developers is not without its trials and tribulations. Source code control helps us manage this through tracking and isolation, but not without caveats. We can help deal with caveats such as merge conflicts, distributed teams, and offline access through some well-planned practices.

In the next chapter, we will look at some low-level, language-specific practices. Topics like generics, lambdas, iterator members, extension methods, and exception handling will be detailed.

3
Low-level C# Practices

Syntax isn't the only thing that matters when it comes to writing code. We can't get far without getting past the compiler, but not everything that compiles is of acceptable quality. Practices and techniques beyond being "syntactically correct" are so important that there are entire third-party ecosystems devoted to detecting common issues and patterns in source code and in compiled code.

This chapter isn't about many of the issues that code analysis tools detect, but details some practices that can be used with C# to avoid certain pitfalls and improve quality. We'll look at recommended practices in the following areas:

- .NET generics
- Sequences and iterator members
- Lambdas
- Extension methods
- Exception handling

Working with generics

Visual Studio 2005 included .NET version 2.0 which included generics. **Generics** give developers the ability to design classes and methods that defer the specification of specific parts of a class or method's specification until declaration or instantiation.

Generics offer features previously unavailable in .NET. One benefit to generics, that is potentially the most common, is for the implementation of collections that provide a consistent interface to collections of different data types without needing to write specific code for each data type.

Constraints can be used to restrict the types that are supported by a generic method or class, or can guarantee specific interfaces.

Limits of generics

Constraints within generics in C# are currently limited to a parameter-less constructor, interfaces, or base classes, or whether or not the type is a `struct` or a `class` (value or reference type). This really means that code within a generic method or type can either be constructed or can make use of methods and properties.

Due to these restrictions types within generic types or methods cannot have operators.

Writing sequence and iterator members

Visual Studio 2005 and C# 2.0 introduced the `yield` keyword. The `yield` keyword is used within an iterator member as a means to effectively implement an `IEnumerable` interface without needing to implement the entire `IEnumerable` interface.

Iterator members are members that return a type of `IEnumerable` or `IEnumerable<T>`, and return individual elements in the enumerable via `yield return`, or deterministically terminates the enumerable via `yield break`. These members can be anything that can return a value, such as methods, properties, or operators. An iterator that returns without calling `yield break` has an implied `yield break`, just as a void method has an implied `return`.

Iterators operate on a sequence but process and return each element as it is requested. This means that iterators implement what is known as deferred execution. **Deferred execution** is when some or all of the code, although reached in terms of where the instruction pointer is in relation to the code, hasn't entirely been executed yet.

Iterators are methods that can be executed more than once and result in a different execution path for each *execution*. Let's look at an example:

```
public static IEnumerable<DateTime> Iterator()
{
  Thread.Sleep(1000);
  yield return DateTime.Now;
  Thread.Sleep(1000);
  yield return DateTime.Now;
  Thread.Sleep(1000);
  yield return DateTime.Now;
}
```

The `Iterator` method returns `IEnumerable` which results in three `DateTime` values. The creation of those three `DateTime` values is actually invoked at different times. The `Iterator` method is actually compiled in such a way that a state machine is created under the covers to keep track of how many times the code is invoked and is implemented as a special `IEnumerable<DateTime>` object. The actual invocation of the code in the method is done through each call of the resulting `IEnumerator.MoveNext` method.

The resulting `IEnumerable` is really implemented as a collection of delegates that are executed upon each invocation of the `MoveNext` method, where the state, in the simplest case, is really which of the delegates to invoke next. It's actually more complicated than that, especially when there are local variables and state that can change between invocations and is used across invocations. But the compiler takes care of all that.

Effectively, iterators are broken up into individual bits of code between `yield return` statements that are executed independently, each using potentially local shared data.

What are iterators good for other than a really cool interview question? Well, first of all, due to the deferred execution, we can technically create sequences that don't need to be stored in memory all at one time.

This is often useful when we want to project one sequence into another. Couple that with a source sequence that is also implemented with deferred execution, we end up creating and processing `IEnumerable`s (also known as collections) whose content is never all in memory at the same time. We can process large (or even infinite) *collections* without a huge strain on memory.

For example, if we wanted to model the set of positive integer values (an infinite set) we could write an iterator method shown as follows:

```
static IEnumerable<BigInteger> AllThePositiveIntegers()
{
  var number = new BigInteger(0);
  while (true) yield return number++;
}
```

We can then chain this iterator with another iterator, say something that gets all of the positive squares:

```
static IEnumerable<BigInteger> AllThePostivieIntegerSquares(
  IEnumerable<BigInteger> sourceIntegers)
{
  foreach(var value in sourceIntegers)
    yield return value*value;
}
```

Which we could use as follows:

```
foreach(var value in
  AllThePostivieIntegerSquares(AllThePositiveIntegers()))
  Console.WriteLine(value);
```

We've now effectively modeled two infinite collections of integers *in memory*.

Of course, our `AllThePostiveIntegerSquares` method could just as easily be used with finite sequences of values, for example:

```
foreach (var value in
  AllThePostivieIntegerSquares(
    Enumerable.Range(0, int.MaxValue)
      .Select(v => new BigInteger(v))))
  Console.WriteLine(value);
```

In this example we go through all of the positive `Int32` values and square each one without ever holding a complete collection of the set of values in memory.

As we see, this is a useful method for composing multiple steps that operate on, and result in, sequences of values.

We could have easily done this without `IEnumerable<T>`, or created an `IEnumerator` class whose `MoveNext` method performed calculations instead of navigating an array. However, this would be tedious and is likely to be error-prone. In the case of not using `IEnumerable<T>`, we'd be unable to operate on the data as a collection with things such as `foreach`.

Context: When modeling a sequence of values that is either known only at runtime, or each element can be reliably calculated at runtime.

Practice: Consider using an iterator.

Working with lambdas

Visual Studio 2008 introduced C# 3.0. In this version of C# lambda expressions were introduced. Lambda expressions are another form of anonymous functions. Lambdas were added to the language syntax primarily as an easier anonymous function syntax for LINQ queries. Although you can't really think of LINQ without lambda expressions, lambda expressions are a powerful aspect of the C# language in their own right. They are concise expressions that use implicitly-typed optional input parameters whose types are implied through the context of their use, rather than explicit definition as with anonymous methods.

Along with C# 3.0 in Visual Studio 2008, the .NET Framework 3.5 was introduced which included many new types to support LINQ expressions, such as `Action<T>` and `Func<T>`. These delegates are used primarily as definitions for different types of anonymous methods (including lambda expressions). The following is an example of passing a lambda expression to a method that takes a `Func<T1, T2, TResult>` delegate and the two arguments to pass along to the delegate:

```
ExecuteFunc((f, s) => f + s, 1, 2);
```

The same statement with anonymous methods:

```
ExecuteFunc(delegate(int f, int s) { return f + s; }, 1, 2);
```

It's clear that the lambda syntax has a tendency to be much more concise, replacing the `delegate` and braces with the "goes to" operator (=>). Prior to anonymous functions, member methods would need to be created to pass as delegates to methods. For example:

```
ExecuteFunc(SomeMethod, 1, 2);
```

This, presumably, would use a method named `SomeMethod` that looked similar to:

```
private static int SomeMethod(int first, int second)
{
  return first + second;
}
```

Lambda expressions are more powerful in the type inference abilities, as we've seen from our examples so far. We need to explicitly type the parameters within anonymous methods, which is only optional for parameters in lambda expressions.

LINQ statements don't use lambda expressions exactly in their syntax. The lambda expressions are somewhat implicit. For example, if we wanted to create a new collection of integers from another collection of integers, with each value incremented by one, we could use the following LINQ statement:

```
var x = from i in arr select i + 1;
```

The `i + 1` expression isn't really a lambda expression, but it gets processed as if it were first converted to method syntax using a lambda expression:

```
var x = arr.Select(i => i + 1);
```

The same with an anonymous method would be:

```
var x = arr.Select(delegate(int i) { return i + 1; });
```

What we see in the LINQ statement is much closer to a lambda expression. Using lambda expressions for all anonymous functions means that you have more consistent looking code.

Context: When using anonymous functions.

Practice: Prefer lambda expressions over anonymous methods.

Parameters to lambda expressions can be enclosed in parentheses. For example:

```
var x = arr.Select((i) => i + 1);
```

The parentheses are only mandatory when there is more than one parameter:

```
var total = arr.Aggregate(0, (l, r) => l + r);
```

Context: When writing lambdas with a single parameter.

Practice: Prefer no parenthesis around the parameter declaration.

Sometimes when using lambda expressions, the expression is being used as a delegate that takes an argument. The corresponding parameter in the lambda expression may not be used within the right-hand expression (or statements). In these cases, to reduce the clutter in the statement, it's common to use the underscore character (_) for the name of the parameter. For example:

```
task.ContinueWith(_ => ProcessSecondHalfOfData());
```

The `task.ContinueWith` method takes an `Action<Task>` delegate. This means the previous lambda expression is actually given a task instance (the antecedent `Task`). In our example, we don't use that task and just perform some completely independent operation. In this case, we use (_) to not only signify that we know we don't use that parameter, but also to reduce the clutter and potential name collisions a little bit.

Context: When writing lambda expression that take a single parameter but the parameter is not used.

Practice: Use underscore (_) for the name of the parameter.

There are two types of lambda expressions. So far, we've seen expression lambdas. **Expression lambdas** are a single expression on the right-hand side that evaluates to a value or `void`. There is another type of lambda expression called **statement lambdas**. These lambdas have one or more statements and are enclosed in braces. For example:

```
task.ContinueWith(_ => {
            var value = 10;
```

```
            value += ProcessSecondHalfOfData();
            ProcessSomeRandomValue(value);
            });
```

As we can see, statement lambdas can declare variables, as well as have multiple statements.

Working with extension methods

Along with lambda expressions and iterators, C# 3.0 brought us extension methods. These static methods (contained in a `static` class whose first argument is modified with the `this` modifier) were created for LINQ so `IEnumerable` types could be queried without needing to add copious amounts of methods to the `IEnumerable` interface.

An extension method has the basic form of:

```
public static class EnumerableExtensions
{
  public static IEnumerable<int> IntegerSquares(
    this IEnumerable<int> source)
  {
    return source.Select(value => value * value);
  }
}
```

As stated earlier, extension methods must be within a `static` class, be a `static` method, and the first parameter must be modified with the `this` modifier.

Extension methods extend the available *instance methods* of a type. In our previous example, we've effectively added an instance member to `IEnumerable<int>` named `IntegerSquares` so we get a sequence of integer values that have been squared.

For example, if we created an array of integer values, we will have added a `Cubes` method to that array that returns a sequence of the values cubed. For example:

```
var values = new int[] {1, 2, 3};
foreach (var v in values.Cubes())
{
  Console.WriteLine(v);
}
```

Having the ability to create new *instance methods* that operate on any public members of a specific type is a very powerful feature of the language.

This, unfortunately, does not come without some caveats.

Extension methods suffer inherently from a scoping problem. The only scoping that can occur with these methods is the namespaces that have been referenced for any given C# source file. For example, we could have two static classes that have two extension methods named `Cubes`. If those static classes are in the same namespace, we'd never be able to use those extensions methods as extension methods because the compiler would never be able to resolve which one to use. For example:

```
public static class IntegerEnumerableExtensions
{
  public static IEnumerable<int> Squares(
    this IEnumerable<int> source)
  {
    return source.Select(value => value * value);
  }
  public static IEnumerable<int> Cubes(
    this IEnumerable<int> source)
  {
    return source.Select(value => value * value * value);
  }
}
public static class EnumerableExtensions
{
  public static IEnumerable<int> Cubes(
    this IEnumerable<int> source)
  {
    return source.Select(value => value * value * value);
  }
}
```

If we tried to use `Cubes` as an extension method, we'd get a compile error, for example:

```
var values = new int[] {1, 2, 3};
foreach (var v in values.Cubes())
{
  Console.WriteLine(v);
}
```

This would result in **error CS0121: The call is ambiguous between the following methods or properties**.

To resolve the problem, we'd need to move one (or both) of the classes to another namespace, for example:

```
namespace Integers
{
  public static class IntegerEnumerableExtensions
  {
    public static IEnumerable<int> Squares(
      this IEnumerable<int> source)
    {
      return source.Select(value => value*value);
    }

    public static IEnumerable<int> Cubes(
      this IEnumerable<int> source)
    {
      return source.Select(value => value*value*value);
    }
  }
}

namespace Numerical
{
  public static class EnumerableExtensions
  {
    public static IEnumerable<int> Cubes(
      this IEnumerable<int> source)
    {
      return source.Select(value => value*value*value);
    }
  }
}
```

Then, we can scope to a particular namespace to choose which `Cubes` to use:

```
namespace ConsoleApplication
{
  using Numerical;

  internal class Program
  {
    private static void Main(string[] args)
    {
      var values = new int[] {1, 2, 3};
```

```
        foreach (var v in values.Cubes())
        {
          Console.WriteLine(v);
        }
      }
    }
  }
```

Context: When considering extension methods, due to potential scoping problems.

Practice: Use extension methods sparingly.

Context: When designing extension methods.

Practice: Keep all extension methods that operate on a specific type in their own class.

Context: When designing classes to contain methods to extend a specific type, `TypeName`.

Practice: Consider naming the static class `TypeNameExtensions`.

Context: When designing classes to contain methods to extend a specific type, in order to scope the extension methods.

Practice: Consider placing the class in its own namespace.

Generally, there isn't much need to use extension methods on types that you own. You can simply add an instance method to contain the logic that you want to have.

Where extension methods really shine is for effectively creating instance methods on interfaces.

Typically, when code is necessary for shared implementations of interfaces, an abstract base class is created so each implementation of the interface can derive from it to implement these shared methods. This is a bit cumbersome in that it uses the one-and-only inheritance slot in C#, so an interface implementation would not be able to derive or extend any other classes. Additionally, there's no guarantee that a given interface implementation will derive from the abstract base and runs the risk of not being able to be used in the way it was designed. Extension methods get around this problem by being entirely independent from the implementation of an interface while still being able to extend it.

One of the most notable examples of this might be the `System.Linq.Enumerable` class introduced in .NET 3.5. The static `Enumerable` class almost entirely consists of extension methods that extend `IEnumerable`. It is easy to develop the same sort of thing for our own interfaces. For example, say we have an `ICoordinate` interface to model a three-dimensional position in relation to the Earth's surface:

```
public interface ICoordinate
{
  /// <summary>North/south degrees from equator.</summary>
  double Latitude { get; set; }
  /// <summary>East/west degrees from meridian.</summary>
  double Longitude { get; set; }
  /// <summary>Distance from sea level in meters.</summary>
  double Altitude { get; set; }
}
```

We could create a `static` class to contain extension methods to provide *shared* functionality between any implementation of `ICoordinate`. For example:

```
public static class Coordinate
{
  public static void MoveUp(this ICoordinate coordinate,
    double meters)
  {
    coordinate.Altitude += meters;
  }
}
```

Context: When designing interfaces that require shared code.

Practice: Consider providing extension methods instead of abstract base implementations.

Exception handling

It was pretty sketchy when exceptions were first introduced to programming languages. They've been around in some form or another in languages dating back to the seventies. Smalltalk is likely the oldest language with exception handling abilities. Similarly-aged C includes an ability to *signal* that could be used for general exception communications, but it is intended more to provide *interrupts*. C also includes the ability to "long jump", but this is mostly provided within the library rather than in the language, that is, there is a `setjmp` method to define a destination (for example a handler) and a `longjmp` method to "throw." But `setjmp/longjmp` is no more than a "non-local goto"—there's no decoupling of the handler from the thrower. It's very complex and error-prone to use `setjmp/longjmp` for exception handling. So complex that the intent of the methods using it can easily get lost.

Smalltalk effectively includes syntax for throwing and handling exceptions. Smalltalk included an ability to use types as monikers for exceptions, effectively decoupling the code that *threw* an exception from the code that *caught* the exception. Neither the handler, nor the code raising the exception needed to know about each other or share current execution state information between one another (such as `setjmp`/`longjmp`). Smalltalk effectively builds exception handling on signaling.

The most common exception handling syntax in modern languages builds on `try`/`catch`/`throw`. Some languages have some variants (such as `finally`, `ensure`, `raise`, and so on) but a `try`/`catch` model is the most common.

Despite existing in languages dating back more than 40 years, exception throwing and handling is still commonly misunderstood and misused by many programmers. Exceptions are even misused by "seasoned" programmers.

Exceptions are a way of providing hierarchical error communication from one piece of code to another. Through the use of exception types, rather than line numbers/labels or memory locations, handlers can be entirely decoupled from a code that throws exceptions from everything but the current stack frame.

There are other means of communicating errors between different pieces of code in C#, but they're tightly coupled, limiting, and are not "opt-in". You can easily communicate error information back to the calling code by means of a return code. However, this ensures the calling code must handle the error either by responding to the error code or by passing it along to its caller. Everything up the potential call graph is required to "buy in" to the return code concept. Exception handling is generally an "opt-in" error handling syntax, where only code that is deemed able to handle the exception need to handle or even know about exceptions. This means that a call graph dozens of levels deep can support propagating errors to the highest level from the lowest level simply with one `try`/`catch` and one `throw`.

There are some basic practices about exception handling that I won't detail here other than outline them for completeness.

Context: When designing logic flow.

Practice: Don't use exceptions for normal logic flow.

Now, saying "don't use exceptions for normal logic flow" is different than acknowledging that exceptions exist and can occur. The `finally` keyword provides the ability to acknowledge that exceptions can occur and circumvent yet-to-be-executed code without pulling them into normal logic flow. The `finally` keyword allows programmers to acknowledge that exceptions occur without a need to handle exceptions and to perform logic that is necessary both when exceptions do occur and when they don't.

For example, when I instantiate a `StreamWriter` object, I'm actually opening a file. Regardless of whether I have an exception or not, I want to make sure I close this file as soon as possible when I know I'm no longer using it. The garbage collector will be kind enough to clean up for me, but on its own timeframe. If I don't explicitly close my stream writer before the object goes out of scope, I run into a possibility of opening the file twice at one time, possibly with dire consequences. I can use `finally` to accomplish my goal:

```
StreamWriter writer = new StreamWriter("file.txt");
try
{
  writer.Write("some text");
}
finally
{
  writer.Close();
}
```

This ensures that regardless of whether the `Write` of `"some text"` succeeded, I close my file and flush any potential buffer that `StreamWriter` might be using.

Context: When writing code that requires execution in the presence of exceptions or not.

Practice: Use a `try/finally` variant.

Of course, in this example, `StreamWriter` implements `IDisposable` and has a `Dispose` method. I could have written it as follows and gotten the same effect as the previous example:

```
StreamWriter writer = new StreamWriter("file.txt");
try
{
  writer.Write("some text");
}
finally
{
  writer.Dispose();
}
```

But there is a built-in keyword in C# as a shortcut for this particular pattern of using an `IDisposable` object and calling `Dispose` when it goes out of scope: the `using` keyword. For example:

```
using (StreamWriter writer = new StreamWriter("file.txt"))
{
  writer.Write("some text");
}
```

Context: When writing code that requires an object be disposed in the presence of exceptions or not.

Practice: Prefer the `using` statement.

At this point I think it's important to define what *handling* exceptions really means. A `catch` block is technically an *exception handler*, but **exception handling** is the process of catching an exception and not letting it escape to a point higher-up the call stack.

So far this may seem fairly simple, and you might be wondering "okay, but how do I *handle* exceptions?" Handling exceptions and catching exceptions are really two different things (much the same as fruits are vegetables, but all vegetables are not fruits). You must catch an exception to handle it, but catching an exception isn't the only part of *handling* the exception.

Sometimes you might want to catch an exception, but not *handle* it. For example:

```
using(StreamWriter streamWriter =
  new StreamWriter("FirstFile.txt"))
{
  streamWriter.WriteLine(FirstFileText);
}
try
{
  using (StreamWriter streamWriter =
    new StreamWriter("secondFile.txt"))
  {
    streamWriter.WriteLine(SecondFileText);
  }
}
catch (IOException)
{
  // delete the first file if
  // we had a problem with the second.
  File.Delete("FirstFile.txt");
  throw;
}
```

The example we just saw basically models a transaction. We have a transaction, that means the first file can't exist without a correct second file. If the second file cannot be created, we can't have the first file. It is an example of wanting to catch but not *handle* an exception. We pass the exception up the stack to something that might be able to catch it and do something useful with it, like inform the user of the problem (which we can't do in this code as it's too low-level). The previous example shows the use of the `throw` statement without an `IOException` or `Exception` instance. This is an example of *re-throwing* the current exception. This should not be confused with throwing an instance of a caught exception. For example:

```
StreamWriter writer = new StreamWriter("file.txt");
try
{
  writer.Write("some text");
}
catch(IOException ioException)
{
  Logger.Error(
    String.Format("trying to write to {0}", "file.txt"),
    ioException);
  throw ioException;
}
```

The previous example takes the exception instance that was caught (`ioException`) and *passes* it to the `throw` statement. This isn't re-throwing an exception, this is throwing a new exception by re-using an existing exception. This statement is saying that an `IOException` occurred in this block, not that we want to "re-throw" the existing exception.

This has the distinct drawback of completely losing the context of the original exception (the stack trace) and tells exception handlers higher up the stack that the exception occurred here, but not in the original place. While this propagates an exception, you have no way of figuring out where the original exception occurred and what to do about it if you are trying to debug your code. If you aren't at or before `throw ioException`, you'll need to restart the program and try to reproduce the exception to figure out what the real problem is. This is almost always not what you want.

Context: When attempting to catch and pass along caught exceptions.

Practice: Re-throw exceptions correctly.

Of course, sometimes you may want to still communicate runtime errors further up the stack, but not re-throw or re-use the current exception context. One possible scenario is that you want provide more, or extra, information. Given the context of your code *and* the fact that a particular exception occurred, that combination may have more implicit information than the existing exception alone. Despite thousands of person-hours invested into the .NET Framework, not all exception types, and not all thrown exceptions, may provide explicit enough information on their own for an exception handler to act upon a particular exception. There are probably various examples of this in the framework with exceptions such as `InvalidOperationException` or `ArgumentException`. Usually these exceptions are very contextual to a specific implementation.

An example of this technique could be in the following form:

```
public char GetCharacter(int offset)
{
  try
  {
    return text[index];
  }
  catch (IndexOutOfRangeException indexOutOfRangeException)
  {
    throw new ArgumentException("Offset is out of range",
      "offset",
      indexOutOfRangeException);
  }
}
```

The fact that we're using a `string` object is a bit of an implementation which means `offset` makes for a leaky abstraction. It may not be clear that the `offset` parameter is an index, making `IndexOutOfRangeException` potentially unexpected. In this case, we can simply catch the implementation-specific `IndexOutOfRangeException` and translate it or adapt it to another, more apt exception. In this case, we chose `ArgumentException`. It tells the caller that a particular argument (`offset`, in our example) was invalid. You could go so far as to create your own application-specific exception to communicate this, or more, information to the caller. But for our example, we'll just use one of the system exceptions.

Context: When using implementation-specific code.

Practice: Don't let confusing implementation-specific exceptions leak your implementation details.

At this point, I hope it seems clear that catching an exception should be an explicit act. You're either handling the exception or re-throwing the exception. But I think it's important to point out that you shouldn't be using `catch` if you are not handling an exception or re-throwing it. I can't think about a reason why you'd use `catch` if you weren't doing one of these two things, but I've seen my fair share of the following lines of code:

```
catch (Exception)
{
  throw;
}
```

I don't know why I've seen this so often, but don't do it.

Context: When thinking about using `catch`.

Practice: Don't catch exceptions you don't handle or re-throw.

Handling an exception means not allowing the exception to propagate up the stack to other handlers of that exception, to its bases, or to the top-level exception handler. Another name for this is **exception swallowing**. It's important that if you do catch an exception and swallow it, that you are truly handling the exception. For example:

```
public void DoLittle(Stream stream)
{
  try
  {
    stream.Write(myData, 0, myData.Length);
  }
  catch (Exception exception)
  {
    GetLogger().Error("", exception);
  }
}
```

The programmer probably thought it was fairly innocuous to not allow any exceptions to escape from this method. It presumably had the context to log things to some destination, so he probably figured logging the error and "swallowing and forgetting" it seemed like the best option.

Unfortunately, in this case, this method doesn't own the `Stream` object, so swallowing the exception keeps any callers further up the stack from knowing that there's a problem. This means they're free to use their `Stream` instance that may be in a really bad state. The best case is that the same type of exception, with the same details, is thrown when they try to use stream again. But the worst case is that another exception is thrown that provides no detail as to why (because that was swallowed elsewhere), leading the developer on a wild goose chase to figure out what went wrong when, had they simply gotten the original exception, they may have had all of the information at their fingertips.

Context: When designing whether or not to catch exceptions.

Practice: Don't swallow and forget.

Exception handling is about knowing what exception occurred and compensating for it. Being able to compensate for exceptions generally requires some specific knowledge. Some times compensation is usually delegated to the end user. For example, while writing to a file I may get an `IOException` because I have run out of disk space. I could, of course, not handle that exception and let the application terminate abnormally losing any in-memory data. Most end users I deal with don't like this for some reason. While it's difficult to specifically tell if an exception is due to out of disk space conditions (and more difficult to actually do anything about lack of disk space programmatically), it's fairly easy to inform the user of the problem and let them retry the action in question. For example:

```
private void saveButton_Click(object sender, EventArgs e)
{
  bool retry = false;
  do
  {
    try
    {
      using(Stream stream =
        new FileStream(filePath,
          FileMode.OpenOrCreate,
          FileAccess.Write))
      using(BinaryWriter streamWriter =
        new BinaryWriter(stream))
      {
        streamWriter.Write(applicationData);
      }
    }
    catch (IOException ioException)
    {
```

```
            retry = DialogResult.Retry == MessageBox.Show(this,
              "Error",
              String.Format("The following error "+
                "occurred writing to a file:"+
                "{0}{1}{0}If you have fixed the "+
                "problem, press Retry",
                ioException.Message,
                Environment.NewLine),
              MessageBoxButtons.RetryCancel);
          }
        } while (retry);
      }
```

This code recognizes the fact that `BinaryWriter.Write` can fail for a number of IO problems, all of which are abstracted within a single `IOException` class. This code just passes along the message to the `IOException` class that contains and asks the user to press the **Retry** button if they have fixed the problem. The code itself doesn't really do anything to *handle* the exception. Instead, it delegates to the user then trusts the user to press **Retry** to signify that the problem was "handled."

The ability to do things such as this hinges on the ability to discern specific types, and thus specific contexts of exceptions. You cannot do this if your `catch` block catches `Exception`.

Context: When catching exceptions.

Practice: Don't catch all exceptions (that is `Exception`).

Wow, you might be thinking exceptions are all about how to correctly handle exceptions. But people are prone to errors when they throw exceptions too. As with many other tools, exceptions can help you only if they're used properly. Exceptions are used to provide actionable error information to indeterminate code further up the call stack. The key point here is *actionable*. Providing code with the fact that something went wrong as an exception without details of how they could possibly compensate for the problem really means the code must simply pass the exception along to eventually let the application terminate abnormally. For example:

```
if(x != 42)
{
  throw new Exception("something went wrong");
}
```

Not being able to programmatically take action on an exception doesn't provide much value to the end users (lost data, lost progress, lost time, and so on, doesn't generally make them happy).

Context: When designing code that throws exceptions.

Practice: Create explicit exception types to model situations that require explicit handling.

Probably one of the best examples of violating everything that exceptions stand for is this simple snippet of code: `throw new Exception()`.

In order to catch this exception, a handler would be required to write `catch Exception exception` (or simply `catch`), which seems innocuous, but this also means that it will also catch every single other possible exception.

The `throw new Exception()` snippet of code provides no intent, which means catching it can infer no intent either. The handler cannot know if it was your `throw new Exception()` intent that it's catching or some other intent such as `FileNotFoundException`. In which case, the handler cannot know, based on the type alone, that it's truly *handling* an exception correctly or hiding an exception. Throwing `Exception` is usually just hiding the fact that exceptions are being used for normal program flow.

Yes, you could use the `Exception` instance's `GetType()` method to figure out if the type is actually `Exception` or not, or you could use the `Exception` instance's `Message` property to textually compare to a string literal, but don't. You're only limiting the possible miscaught exceptions, or not illuminating them (for example, someone else used `throw new Exception()` or used `"something went wrong"` as the exception message).

Context: When writing code to communicate runtime errors.

Practice: Don't throw `Exception`.

One of the huge benefits of exception handling in C# is the ability to decouple the code raising the runtime error, from the code handling the runtime error, based on an `Exception`-derived type. This means that you can communicate common runtime errors, or you can communicate specific runtime errors. If you perform an action whose runtime error is best abstracted by throwing `FileNotFoundException`, you can simply throw a `FileNotFoundException` and handlers further up the stack will know what you mean. If you have a specific circumstance that is specific to your application and a specific context, then you can create a unique exception type to model that runtime error. That way, only things that catch `Exception` or your specific exception can handle the runtime error condition.

This ideally means that the condition by which a handler decides to handle an exception is based solely on the type of the exception. Everything within the `catch` block is devoted to handling the exception, and nothing else.

If you need to resort to some state on the exception instance (such as `Message`), then the exception isn't designed properly, or the faulting code isn't throwing the right exception. Your exception handler is forced to take on too much responsibility and you're not using C#'s exception abilities to their greatest potential. You've effectively created two places where the decision to handle an exception is made.

Context: When designing exceptions.

Practice: Prefer to rely on exception type rather than exception state.

Exceptions to the exception practices

As with any practices, they're contextual. We've detailed some really useful exception practices, but most don't have a universal context. There are places where you do "violate" these practices. Let's have a look at a few.

There's at least one place in every program that relinquishes control back to the system and never comes back. In .NET, this is generally the return from the `Program.Main` method. Whatever exception is allowed to be thrown out of `Program.Main` exits the application. The system might do something unspecific with it, such as dump it to a console, but from the application's point of view, this means we're done. None of our code is generally going to run again for this invocation.

This is a unique situation. This effectively means that there aren't any other handlers further up the call stack, so any practices we have that are meant to alleviate problems with handlers further up the call stack are moot. I call this situation the **top-level exception handler** or the **last-chance exception handler**. This handler has some special status. It can do things we'd normally not want to do in any other exception handler.

The best example is catching `Exception`. In a top-level exception handler, we have a good reason to catch `Exception`. We may want to log that exception before we terminate. This is the last chance we have to do anything with the exception, such as track it. For example:

```
static void Main(string[] args)
{
  try
  {
    DoAllTheThings(args);
  }
```

```
    catch (Exception exception)
    {
      using(StreamWriter writer =
        new StreamWriter("log.txt"))
      {
        writer.Write(
          string.Format(
            "Exception:{0}{1}{0}{2}",
            Environment.NewLine,
            exception.Message,
            exception.StackTrace));
      }
    }
  }
```

In this example, we delegate from the `Main` method, to `DoAllTheThings`, presumably to do all of the work and leave `Main` responsible to be the top-level exception handler. Then, we catch `Exception` and dump the details that we find important out to a text file called `log.txt`.

Context: When considering designing reliable applications.

Practice: Consider thread/process entry-points as last-chance exception handlers.

The `Program.Main` method isn't the only place where we have a top-level exception handler. The entry-points of other threads are also top-level exception handlers. I detail "other" because every process has at least one thread, and with .NET, the entry-point for that thread is really `Program.Main`.

By default threads in .NET are actions rather than functions. They don't communicate results back to the invoking thread. There are all sorts of application-specific magic that you can write to communicate *results* back from a newly spawned thread, but there are better ways of doing that nowadays. Suffice it to say that if you're not communicating results from one thread to another, you probably don't have an infrastructure to communicate any exceptions that occurred during processing of that action. To that end, it's useful to consider entry-points such as this as last-chance exception handlers and do what you need to do to make your application robust and reliable, such as log the problem. The following code is very much similar to what we did in `Program.Main`:

```
  private static void ThreadEntry()
  {
    try
    {
      DoAllTheThingsInBackground();
```

```
    }
    catch (Exception exception)
    {
      GetLogger().Error("Oops, ran into a problem.",
        exception);
    }
  }
```

For interest's sake, you may invoke this thread entry on its own thread with code similar to the following:

```
var thread = new Thread(new ThreadStart(ThreadEntry));
thread.Start();
```

You may not want to simply catch `Exception` and log it with all thread "entry-points." The framework provides the ability to spawn threads in order to calculate results asynchronously. In these circumstances, the ability to communicate the results back to the calling thread (or back to a specific thread) usually includes the ability to throw these exceptions asynchronously.

Context: When considering top-level exception handlers in "thread entry-points."

Practice: Avoid swallowing exceptions in situations where asynchronous exceptions are supported.

In these cases I generally recommend using thread pool threads and parts of the framework such as the **Task Parallel Library** (**TPL**), instead of manually creating threads.

Summary

As we've seen, there are many practices that we can use in our everyday programming and design that go a level beyond just the syntax of the language we're using. Syntax is often is added to a language for specific reasons. It's useful to know the principles behind why the syntax changed or was added to. This chapter covered some more recent additions to the language, such as lambdas and extension methods. With some simple practices we can make better use of this syntax.

In the next chapter, we'll look at some architecture-specific practices. These practices will include things such as decoupling, data-centric applications, and we'll take a brief look at some recommendations for distributed architectures.

4

Architectural Practices

Any software project with any level of complexity is generally built on some sort of architecture. This architecture is effectively the design vision of the system. It provides a high-level design view of how the system will be put together and how it fulfills requirements at that level.

It's one thing to simply document or communicate a system's architecture; it's another thing to base an architecture on sound practices that re-use tried-and-true techniques, practices, and technologies among others.

For the most part, this chapter deals with low-level architecture practices and details some of the practices that are generally accepted in the industry that I frequently see people having problems with, or "forgetting the principles" behind them. After a brief list of terms, we'll look at the recommended practices involving the following topics:

- Decoupling
- Data-based applications
- Distributed architecture

Terms

Top-level architecture is a high-level, system-wide, all-encompassing architecture that describes the top-level components in the system. Depending on the requirements, this architecture might detail certain things such as communications methods, distribution of components, platform types, technology types, and so on.

Low-level architecture is a high-level description of a subsystem or a part of a larger system. Low-level architecture should describe external interfaces, internal components, and other aspects that describe how certain requirements are fulfilled.

Impedance Mismatch came out of the **Object-Relational Mapping** (**ORM**) movement, and attempts to describe the inherent disparity between what a relational database can model and what an OO language can model. This type of mismatch occurs outside the relational databases and can rear its head anywhere two different types of systems integrate.

Decoupling is the process of reducing dependencies, or changing the type of dependencies, between two components.

Decoupling

To a certain extent, any architecture, whether it is a low-level or a high-level architecture, is a form of decoupling. An architecture's intention is to detail logical and physical abstractions to a certain level. Abstractions are the most common method of decoupling. Something that depends on an abstraction instead of something that is concrete is said to be loosely coupled since it does not directly depend on certain implementation details.

In any system that requires two components, you can never completely decouple the two. At the very least, the system won't work without both components. Decoupling isn't about removing a component from a system, rather it's about distilling dependencies down to depending on components that are more stable. Ideally, abstractions should be the most stable, so an idea dependency is upon an abstraction.

To a certain extent, an architecture is the decoupling vision of an application or system. Most of the decisions about decoupling should be made at the architectural level. The impetus for these decisions is generally influenced by how the application or system needs to be deployed, what types of technical resources are available or required, and certain non-functional requirements.

Command Query Separation

Bertrand Meyer coined the acronym **CQS** (**Command Query Separation**) when he defined the principle of separating actions (methods that modify state) or queries (methods that only query state). He went on to detail that a *command* is an action. He suggested that methods should either be a command or a query, but not both. This concept is detailed in other areas with concepts such as "side-effect-free" functions.

The ability to break down responsibilities to their lowest granularity is generally useful in software design. It reduces coupling and can introduce better explicitness, which improves maintainability.

Principle: Methods should either be a command that performs an action and modifies state, or a query that returns the current state to the caller.

More specifically, it is generally accepted that methods should be side-effect free whenever possible.

Of course, this general concept introduces some complexity in certain areas. Martin Fowler exemplifies this with the following stack example:

A `Pop` method on a stack ideally both pops something off the stack (thus mutating observable state) and returns what was popped off the stack. For example:

```
var elementCount = stack.Count;
var element = stack.Pop();
Debug.Assert(elementCount - 1 == stack.Count);
```

It would become complex, and arguably confusing, for the last element that was popped off to be a state of the stack. Arguably, you could implement a stack in the following way:

```
var stack = new MyStack<int>();
var elementCount = stack.Count;
stack.Pop();
var element = stack.LastPopped;
```

However, this would be confusing. Plus, it would potentially introduce an invariant into the code that used this type of stack in the context of multiple threads. The last-popped element changes from private data (local to the `Pop` method and returned) to shared data (an instance member of the stack class). Being shared data means it needs to be protected in a multi-threaded context. Using `Pop` in this context would require some sort of synchronization, likely right on the stack instance itself, depending on how it is used. For example:

```
lock (stack)
{
  var elementCount = stack.Count;
  stack.Pop();
  var element = stack.LastPopped;
  Debug.Assert(elementCount - 1 == stack.Count);
}
```

Note that `Count` is also shared and would also require protection, which is why it is included in the `lock` block.

Context: When considering CQS.

Practice: Only separate commands from queries, where appropriate.

Data Transfer Objects (DTO)

Martin Fowler created the First Law of Distributing Objects in which he stated, "*Don't distribute your objects.*"

Unfortunately, this law has been misinterpreted in many ways. This law is not meant to imply that the data related to an instance of a class shouldn't be distributed to another node and utilized with other logic (potentially with the same class definition). What it is trying to communicate is that you shouldn't wrap these objects in some sort of object-distribution framework and expect that a method call on such an object would be magically distributed to some other node.

Distribution requires much more thought (as we'll see shortly). This thought almost always results in the packaging of the data that needs to be operated on, and shipping it to a remote location. You want to be able to use your classes in a way that makes sense to you. A remote call to some other node is not something you want done implicitly.

Another problem with directly using your domain objects as the source of the data being transmitted stems from the ability of these domain classes to take on the responsibility of serialization themselves (typically, classes serialize themselves, or are serializable in .NET). This tightly couples the domain class to *that* data transfer implementation detail. Throughout a system, there may be multiple reasons for data to be serialized. One reason may be to transfer object data to distribute an action (think `System.Action<T>`). Other reasons may be to store the current state to the file system for later retrieval, or to store state into a database, and so on. The need for these various serializations is independent of what the domain does (the business logic), and how the serialization implemented is generally less stable than the business logic. (That is, user interfaces, number of components in the system, interaction of components, how the system is distributed, and more, are all independent of the business logic). To push that instability indirectly into domain classes, by forcing them to take on the responsibility of various forms of serialization at the whim of other components increases the risk of error. That is, every time a class is changed to support external serialization, the risk of introducing a bug increases, despite the business rules not changing.

The recommended practice of dealing with this, in the general case, is to use a pattern called **Data Transfer Object** (**DTO**). This pattern details creating a type to encapsulate only the data that is required to be transferred. This generally goes against the object-oriented design because we're effectively creating a "struct" (in C++ terms) or a "value object" (in Domain Driven Design terms), that has no behavior. However, that DTO can *only* be used for transferring data, it cannot be used with business logic (behavior).

Context: When transferring domain data.

Practice: Use the DTO pattern.

Using DTOs can get somewhat complex because (once you have a need for a particular DTO) you need to do the following:

- Create the DTO class
- Create an ability to serialize and deserialize a DTO instance
- Create code to transfer a serialized DTO data
- Create code to translate from the domain object to the DTO (and create the DTO)
- Create code to translate from the DTO to the domain object (and create the domain object)

You can imagine that in a complex domain with dozens or hundreds of domain classes this could be quite a bit of work.

Fortunately, there are techniques and frameworks available that allow us to mitigate the work involved in supporting this. One technique is to create a general mapper that automatically maps DTOs and domain objects. The simplest form of this is to use convention to match property types and names, and copy data implicitly. As DTOs and domain objects evolve independently, the mapper will need to be configured to be able to perform that custom translation. There are existing frameworks, such as AutoMapper, available that perform this very task.

Context: When designing the ability to convert DTOs and domain objects back and forth.

Practice: Use a framework to map DTOs and domain objects back and forth.

More information about AutoMapper can be found at `https://github.com/AutoMapper/AutoMapper` (`http://bit.ly/LeVhD0`).

Single responsibility

Single Responsibility Principle (SRP) states "a class should have one, and only one reason to change". While this principle is generally viewed as applying to classes, it can be applied to many other aspects of software design. For example, individual components of a system should exhibit high cohesiveness, and therefore should have related responsibilities and reasons for change.

I try to apply this principle through all levels of my applications and systems. Aspects of a system that has single responsibility are more cohesive and have the benefits of cohesion, such as readability/understandability, eased maintenance, and reduced duplication. Components of a system or components of source code that take on a single responsibility are more easily used in situations that call for that responsibility. SRP also means there are generally less things going on at once (or in one place), making it easier to understand and modify.

Context: When designing and implementing any logical or physical component.

Practice: Ensure SRP in that the component is cohesive and has one reason to change.

Layering

Layers are a design technique to logically group similar functionalities. Specifically, layers group together subtasks at a particular level of abstraction. You could say layering is a form of grouping by responsibility (see SRP in previous section). Grouping related functionalities into layers has some specific attributes over and above simply conceptually thinking of a group of classes as one particular layer.

A real-world layer is something that is laid atop another layer. Physically, one layer can at most contact two other layers (the layer above and the layer below). It cannot contact any other layers. Logical layers in software design are similar. When we create layers and implement them, we organize them from lower-level concepts to higher-level concepts. Logical layers differ slightly from real-world layers in that they "contact" (or take dependencies) only in one direction: downward.

In other words, lower-level layers never know about higher-level layers even though logically they're adjacent. Take the following diagram, for example:

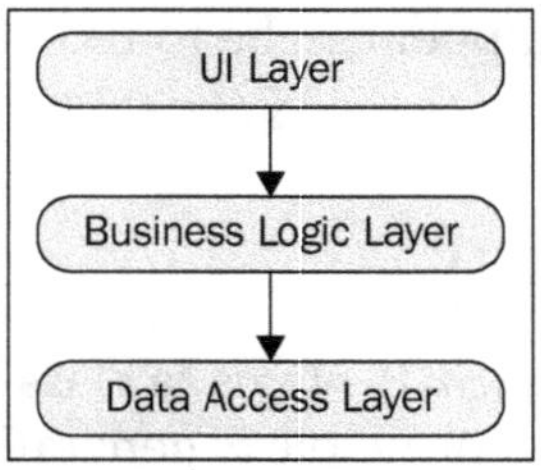

This diagram details that the **UI Layer** makes use of the **Business Logic Layer**, and the **Business Logic Layer** makes use of the **Data Access Layer**. This shows that the lower-level layers are not dependent on higher-level layers (the arrows point downward). For example, the **Data Access Layer** would never take a dependency on, or use, the **Business Logic Layer**, and the **Business Logic Layer** would never take a dependency on the **UI Layer**.

In reality, this three-layer architecture isn't fine-grained enough. Implementing a three-layer architecture like this means there are concerns that don't necessarily belong in any of the three layers, and have no place to live, therefore often getting shoe-horned into one of the three layers. This often leads to violations of the abstraction-between-layers and unidirectional-dependency rules since there are various concerns in a software system that are used by multiple layers.

Choosing to design layers into a software system could be driven by several motivations. As with our class-level abstractions, we gain componentization and independence. One motivation for a layered design may be that of robustness and quality. As we further increase the componentization of a system, we increase its ability to be changed and decrease its fragility.

Layers can help make the relationship between types relate by level abstraction and their subtask explicit.

Context: When dealing with many subtasks related by level of abstraction.

Practice: Consider using the layering pattern.

Data-based applications

It's hard to write software that doesn't deal with some sort of data that needs to be processed, stored, retrieved, and displayed in some form or another. While technologies that store data have only begun to change recently, frameworks to access these technologies change very frequently. Someone once quipped that Microsoft data development technology changes every four years. While this trend seems to have slowed in recent years, there's a trend away from relational data (the type of data these data development technologies interface with) towards non-relational data and "big data." One could argue that we're in the shadow of yet another data access framework from Microsoft. Regardless, we want to decouple our dependence on a particular framework or a particular data storage technology in as many places as possible.

While we're not particularly designing or architecting a system to support changing a data framework or changing a data store on-the-fly, we want to decouple components with data access responsibility away from other components. If your choice of data store or data framework isn't stable, you would want to decouple things that are more stable (or stable differently) from that instability. The stability of any one component is only as high as its least stable dependencies. A component changes as long as any dependency changes. Like SRP, there should be a limited number of reasons for a component to change. Having unstable dependencies gives it the wrong reasons to change, or the wrong reasons to be unstable.

When we start to deploy applications that use data and databases, we start to see how the data is used and how that usage affects the database and the rest of the system. Depending on the architecture and the design, we can start to see that, despite a certain level of decoupling through abstractions, those abstractions are leaking dependencies.

Let's look at a typical data-based architecture. The most frequent architecture that I've encountered which deals with data is the single-database architecture. All features of the system access a single database and this is usually a single catalog (in connection string parlance). When you have any sort of data in a system, you generally have requirements to report on that data. Reporting can have a huge impact on the data changes that a database will allow at any given time, and also the load on the database. When generating a report, the query for the report may put columns or rows into a read-only state. If that query takes a long time, that read-only state might be in place for a long time (in computer timeframes, a "long time" may be several seconds). While in a read-only state, the rest of the application will be blocked from writing to those columns or rows. If the data is locked for a long time, this leads to responsiveness problems in the best case, and timeouts in the worst case.

The basic problem is that write-heavy components access the same data as read-heavy or read-only components. In other words, commands to modify data happen on the same data that is being queried. The concept of CQS can be expanded here to segregate read responsibility from write responsibility. The pattern is called **Command/Query Responsibility Segregation** (**CQRS**). We can apply this pattern at the class level, but separating write-heavy components from read-heavy, or read-only components from each other at the data level can also have many benefits.

Object Relational Mappers (ORMs)

Within a platform, there are generally classes available to communicate with a range of relational database implementations. In the Windows arena, we've had things such as ODBC, ADO, ADO.NET, MDAC, OLEDB, among others. In .NET we have various wrappers around ADO.NET to provide access to various brands of databases.

In order to get data in and out of a database with ADO.NET, we had to write quite a bit of code to map from the data model to our domain model. For example, if we wanted to read and map customer data from a customer table in a relational database, we could use ADO.NET as follows:

```
public Customer FindCustomer(int id)
{
  using (var connection =
    new SqlConnection(connectionString))
  {
    var command = new SqlCommand(
                         "SELECT ID, Name, Phone, " +
                         "Street, City, Province, " +
                         "Country, PostalCode " +
                         "FROM Customer" +
                         "WHERE ID = @ID",
                         connection);
    command.Parameters.Add("@ID", SqlDbType.Int);
    command.Parameters["@ID"].Value = id;
    connection.Open();
    var dr = command.ExecuteReader();

    while (dr.Read())
    {
      return new Customer(
                (int) dr["ID"],(string) dr["Name"],
                (string) dr["Phone"],(string) dr["Street"],
                (string) dr["City"],(string) dr["Province"],
                (string) dr["Country"],
    }
    return null;
  }
}
```

With this, we need to create a `SqlConnection` that models our connection to that database based on a `connectionString`. We then create a `SqlCommand`, which encapsulates our SQL query which will be executed in the context of the `SqlConnection` and the parameter customer ID we're looking for. We then execute the command in the context of a "reader" that returns rows of data as a `SqlDataReader`. We then `Read` the first (and only expected) row, and then use that reader's indexer to access each column in the resultant row as parameters to the `Customer` constructor.

Imagine needing to do this for dozens of tables and domain classes. Imagine if there wasn't a class-per-table mapping and joins were necessary! A scary prospect, indeed. Even if we did take that task on and completed it, now our code is tightly coupled to the schema of the database. I have magical strings that represent queries into the database (a DBAs nightmare). Any tuning or design changes could result in recompilation of the code and redeployment.

With LINQ to SQL or Entity Framework, you could define the relationships between tables and classes within a designer, effectively as configuration, and offload the mapping heavy lifting to a framework. Then the only code we'd need to write is the code that accesses the context, for example:

```
public Customer FindCustomer(int id)
{
  using (var database =
    new DatabaseDataContext(connectionString))
  {
    var q = from cust in database.Customers
          where cust.ID == 1 select cust;
    return q.SingleOrDefault();
  }
}
```

Here we access the `Customers` IQueryable on the database context, use LINQ syntax to define a filter (`cust.ID == 1`), and return the single result or default (`null`). We've removed the configuration from `FindCustomer` (the SQL text, the command, the parameter, and others) and pushed it off to a DBML file. Even with this solution we need to recompile and redeploy. The only code that is recompiled is effectively generated from the DBML configuration file. This particular example is a data-first scenario, where the classes used to get data from the data access technology to our code are all generated. Because these classes are completely generated, we don't have as much flexibility with what types of data is used since we're limited by our Impedance Mismatch. Due to this, it's a good idea to treat these generated classes like any transfer of data to an external source, use DTOs. Once you run into a problem with Impedance Mismatch, you need to create an abstraction (DTO) to hide the implementation details of that mismatch.

Context: When dealing with data access technology generated classes.

Practice: Consider abstracting the Impedance Mismatch logic in DTOs.

A code-first model is also possible. Code-first is when the data schema is created from code, rather than code being generated from a data schema. Code-first is a more typical example with technologies such as nHibernate, where a class definition is a part of the configuration of the destination of the data. You'd then create configuration about mapping in an nHibernate mapping file. This mapping file may look like the following:

```
<?xml version="1.0" encoding="utf-8"?>
<hibernate-mappingxmlns="urn:nhibernate-mapping-2.2"
  auto-import="true">
  <classname="Customer, MyAssembly"lazy="true">
    <idname="id"><generatorclass="native"/></id>
    <propertyname="Name"/>
    <propertyname="Phone"/>
    <propertyname="Street"/>
    <propertyname="City"/>
    <propertyname="Province"/>
    <propertyname="Country"/>
    <propertyname="PostalCode"/>
  </class>
</hibernate-mapping>
```

Accessing data can be done with LINQ, for example:

```
public Customer FindCustomer(int id)
{
  using (var session = factory.CreateSession())
  {
    var q = from customer in session.Linq<Customer>()
            where customer.Id == id
            select customer;
    return q.SingleOrDefault();
  }
}
```

Here, we use a precreated and preconfigured nHibernate `factory` to create `ISession`. That session then creates a queryable which we will use to perform the LINQ query and filter, returning the found object or null.

Regardless of whether you choose nHibernate, Entity Framework, LINQ to SQL, some other ORM, or code- or data-first, using ORMs offloads some of the work to configuration, which can evolve independently of your code to a certain degree. Just as with any decoupling, we don't have a complete separation, so some changes to the database will impact your code. However, with ORM, many changes to the database are abstracted within the configuration.

Context: When dealing with relational databases to store object-oriented data.

Practice: Consider offloading the mapping between the two to an Object Relational Mapper.

NoSQL

NoSQL, or **non-relational** databases have come to the forefront lately. They're typically used in situations where very large amounts of data are being used, and where that data needs to be distributed to potentially, many places. Typically, relational databases have not been good at this because they need to maintain certain consistency guarantees. These guarantees introduce latency into the system and can drastically affect the performance of a distributed system.

Eric Brewer came up with the **CAP Theorem** (**Consistency**, **Availability**, and **Partition Tolerance**). This theorem detailed that of these three attributes, at most only two can be guaranteed in a distributed system. That is, you can have consistency and availability (CA), availability and partition tolerance (AP), or consistency and partition tolerance (CP). Realistically, there are two options CA/CP and AP because CA isn't tolerant of network partitioning, and thus, cannot be available.

Consistency in this context does not mean data integrity. The integrity of data is maintained atomically, but whether or not every single node in a system has the *same data* is what is meant by consistency. In some systems, it's perfectly fine for one node to be working with data that is older, compared to the data on another node. Search engines, for example, are highly distributed systems. Data is effectively replicated across many nodes so that each node can get results very, very quickly. The fact that one node may return five results, while another node may return four results, is likely of little consequence. Eventually, both nodes will have the same results. The act of asking for those results shouldn't be blocked on waiting for both nodes to be synchronized to produce the same results. The concept that each node will eventually have the same data is called **Eventual Consistency**.

NoSQL and Eventual Consistent models work well in situations that are read-heavy and modification-light, that is, data doesn't change that often and is read very frequently.

Context: When dealing with huge amount of data with loose consistency requirements.

Practice: Choose a non-relational database.

Context: When choosing a technology for reporting data.

Practice: Avoid NoSQL databases.

Document databases

Dealing with storing data in a relational database compared to our domain model often results in mappings that aren't one to one. The requirements and practices in the relational world are different than those in the object-oriented world. Things like "third-normal form" don't make sense in object-oriented. We just deal with hierarchical data directly in our object-oriented code. We have collections instead of relations, and instances instead of keys. As we've seen earlier in this chapter, knowing about, and mapping back and forth from a relational model to a hierarchical model is time consuming and requires a lot of code that needs to be maintained.

ORMs can help alleviate this, and while this alleviates a lot of coding, it introduces configuration. It also doesn't alleviate the inherent problems of two different forms of data (relational and hierarchical) that is, Impedance Mismatch.

Document database are a form of database that stores "documents." A document is some sort of structure data. Many implementations use JSON (or its binary counterpart BSON) which is specifically designed to store object-oriented data. Many document databases have drivers which simply automatically map from your classes right into the structured data stored in the database.

Mongo is one such database that includes a C# driver (there are a few third-party OSS drivers as well) which does this mapping. For all intents and purposes, these drivers let you store instances of your class in the database. An example of using Mongo in the same way we've already shown may look like this:

```
public Customer FindCustomer(int id)
{
  MongoServer server = MongoServer.Create(connectionString);
  {
    var database = server.GetDatabase("Database");
    MongoCollection<Customer> customers =
```

```
        database.GetCollection<Customer>("Customer");
      return customers.FindAs<Customer>(Query.EQ("Id", id)).
        SingleOrDefault();
    }
  }
```

Here, we create a `MongoServer` and Mongo database objects (`server` and `database`). We then create a Mongo collection object to model a `Customer` table that we will query using its `FindAs` method. We then return the single result or null if it wasn't found.

Adding objects to the database is even easier, given our server and database object. We'd simply invoke the following code to add data to the database:

```
customers.Insert(customer);
```

The configuration is the actual class (other than the connection string, name of the database, name of the collections in the database, and others). The Mongo driver does the rest for us.

Context: When object-oriented data is the only data storage requirement.

Practice: Consider a document database.

Pulling it all together

We've seen that there are many reasons to have data, many types of ways to store data, and many reasons to pick a type of data storage. How do we consolidate all of these things?

Fortunately, if we look at what's going on in our system, we can make some specific decisions about what to do. Firstly, reporting is an inherently time-insensitive task. We know that as soon a report is generated, the data it displays is out of date. Any work attempting to get real-time reporting is futile.

Secondly, we know we want to have a decent granularity of data to its responsibility. For example, application data and reporting data. We know we want to make sure a report that requires lots of power and data doesn't adversely impact the application writing data.

Based on these observations, the one design that fulfills these types of requirements is the one that stores application data in a document database, and reporting data in a relational database. This can further be optimized so that the relational reporting data can act as a warehouse and be transferred to more applicable technologies, such as a Business Intelligence tool, for greater flexibility and power in reporting.

Context: When considering implementing reporting.

Practice: Consider using technologies that report on separate data, such as BI tools.

Context: When considering application data store technology.

Practice: Consider non-relational.

Distributed architecture

With the advent of big data and multi-core machines, it becomes apparent that in order to keep up with the amount of data, we need to begin scaling our systems out.

Although making use of multiple cores simultaneously (that is, in parallel) is effectively considered scaling up (or vertical scalability), some of the principles we can use to reliably do this can be applied to scaling out (or horizontal scalability).

One of the difficult parts of multithreaded programming is the synchronization of shared data. Data that can be read and written in two different places at the same time needs to make sure those operations don't overlap across threads and corrupt data. This is the act of making something **Thread Safe** or writing code for **thread synchronization**. This process is tricky and sometimes hard to get right. More detail on this can be found in *Chapter 8, Parallelization Practices*.

Another difficult part of multithreaded programming and distributed design is the separation of work so that it can be executed in parallel or distributed. There is a pattern called the **Parameter Object** pattern, which encapsulates all of the parameters (and data) that are needed for a particular invocation of a method.

We can use a specialization of the Parameter Object pattern to encapsulate parameters required to perform an action or to modify state (that is, a command). Effectively, we create a command class to encapsulate the parameters, as well as the command (and thus its intent, the name of the class, explicit). By providing an explicit instance of a class to encapsulate all of the data required in what needs to be actioned, we've effectively broken work down at a per-action level. That's not to say that all of the methods you already have that modify state and only operate with given parameters is at an appropriate break down. You likely need to step back and put some thought into commands of your system. But, that's application-specific, so I'll leave that as an exercise of the reader.

This partitioning of work allows the work to be scheduled, parallelized, balanced, assigned, and executed independently. For example, look at the following method:

```
private BigInteger CalculateSum(int blockSize,
  IEnumerable<int> source, int start)
{
  Var subset = source.Skip(start).Take(blockSize);
  BigInteger sum = new BigInteger(0);

  return subset.Aggregate(sum, (current, n) => current + n);
}
```

And it's invocation:

```
var sum = CalculateSum(chunkSize, values, i*chunkSize);
```

`CalculateSum` is a simple method, which takes an enumeration of integers (that could be from deferred execution via something such as `Enumerable.Range`) and sums all of the values, storing the result in a `BigInteger`.

We could easily encapsulate the parameters `blockSize`, `source`, and `start` into their own type (class), for example:

```
public class CalculateSumCommand
{
  public IEnumerable<int> Source;
  public int Start;
  public int BlockSize;
}
```

We could then slightly change the method that calculates the sum, and change it to a command handler:

```
private BigInteger HandleCommand(CalculateSumCommand command)
{
  var subset = command.Source
    .Skip(command.Start)
    .Take(command.BlockSize);
  var stopwatch = Stopwatch.StartNew();
  BigInteger sum = new BigInteger(0);

  return subset.Aggregate(sum, (current, n) => current + n);
}
```

This lightweight command object can now be passed around as a container for all of the data required to perform this particular action. The data becomes private to the method through its encapsulation in the command, and we no longer need to deal with shared data, and the synchronization and thread-safety issues that go along with it.

This simple design change makes it so that we can distribute work amongst multiple threads and, by extension, distribute amongst multiple processors or cores.

This distribution of commands is simply a scheduler, with a queue of commands that are invoked with some level of load balancing, or something that just takes the command and executes it either synchronously, or asynchronously.

Messaging

Essentially, distributed architectures can't operate on shared data. Sure, two nodes in a system could write data to a single database and each node would effectively share that data, but in reality they would both be working with their own copy (in memory) of the data. The database would be the mode by which synchronization occurred (assuming transactions were used).

We can make the copying of data explicit through the use of a **command class**. The command class encapsulates the data required for the required action (command) and thus cannot be shared (unless the instance of the command class is shared), and therefore does not require synchronization.

Within various refactoring tools, there is an ability to refactor parameters to a parameter object, sometimes called Extract Class from Parameters. Although this may be a good method of refactoring code to use a parameter object, what is and isn't a command may require more thought, analysis, and design than simply accepting that the current method model's a command processor exactly.

Context: When dealing with data that needs to be actioned independently and asynchronously.

Practice: Consider command classes.

Messaging doesn't need to involve the packaging, transmitting, and unpackaging of data going over the wire. Messaging can simply be a design style of invoking code.

Data synchronization and events

When we start dealing with asynchronous operations, either in a multi-threaded environment, or within a distributed environment via messages, we begin to realize that we simply can't use return values.

In our command handler example, despite processing a command parameter object to calculate a sum asynchronously, the return value of that method has nowhere to go. One way of dealing with this is to have code that blocks (or is synchronous) and waits for the result. However, this has many problems.

Code that is synchronous, by definition, is on another thread running independently. There's no guarantee that one thread will continue to execute while the other executes, if one blocks the exits before the other completes. The result is completely lost. The same thing happens with distributed, if the initiating node becomes partitioned in some way (get severed from the network, hangs, shuts down, reboots, and so on) the result of the request can become lost.

```
private SumCalculatedEvent ProcessCommand(CalculateSumCommand command)
{
  var subset = command.Source
    .Skip(command.Start)
    .Take(command.BlockSize);
  var stopwatch = Stopwatch.StartNew();
  BigInteger sum = new BigInteger(0);

  sum = subset.Aggregate(sum, (current, n) => current + n);
  return new SumCalculatedEvent
  {
    Sum = sum,
    TimeSpan = stopwatch.Elapsed
  };
}
```

In the modified `ProcessCommand` method we just saw, we now return an event to encapsulate the fact that a sum has been calculated. Included in this event is a `TimeSpan` field to include the amount of time take for the calculation (for metrics):

```
public class SumCalculatedEvent
{
  public BigInteger Sum;
  public TimeSpan TimeSpan;
}
```

This allows us to simply use this event as a message that can be sent from the node that handled the command, to any node that requires knowledge that the calculation has occurred.

DTOs Revisited

If you've noticed, with this general messaging design, all of the data going back and forth between nodes is either a command or an event. These commands and events are simple, flat, behaviorless data containers. Isn't this what a Data Transfer Object is? Commands and events are exactly that, just DTOs.

Once you have a model where asynchronous communication between two things (threads or nodes) is done with commands or events, then you're spared the need to create other DTOs. The DTOs effectively become commands and events.

When we deal with commands and events, we deal with the concept of commands and events and we're not directly mapping data from domain to DTO. We are actually making requests and responding to things. We introduce something with a little more meaning than just a mapper. Regardless, this generally also means that the act of mapping is alleviated and, at most, we need to deal with serialization of these commands and events.

Depending on how we want to communicate these commands and events between nodes, this process may also be off-loaded as we can use third-party tools and frameworks such as message queues or services buses to do this communication for us. We'll see more detail on these concepts in *Chapter 9, Distributed Applications*.

Summary

The ability re-use concepts and patterns is not limited to design. As we've seen, we can apply it to architecture as well. By using known and recommended practices in the correct contexts, we can alleviate some of the burden of analysis and design. We can also focus more on the value that the system will provide, rather than the infrastructure needed to support it. Supporting data within a system comes at a price. We can use tools and frameworks, such as object relational mappers, to map the data in our system to a particular database, and back, without being forced to write and support a bunch of vendor-specific code. The burden of knowing whether or not a system needs to be distributed at the onset of a project can be alleviated to a certain extent by making some architectural-related decisions, such as preferring Command Query Separating and to model actions as Commands, and to communicate state change through events.

So, as we can see, applying practices to how we architect and design software allows us to achieve expected results at the architecture level. Using generally accepted practice in the architecture allows communication about the architecture to be smoother because it's based on a shared vocabulary.

In the next chapter, we'll look at some practices related to deploying applications, components, and systems. We'll look at the recommended practices involving Visual Studio Setup and Deployment projects and Windows Installer XML.

5
Recommended Practices for Deployment

There comes a time in any complex application's life when it needs to be deployed onto a computer for use by the users or by customers. With simple apps, this process can be as easy as copying a ZIP file, unzipping it to a directory, and running the app.

Installation technologies are very rich in their features and vast in their flexibility. A single chapter can't possibly cover all of their features. This chapter will cover some of the more common features required by the majority application installations.

With Windows®, users expect a certain level of integration with the system; from installing icons in the submenu of the Start menu, icons on the Desktop, configuration of the Registry, and so on. This chapter doesn't attempt to detail with how applications can integrate with Windows®, but it details deployment practices with regard to deploying applications integrated into Windows.

This chapter's various recommended practices for deployment and working with deployment technologies will include the following topics:

- Working with installers
- Visual Studio Setup and Deployment projects
- ClickOnce
- Windows Installer XML (WiX)
- Silent installations
- Testing

Working with installers

This chapter can't possibly list all of the possible integration points in Windows that an application can take advantage of. Each integration point has its own requirement, which may vary from run-time calls into APIs, or one-time calls into configuration APIs.

Windows' design guidelines include guidelines for installation and removal of applications. The requirements of each application are different, depending on how it integrates into Windows, but the general guideline for removal is to remove any artifacts required by the application to run or integrate into Windows, and leave user-created files on the computer (or prompt the user to remove user-created files).

Much beyond hooking into **Add/Remove Programs** or **Programs and Features,** it is up to the application to decide how to configure and remove. This could entirely be written by the application developer (calling into the APIs to create registry entries, copy files to Windows system directories, and so on).

Context: When contemplating deploying an application in Windows that isn't merely copying a file or two.

Practice: Choose an installer technology to perform the install and uninstall actions.

The history of installation technology for Windows has been long and varied. Windows has had guidelines for installers and uninstallers for a long time. Windows has hooks for these installers to register applications and their uninstallers. All good installation technologies have this ability. There are some basic requirements for uninstallation that these technologies will take care of for you.

Context: When choosing a Windows installation technology.

Practice: Be sure to evaluate alternatives and choose a technology that fulfills your needs.

Working with Windows Installer

Sometime around 2000, Microsoft introduced **Windows Installer**. This Windows component provides abilities for processing various installation and uninstallation actions, and dealing with various interactions with the system. This component was formerly called Microsoft Installer, and the information about the actions a particular installation requires are contained in an **MSI (MicroSoft Installer)** file.

Making use of Windows Installer covers various Windows Logo requirements. Although most installation technologies on the market would likely cover the same requirements, making use of any of these technologies, rather than writing your own, means less work testing.

MSI support is available for every supported version of Windows. While there are various other technologies that can be used, for simplicity I'm going to focus on technologies that support or produce MSI files (that is, support Windows Installer). A single chapter can't possibly cover even the most important parts of installation, the wide-variety of technologies, and still be informative. My choice of focusing on MSI shouldn't be the only criteria that you use when evaluating technologies.

There are already existing, fairly technical, best practices for Windows Installer developers. For the most part, I won't cover those because they're easy to find and fairly low level. These practices will be geared more towards the average developer and project, and focus on getting them up and running writing an installer quickly.

Uninstalling

The more integrated an application is into Windows, the more that application is required to perform during deployment, and therefore the more the application is responsible for during uninstallation. For the most part, each action that is required by the application during install leaves something on the system (registry entries, files, among others). The process of uninstalling is the process of reversing all of the changes made by the installer to the system. This is generally supported directly by the installation technology as it simply "reverses" an action.

This assumes, of course, that all of the changes to the system were done by the installer or during installation. To support the uninstallation of things that the application might do to the system (create files or create a registry entry) those changes can be removed during uninstallation if the installer is configured to perform those changes (the application can still perform these actions, just now, if the installer does them too, the uninstaller will remove them).

Context: To uninstall artifacts of actions performed by an application.

Practice: Perform similar actions in the install script.

Visual Studio Setup and Deployment projects

Visual Studio 2003 introduced **Setup and Deployment** projects. These projects were simply a means to contain the definition of *how to build an MSI file*. The process of building these projects effectively builds an MSI file for the distribution and deployment of an application.

These projects were simple. They allowed wizard-creation of projects and designer-like configuration, and editing. In the **Add New Project** dialog, you will find an **Other Project Types | Setup and Deployment | Visual Studio Installer** category that includes five different project types: **Setup Project**, **Web Setup Project**, **Merge Module Project**, **Setup Wizard**, and **CAB Project**. The following is a screenshot of these templates:

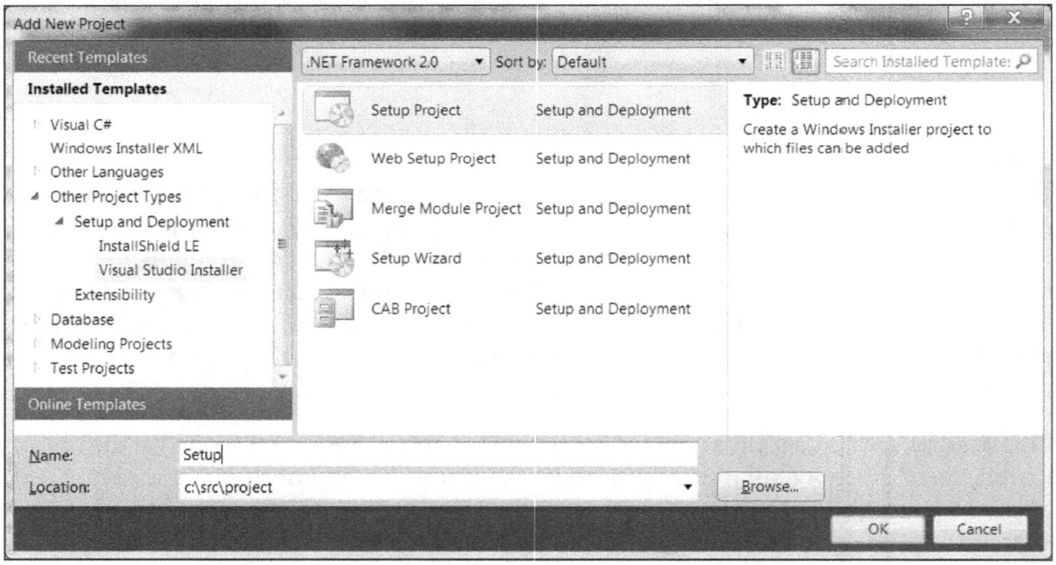

Setup Wizard

The Setup Wizard project type guides you through the process of creating a Visual Studio Installer project, and will create one of the other four project types, depending on the options you choose. It will also automatically include different types of files from other projects in the solution that you are presumably deploying with this setup.

Context: When creating setup projects with Visual Studio Installer.

Practice: Prefer to create the project with Setup Wizard to guide you through which type of setup project to create, and automatically include files from other projects.

Setup Project

This creates a blank setup project with a user interface (normal and administrative) typical of a local application install. It requires that you manually add all of the artifacts, such as files, registry, and more, as well as specific *launch conditions* that you would like this setup to perform.

Web Setup Project

This project type lets you create an MSI preconfigured with a *Web Application Folder*, which is a special folder in the **File System** properties of the setup, and a UI, which is specific to be deployed to web applications or websites.

It's fairly uncommon to require that a web project be deployed in this way. It assumes the web project will be provided to many clients or customers, for individual and independent usage. My experience has been that web projects are generally used by only the organization developing them.

Context: If not developing a web project for multiple customers.

Practice: Prefer Visual Studio's **Publish Web** feature to manually deploy a web project to a server.

Many things have changed since the Web Setup project was created in the Setup and Deployment project set. Although *Publish* is a better choice to manually get a website/application up on a server, in many cases this needs to be an automated process. In cases where you want to automate the deployment of a website/application, use the Web Deploy extension. This extension supports command-line scripting and integrates into MSBuild. This allows continuous integration servers to easily deploy your site/application automatically.

Context: When considering automated deployment of a website/application.

Practice: Choose the Web Deploy extension.

Merge Module Project

This project creates a blank Merge Module project to build an MSM (instead of a MSI) file that contains shared files, resources, registry entries, and setup logic that, presumably, will be merged with other setup projects to create MSI files. Merge Modules do not contain a user interface and do not have their own launch conditions. Merge Modules also cannot be installed on their own. They must be merged into an installation package to produce an MSI (or another MSM) file.

While Merge Modules allow you create a packaged grouping of setup files, resources, registry entries, and setup logic, it's rare that producing an MSI with files under the same control as the organization producing the MSI will require any Merge Modules. It's conceivable that, if there are two different teams, with different delivery schedules, one team produces files that will be used by the other to create an MSI file. The first team could also package those files within Merge Module, which the other team could then merge into their MSI file, at their leisure. However, it's more common that Merge Modules are used only to provide setup components to third-parties to merge into an unrelated (although, typically dependent upon) component.

Context: When considering how to package components for installation by third-parties.

Practice: Consider creating a Merge Module project.

If possible, it's recommended to use the Setup Wizard template to create a Merge Module project, rather than creating this project through the Merge Module Project template. This would facilitate the automatic gathering of information about other output files and dependencies from other projects.

CAB Project

CAB installation is generally reserved for installing ActiveX components via a web browser. But a CAB project can effectively work as an archive of files (like a ZIP file).

If possible, it's recommended to use the Setup Wizard template to create a CAB project, rather than creating this project through the CAB Project template. The Setup Wizard template automatically gathers information about other project output files and dependencies.

Setup and Deployment projects allowed developers to deploy their applications and dependencies with minimal support for the MSI features. Setup and Deployment projects supported deploying files to specific directories, adding icons/shortcuts to the user's desktop, adding keys and values to the registry (including file types), launch conditions, a user interface, and custom actions.

Each Visual Studio Installer project has settings for the filesystem, registry, file types, user interface, custom actions, and launch conditions. This is true except for the Merge Module project, which doesn't have a user interface or launch condition options, and CAB projects that really only contain files.

File System

These settings define the files and directories that will be installed onto the target computer. These settings also include where the files and directories will be deployed. The settings are generally flexible regarding where the files and directories can be deployed (from `Windows System` folder, to `Program Files` folder, to custom hard-coded directories). Typically, an application will deploy to a target directory that defaults to Program Files, but is either accepted or changed by the user during the installation process. This is typically the **TARGETDIR** property.

Most installation technologies default to a property name of TARGETDIR. You can use any name you like within your installation, as long as you use that name wherever the target directory is needed. This property is publicly available to the MSI subsystem and can be set via the command-line for purposes, such as a silent (or quiet) install. So, for your install to work as expected in situations such as a silent install, it's best to keep the property name as TARGETDIR. It is important that all of the letters be in upper case, as that is what signifies that the property is public.

Context: When considering what to name the target directory property, or whether to use built-in names such as TARGETDIR.

Practice: Consider using the standard property name TARGETDIR.

The File System settings also includes files such as icons on the user's desktop, or in the user's Program Menu. The File System settings are smart enough to know about any "special folder" such as the `Common Files` folders, user's `Application Data` and `Favorites` folders, among others.

Context: When designing your setup's File System.

Practice: Consider including expected components such as Desktop and Program Menu icons, which are shortcuts to installed executable or "runnable" files.

File types

Many applications work with specific file types. Therefore file types are registered with Windows. An application can register these file associates at run time, and may very well need to update or change this registration while running. However, it's best to register these file associations during installation so the user can execute associated applications through the file associations.

Context: When file associations are used by an application.

Practice: Consider registering those associations during installation.

User interface

Most installations contain a user interface that interacts with the user to collect typical information such as destination directory as well as a welcome, confirmation, and progress.

Context: When designing an installation.

Practice: Consider using standard series of installation steps to reduce surprises for your users.

Launch conditions

This contains the mandatory conditions required by the application being deployed to execute. These are detected during setup and are conditions of completing setup. Detection of the .NET Framework version is built-in, but other conditions such as existence of files on the destination computer, existence of registry keys, and registry values, or Windows Installer prerequisites. Windows Installer prerequisites search a specific version of other components installed with an MSI that exists (or doesn't exist) by Component ID.

Typically, launch conditions are validation of specific values of the result of a search, that is, you usually create an entry in Search Target Machine to get a *value* and you then compare it to a known value in launch conditions.

When using the Setup wizard, the version of the .NET Framework required will automatically be detected. All of the other conditions will need to be manually created. It's fairly rare that other conditions are required during install. When including a Merge Module for a prerequisite, the conditions to install that prerequisite are included. There's no reason to manually create a launch condition for prerequisite libraries included in your setup project.

Custom actions

Custom actions are not created via Setup and Deployment project templates. Custom actions are simply *class libraries* that contain one or more `System.Configuration.Install.Installer`-derived classes.

Custom action class libraries are then added to the File System configuration of a Setup project. The Setup projects are then configured to use custom actions through the custom actions designer by right-clicking the **Custom Actions** node and then selecting the appropriate file from the **Setup Projects File System** files.

Drawbacks of Setup and Deployment Project

In July 2010, Microsoft announced that it would no longer be developing Setup and Deployment projects beyond Visual Studio 2010. True to their word, Visual Studio 2012 did not have Setup and Deployment projects. Their stance was that third-party software would need to be used to deploy applications developed with Visual Studio.

In Visual Studio 2010 and earlier, Setup and Deployment projects also do not support creating patches (minor updates or MSP files), do not have MSBuild integration, do not support configuration of users and groups, cannot create new Web Sites, cannot install/configure IIS certificates, cannot install/configure SQL databases, or are unable modify XML file.

Context: If considering an installation technology beyond Visual Studio 2010, or considering an installation technology to be used by automated builds.

Practice: Avoid Setup and Deployment projects.

ClickOnce

Generally, ClickOnce is used when centralized deployment or execution of applications are required. ClickOnce deployments are auto-updating and do not require users to have administrative access on their computers. ClickOnce does nothing application-specific with the registry or the desktop, and really only installs (and uninstalls) Start Menu shortcuts and files related to the application.

ClickOnce packages are created with the Visual Studio Publish wizard to publish an application project to a website or network file share. A new project is not created and the options used to publish are stored with the project that is being published. Settings for ClickOnce deployment can be found in the **Publish** tab of most Visual Studio application projects, where options such as **Application Files**, **Prerequisites**, whether the application automatically checks for updates, and other options can be fine tuned from the detected defaults.

Context: When publishing an application to a centralized location from which users will install or run the application.

Practice: Prefer ClickOnce.

Context: When distributing an installer (MSI) that users will use to install an application.

Practice: Prefer Windows Installer (MSI).

Windows Installer XML (WiX)

Windows Installer XML (WiX) is a powerful XML-based definition language for defining how to build an MSI file. WiX is currently the only Microsoft-backed (they support all installer technologies, but they pay people to work on WiX) installer technology. Clearly it supports Windows Installer and MSI files. WiX, although backed by Microsoft, is open source and freely available.

Based on its name, WiX sounds like it would be a lot of manual editing of text (for example, XML) and doesn't sound very friendly. WiX (pronounced as *wicks*), as it is commonly known now, is a toolset. While WiX brings the concept of themed code-names to an all-time high, its core contains various components such as Candle, Light, Heat, Burn, Votive, Dark, Lit, Torch, Pyro, Melt, Smoke, and many more. This section describes the least advanced of these various components.

At the very least, using WiX involves compiling a *source WiX* file (`.wxs`) with Candle to *produce* intermediate files, and using Light to *link* intermediate files into MSI files. Fortunately though, there are other tools (as well as a vibrant community and third-party tools) that help in the generation and validation of WiX source files.

The WiX XML is very powerful, but doesn't always follow a specific structure. WiX generally starts with a root WiX element. That WiX element can contain a `Product` element that describes the product and its packages. A WiX element can also contain a `Fragment` element that describes a source unit to share between projects to make maintaining a single project easier. A fragment is often compared to a *source code unit* when comparing WiX to developing software. You could have your entire MSI defined in one file just like writing software, but it can also be broken into multiple files with fragments. A typical WiX source file may be similar to the following:

```
<?xml version="1.0" encoding="UTF-8"?>
<Wix xmlns="http://schemas.microsoft.com/wix/2006/wi">
  <Product Id="YOUR-PRODUCT-GUID"
          Name="My Product Setup"
          Language="1033"
          Version="1.0.0.0"
          Manufacturer="My Corp">
    <Package InstallerVersion="200"
            Compressed="yes"
            InstallScope="perMachine" />

    <Directory Id="TARGETDIR" Name="SourceDir">
      <Directory Id="ProgramFilesFolder">
        <Directory Id="INSTALLFOLDER"
            Name="My Product">
          <Component Id="ProductComponent">
              <!-- TODO: Insert files,
              registry keys, and other resources here. -->
          </Component>
        </Directory>
      </Directory>
    </Directory>

    <Feature Id="ProductFeature" Title="My Product"
            Level="1">
      <ComponentGroupRef Id="ProductComponents" />
    </Feature>
  </Product>

</Wix>
```

Of course, when you need to deal with multiple features, each containing multiple files, directories, registry entries, and others, this single file can become tedious very quickly. In this case, you might break it up into multiple fragments. For example, the following three code snippets.

First code snippet:

```
<?xml version="1.0" encoding="UTF-8"?>
<Wix xmlns="http://schemas.microsoft.com/wix/2006/wi">
  <Product Id="YOUR-PRODUCT-GUID"
          Name="My Product Setup"
          Language="1033"
          Version="1.0.0.0"
          Manufacturer="My Corp">
    <Package InstallerVersion="200"
            Compressed="yes"
            InstallScope="perMachine" />

    <Feature Id="ProductFeature"
            Title="My Product" Level="1">
      <ComponentGroupRef Id="ProductComponents" />
    </Feature>
  </Product>
</Wix>
```

Second code snippet:

```
<?xml version="1.0" encoding="UTF-8"?>
<Wix xmlns="http://schemas.microsoft.com/wix/2006/wi">
    <Fragment>
    <Directory Id="TARGETDIR" Name="SourceDir">
      <Directory Id="ProgramFilesFolder">
        <Directory Id="INSTALLFOLDER"
                  Name="My Product" />
      </Directory>
    </Directory>
  </Fragment>
</Wix>
```

Third code snippet:

```
<?xml version="1.0" encoding="UTF-8"?>
<Wix xmlns="http://schemas.microsoft.com/wix/2006/wi">
    <Fragment>
    <ComponentGroup Id="ProductComponents"
                    Directory="INSTALLFOLDER">
```

```
        <Component Id="ProductComponent">
          <!-- TODO: Insert files,
          registry keys, and other resources here. -->
        </Component>
      </ComponentGroup>
    </Fragment>
</Wix>
```

While it's easy to simply open up a text file and start typing in WiX tags and elements to define what and how you want to install files and configure Windows, this is a daunting task for anything but the simplest of systems. Luckily, the WiX toolset includes a tool called **Heat** to "harvest" a lot of information about a deployment, and generate a `.wxs` file. Heat supports having information about the files and directories, Visual Studio Project registry, website, and performance counter, information. So, the creation of `.wxs` files for the deployment of your application can be easily automated without needing to know much about the structure of `.wxs` files or the semantics of WiX XML.

Context: When wanting to create `.wxs` files with already existing resources.

Practice: Use Heat to generate the bulk of the information in `.wxs` files.

Include files

WiX has a concept of *include* (`.wxi`, although it's not mandatory) files. These files have a root `Include` element; for example:

```
<?xml version="1.0" encoding="utf-8"?>
<Include>
  <!-- TODO: Put your code here. -->
</Include>
```

The file can then be included within another as follows:

```
<?include MyInclude.wxi ?>
```

The content of the `Include` element is simply placed, verbatim, into wherever the `<?include` tag is placed. This means that the contents aren't syntax checked until it's included since the parent element influences the validity of child elements. You could very well create a WiX `include` file, which when included in one place works fine but fails in another.

Context: If you have WiX source elements that are repeated several times or shared.

Practice: Consider placing the elements within a WiX `include` file.

This offers a level of decoupling so `include` files can change independently. It also means that different `include` files can be included conditionally. WiX has a preprocessor conditional syntax, which it uses to ignore parts of the source based on some condition. This syntax basically has the form `<?if condition ?>...<?endif ?>`. This is often used to compare environment variables, WiX variables, literal values, and so on. For example, if we wanted to include a particular file based on the WiX variable, we could have the following snippet of code:

```
<?if $(var.Type) = FreeWare ?>
    <?include FreeWareComponents.wxi ?>
    <?endif ?>
```

Fragments

Fragments are a way of grouping WiX source units together. Many WiX elements rely on being within specific elements. `ComponentGroup`, for example, is a child element of `Product`, it defines what component groups a product contains. Including a `ComponentGroup` within defines the specific components (within the group) that are part of the install. A `ComponetGroup` element can also be a child of a `Fragment` element, and not be directly contained within a `Product`. The `ComponentGroup` element can then have an ID attribute and be referenced by a `product` element (via the `ComponentGroupRef` element). This allows the `Fragment` element's supported child elements to be more readily shared amongst multiple elements. In our `ComponentGroup` example, the `Product` element could contain two `Feature` elements that reference the same `ComponentGroup` (this assumes that one `Feature` element includes a `ComponentGroup` that the other doesn't, otherwise the features would be the same).

Fragments introduce a level of decoupling which allows elements to be coupled by ID, and not by hierarchy. The elements referencing to another element contained in a `Fragment` element, can remain within the same file, or that `Fragment` element can be moved out to another file to reduce coupling further.

Fragment files are WiX XML files that contain a single `fragment` element with child elements, presumably related, grouped as an atomic unit, for example:

```
<?xml version="1.0" encoding="UTF-8"?>
<Wix xmlns="http://schemas.microsoft.com/wix/2006/wi">
  <Fragment>
    <!-- TODO: Put your code here. -->
  </Fragment>
</Wix>
```

Although fragment files can be organized in much the same way as include files, they're not included when the setup is built. Fragment files are simply one of the many `.wxs` files given to Candle for compilation. Candle basically merges all of the XML from the `.wxs` files into one, and compiles that into a WIXOBJ file. Fragments within these fragment files are usually given an ID, and referenced by something else.

Fragment files are useful in much the same way as include files, in that they can contain shared or repeated source elements that need only live in one file. Another use of fragment files is to replace source elements based on some condition. This condition would be external to the WiX source, and would manifest itself by the choice of `.wxs` files given to Candle when it is executed. For example, based on some condition you may pass different parameters to `candle.exe` (such as different fragment file names). A similar thing can be done with include files, but the value would need to be passed on the command line to Candle. Somewhere in the `.wxs` files, a conditional would test this value and include different files. See the *Include files* section for an example.

There's greater support for fragments within WiX. For example, the Heat utility will harvest information and create a fragment file (or a file with a `Product` or `Module` element).

Migrating from Setup and Deployment projects

At the very least, a Setup and Deployment project generates an MSI file. This file can be decompiled into a `.wxs` file with the Dark utility; for example, `dark setup.exe`.

This generates a default `setup.wxs` file that can be built with WiX to generate the same installation. This effectively allows you to transition to WiX very quickly. Depending on how the MSI file was created, this may result in a .wxs file that basically has its own UI definition. It doesn't re-use any definition contained in another `.wxs` file or another `.wixobj` file. This isn't generally bad, but if you want to use a common WiX UI or deal with any of the common WiX UI, then you'll need to modify the `.wxs` to work with those WiX UI elements.

This method also doesn't really take into account default settings or values. Everything that was in the previous MSI file is included in the `.wxs`, regardless of whether they're default values or not. For example, the `package` element may contain languages and platform elements that weren't in the original source code, and default values were used.

Heat will get you up and running with WiX fairly quickly based on the results of a Setup and Deployment project. WiX also integrates very nicely into Visual Studio to allow you to create setup projects that have references to other projects, and build them from within Visual Studio much in the same way Setup and Deployment projects would.

Integrating into Visual Studio

If you do any amount of work in Visual Studio, you'll want to use the Visual Studio WiX integration. This integration is done with the Votive package. Finding help about this integration is sometimes easier when you include *votive* in your search.

Once WiX is installed, there is the additional **Windows Installer XML** in the **Installed Templates** category, with six new project types that can be added to a solution: Setup Project, Merge Module Project, Setup Library Project, Bootstrapper Project, C# Customer Action Project, and C++ Custom Action Project. Following is a screenshot of the WiX project templates:

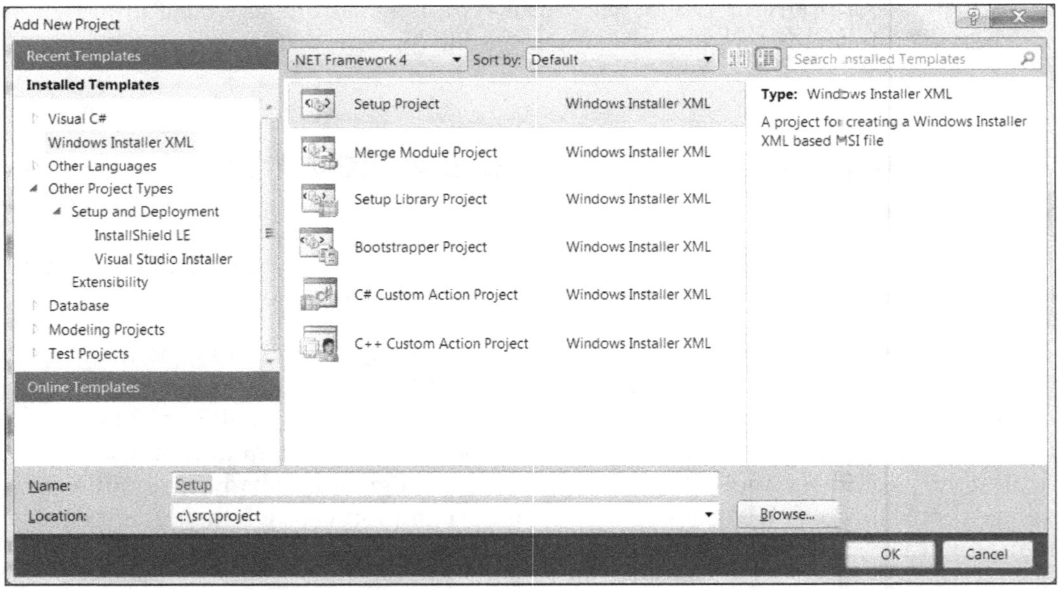

Setup Project

Effectively the same as the Setup and Deployment projects' Setup project, this creates an empty setup project, creating a `.wxs` file with the default `Product` and `Fragment` elements/attributes within a newly created `.wixproj` project.

The generated .wxs file included in the .wixproj should be very similar to:

```
<?xml version="1.0" encoding="UTF-8"?>
<Wix xmlns="http://schemas.microsoft.com/wix/2006/wi">
  <Product Id="*" Name="Setup" Language="1033"
      Version="1.0.0.0" Manufacturer="Microsoft"
      UpgradeCode="c0bdfa74-b14f-40ea-9016-a99f09e6990b">
    <Package InstallerVersion="200" Compressed="yes"
            InstallScope="perMachine" />

    <MajorUpgrade
      DowngradeErrorMessage=
        "A newer version of [ProductName] is already installed." />
    <MediaTemplate />

    <Feature Id="ProductFeature" Title="Setup" Level="1">
      <ComponentGroupRef Id="ProductComponents" />
    </Feature>
  </Product>

  <Fragment>
    <Directory Id="TARGETDIR" Name="SourceDir">
      <Directory Id="ProgramFilesFolder">
        <Directory Id="INSTALLFOLDER" Name="Setup" />
      </Directory>
    </Directory>
  </Fragment>

  <Fragment>
    <ComponentGroup Id="ProductComponents"
                    Directory="INSTALLFOLDER">
      <!-- TODO: Remove the comments around this
      Component element and the ComponentRef
      below in order to add resources to
      this installer. -->
      <!-- <Component Id="ProductComponent"> -->
        <!-- TODO: Insert files,
        registry keys,
        and other resources here. -->
        <!-- </Component> -->
    </ComponentGroup>
  </Fragment>
</Wix>
```

What differentiates a setup .wxs file is the Product element.

Merge Module Project

Effectively the same as the Setup and Deployment projects' Merge Module Project, this creates an empty setup project, creating a `.wxs` file with the default `Module` elements/attributes within a newly created `.wixproj` project. Creating this type of project should create a `.wxs` file similar to the following:

```
<?xml version="1.0" encoding="UTF-8"?>
<Wix xmlns="http://schemas.microsoft.com/wix/2006/wi">
  <Module Id="WiXMergeModule" Language="1033"
          Version="1.0.0.0">
    <Package Id="96387d2c-3bf6-49af-be4e-772fdae0bdc7"
             Manufacturer="Microsoft"
             InstallerVersion="200" />

    <Directory Id="TARGETDIR" Name="SourceDir">
      <Directory Id="MergeRedirectFolder">

        <!-- TODO: Remove the comments around
        this Component element in order to add
        resources to this module. -->
        <!-- <Component Id="ModuleComponent"
        Guid="a0e959c5-cfea-4999-9102-926f9538e689"> -->
        <!-- TODO: Insert files, registry keys,
          and other resources here. -->
        <!-- </Component> -->

      </Directory>
    </Directory>
  </Module>
</Wix>
```

The `Module` element differentiates this as a Merge Module `.wxs` file.

Setup Library Project

This creates a WiX library project that builds a `.wixlib` project. WiX libraries are compiled setup functionalities that can be shared across multiple WiX projects. They seem to effectively be a compiled WiX `Fragment`. For example, creating a WiX Setup Library generates a `.wxs` file in the project similar to the following:

```
<?xml version="1.0" encoding="UTF-8"?>
<Wix xmlns="http://schemas.microsoft.com/wix/2006/wi">
  <Fragment>
    <!-- TODO: Put your code here. -->
  </Fragment>
</Wix>
```

WiX Libraries are like Merge Modules, but of course, they're shareable only between WiX projects (not used in `.wixproj` projects). The same basic recommendations apply to WiX Libraries as to Merge Modules, except that the audience will be limited only to WiX users.

Bootstrapper Project

Bootstrappers allow the bundling and execution of multiple MSI files that would otherwise not be allowed (you're not allowed to run two MSI files at the same time).

This WiX project template creates an empty bootstrapper project, creating a new `.wixproj` file and a `.wxs` file with a default `Bundle` element. The `Bundle` element is used to define chained packages. Creating a bootstrapper project creates a `.wxs` file with generated code similar to the following:

```
<?xml version="1.0" encoding="UTF-8"?>
<Wix xmlns="http://schemas.microsoft.com/wix/2006/wi">
  <Bundle Name="WiXBootstrapper"
      Version="1.0.0.0"
      Manufacturer="Microsoft"
      UpgradeCode="766260d1-11d2-461e-9cef-83bbdc8fb586">
    <BootstrapperApplicationRef
      Id="WixStandardBootstrapperApplication.RtfLicense" />

    <Chain>
      <!-- TODO: Define the list of chained packages. -->
      <!-- <MsiPackage SourceFile="path\to\your.msi" /> -->
    </Chain>
  </Bundle>
</Wix>
```

To chain to other MSI files, simply read the `TODO` text within the `Chain` element, and place as many `MsiPackage` elements that you require. The `BootstrapperApplicationRef` references a UI, in this case the WiX built-in UI `WixStandardBootstrapperApplication.RtfLicense`.

Bootstrappers are DLLs loaded by the `Burn` component, which is the chainer component (or "bootstrapper" for lack of a better term).

Context: When developing an installer that will be dependent on other MSI packages.

Practice: Consider creating a Bootstrapper project to implement chaining of the MSIs.

You may want to chain together installations if you require independent *prerequisites* or *shared* applications. This is pretty clear when you're dealing with third-party prerequisites, but less clear if you'e dealing with your own prerequisites. Often the need to chain isn't based on the ability to install but the uninstall requirements. If you have shared binaries that are used by separate installs, the ability to uninstall an application but leave the shared binaries on the system might be a requirement. In such cases, chaining might be a good option.

Chaining is very complex and drastically increases the surface area that you need to deal with in your installer, increasing the likelihood of an error. Only chain your own MSI file if you need to.

Context: When developing complex installations.

Practice: Avoid chaining MSIs unless you really need to.

C# Custom Action Project

This creates a new class Library project, with a single class that has a single method (usually `CustomAction1` that is attributed with `Microsoft.Deployment.WindowsInstaller.CustomActionAttribute ([CustomAction])`.

The custom action is used within a `.wixproj` file, by adding a `Binary` element, a `CustomAction` element, and a `Custom` element to an `InstallExecutSequence` element to the WiX XML. Adding a reference to the custom action project to the setup project (or projects) automatically creates a WiX `define` for various attributes about the custom action, including the target path (usually `CustomActionProjectName.TargetPath`). These `define` can be used within the `Binary` element to reference the custom action DLL by alias (for example, it will reference the DLL file regardless of the currently selected project configuration).

Although there isn't a project to create a VB custom action, it would be fairly easy to create a VB Class Library project and implement a class with a method returning `ActionResult` with a single `Session` parameter, and attributed with `CustomActionAttribute`.

Integrating a custom action within a WiX install is a matter of declaring a `Binary` element to reference the DLL file, then declaring a `CustomAction` element referencing the `Binary` elements key (`Id`), declaring the entry (the method name), and any `Execute` and `Return` preferences. If you reference the custom action project in the setup project, preprocessor variables will be declared with information about the referenced projects, such as the path of the binary. For example, to include a custom action in a setup, we could have code similar to the following:

```
<Binary Id="MyCustomAction"
        src="$(var.WiXCustomAction.TargetPath)"/>
```

```
<CustomAction Id="AfterFilesCustomAction"
              BinaryKey="MyCustomAction"
              DllEntry="CustomAction1"
              Execute="deferred"
              Return="check"/>
```

This would assume we created a custom action project named `WixCustomAction`, which had a class in it with a method named `CustomAction1`, for example:

```
public class CustomActions
{
  [CustomAction]
  public static ActionResult CustomAction1(Session session)
  {
    session.Log("Begin CustomAction1");

    return ActionResult.Success;
  }
}
```

C++ Custom Action Project

This generates a project much in the same way that creating a C# Custom Action does, except that it creates a project in native C++.

Context: If you require a custom action that requires some degree of native code.

Practice: Consider a C++ Custom Action project.

Continuous integration

As I mentioned earlier, one thing that WiX has over Setup and Deployment projects is that it has a way to build an MSI file from the command line. This can either be done by directly invoking any necessary WiX executable components, or MSBuild can be used to build the `.wixproj` file. Examples of both are as follows.

WiX executable components:

```
candle.exe setup.wxs -out setup.wixobj
light.exe setup.wixobj -cultures:null -out setup.msi
```

MSBuild:

```
msbuildsetup.wixproj
```

One of the biggest corners some of my clients paint themselves into is through the adoption of Setup and Deployment projects. These cannot be supported with MSBuild or most other automated build techniques. When it comes to perform automated builds (for example, continuous integration) they quickly realize that Setup and Deployment has failed them, and they need to go back to the drawing board. Couple that with Microsoft's announcement to stop supporting Setup and Deployment projects in future versions of Visual Studio, the choice whether or not to start using Setup and Deployment projects is a bit of a no-brainer.

Fortunately, you can harvest information from an MSI file with WiX (see the *Migrating from Setup and Deployment projects* section, in this chapter).

You can build Setup and Deployment projects from the command-line, but you must use `devenv.exe`, which requires the installation of Visual Studio on the computer where the build is being performed. Depending on what you are using for automated builds, Visual Studio may not already be installed. An example of using `devenv` to build a Setup and Deployment project is `devenev.exe Setup.vdproj /build Release.`

This builds the VDPROJ and all dependent projects, with no flexibility. If you have two VDPROJ projects that are dependent on the same project, that project will be built twice.

Silent installations

Windows Installer supports a silent installation (or quiet installation) mode. This is typically done with the `quiet` command-line option, for example:

```
msiexec.exe /i setup.msi /quiet
```

This form of installation basically takes all of the default values of properties, and performs all of the steps with those values. If any of those properties are public (all upper case) then they may be set at the command line.

For example, if we wanted to do a silent install to a specific directory (and the standard public property INSTALLDIR was used for that value), then we could perform a silent install to that specific directory as follows:

```
msiexec.exe INSTALLDIR="c:\specific directory" /i setup.msi /quiet
```

WiX has several other components for advanced MSI topics that a single chapter simply can't do justice to. Some of the components are as follows:

- **Dark**: This is a decompiler
- **Lit**: This is a library tool used to combing WiX object files into WiX library files

- **Torch**: This is a tool to perform a diff on WiX XML to generate MSI transform files (MST)
- **Pyro**: This tool creates the MSI patch files (MSP)
- **Melt**: This tool converts an MSI MSM file into a WiX component group
- **Smoke**: This is WiX's equivalent of FxCop or Code Analysis

Testing

Testing seems fairly straightforward, however, it can be quite complex. Using technologies such as Windows installer provides you reduced testing, as you can assume any of the code you're making use of in Windows installer is already tested. You don't need to test the act of copying files, or the act of setting/changing registry values work, for example.

For the most part, installation technologies take care of a lot of things for you. However, there are some things very specific to your installation that you may want to verify for each edition of your MSI. While copying files and setting registry values work in Windows Installer, you may want to verify that all of the files you want copied get copied during an install, and that all of the registry values you want to set are set during an install.

As with any testing, coming up with a plan and prioritizing what to test often comes with understanding what the user wants out of the installation. Installations can become complex very quickly. Examples of complexities includes the number of permutations, or an install based on the feature groupings, and component groupings, specific requirements for different Windows version, administrative install, uninstall, modify, unattended install, GPO install, and so on.

As with most test plans, it's important to include items that facilitate the verification of an install. Items such as the following:

- Features to be tested
- Features not to be tested
- Schedule
- Responsibilities
- Staffing
- Approach
- Resources (computers, OS versions, servers, and others)
- Deliverables

Although MSI packages have feature groupings, the above list doesn't outline these particular types of features. However, in addition to the aforementioned generalized tasks, *features to be tested*, *features not to be tested*, and (to a certain extent) *approach* may include sub-tasks such as:

- Install features
- Install components
    - Files
    - Directory
    - Registry Keys
    - Registry Values
    - Shortcuts
- Custom Actions
- Unattended install
- GPO install
- Uninstall
- Others

As with any test plan, it's important to include what isn't tested because it details your understanding that these items exist and make it explicit that they're not included or not supported.

It's important to test that you've correctly configured and designed an installation to do what you expect it to do, in the conditions you expect it be exercised in. It may not be enough to simply assume that you've configured the settings correctly in the installation technology you've chosen. You may not completely understand what that configuration means in the interaction of that technology in the various scenarios that you want to support. It's also important to focus your testing on realistic scenarios. You may want to support unattended installation (especially if you want to do any automated testing of your install) but you may not need to support GPO installs (which is Group Policy Object installation within a domain by means of unattended install, so, you may want unattended install to work properly, but if it doesn't work within the context of GPO, it may not matter).

Summary

While this chapter focuses mainly on deployment of applications through Windows Installer, it's clear that the application deployment is complex in its own right and that making use of third-party technologies to get the job done is an important decision for a team to make. It's also important for the team to pick the right technology or product to create that installation. There isn't nearly enough space in a single chapter to cover all of the possible details of installation, even with just Windows Installer. There are several books about Windows Installer and technologies that make use of Windows Installer (MSI) such as WiX or InstallShield. If you find that this chapter doesn't cover all of the topics your installation or setup requires, I recommend you look into a book devoted to installing Windows applications or software. There are several books available, but with the transition away from Setup and Deployment projects, many of those books are a bit dated. There is the *Definitive Guide to Windows Installer* from *Apress*. There is also *Getting Started with Windows Installer XML (WiX)* available from *Packt Publishing*.

The next chapter will cover automated testing practices. Practices regarding test naming and structure, coverage, mocking, and types of tests will be covered.

6
Automated Testing Practices

This chapter serves to detail recommended practices for automated testing. The title of this chapter is careful not to use the term *Unit Testing Practices*. While unit testing is a vital part of developing quality software, it's not the only aspect of developer-oriented testing of software. We'll detail practices related to writing effective tests, designing tests, make effective use of tests, and test maintainability. The chapter will cover the following topics:

- Test coverage
- Testing
- Test naming and project structure
- Design methodologies:
    - Test-driven development
    - Spec-driven development
- Mocking
- Integration tests
- Continuous testing

First principles

Any practice worth its salt in terms of its applicability and correctness are often guided by a set of principles or goals, as it were, that the practices are trying to adhere to or accomplish. Automated testing is no different. Automated testing has certain goals that it is expected to accomplish and our practices revolve around accomplishing those goals.

Related terms

In any effective conversation, a consistent vocabulary is vital to communication. So, let's quickly get some terms out of the way:

- **Unit test**: An automated test that tests a single *unit* of source code. Unit is a bit subjective and often means *module* in many circles, but could be as narrow as a class or a method.
- **Integration test**: An automated test that validates the interaction of combined modules.
- **Test fixture**: In the context of automated testing and unit testing frameworks, this is the class or the class hierarchy where test methods live.
- **System under test** (**SUT**): What is being tested? This could be a unit, a subsystem, or the whole application.
- **Test-driven development** (**TDD**): A form of test-first software design where the design is driven by tests and code is written to pass a unit test.
- **Behavior-driven development** (**BDD**): An approach to defining acceptance criteria and acceptance tests that facilitates collaboration between technical and nontechnical business participants.

Test-driven development

I feel it's important to provide some detail about TDD if we're going to talk about automated testing at all. TDD is a form of software design. It's primarily used from the ground up to flush out a design based on the usage of the API being created. In other words, the use of the API would be developed within tests to provide a real-world usage of the API (rather than being "academic"), and ensures that each and every piece of code is covered by one or more tests.

Coming more from a "Brownfield" type of a project where you've already got lots of code that "works," you may have the need for some small refactorings, bug fixes, or feature enhancements. A TDD-style of design can be used for feature enhancements.

The common mantra or *mnemonic* of sorts, with TDD is "Red, Green, Refactor". **Red** signifies a failed test in a test runner, **green** signifies the same test passing, and **refactor** means now that the test passes, you're safe to refactor.

Red, Green, Refactor

TDD has the mantra "Red, Green, Refactor", which means you first create failing tests (red), then update the code to pass the test (green), then you can be confident that changes (refactor) aren't going to introduce problems or cause regressions. It could be better detailed as "Red then Green the Refactor with confidence." The fact that a test was written and proven that it does catch problems (red) means you can be confident that if you change the internal workings of the software without affecting how it acts externally (refactoring), then it is most likely that any problems you might introduce will be detected by a test.

With TDD, this generally means you write a test before you write the code that the test verifies. But we can leverage this technique with existing code as well. For example, when we find (or are told of) a bug, we can write a test that fails which *proves* the bug, and then fix it so that the test passes.

I'm not a tester

I hear this comment quite a bit from various developers. This chapter is by no means a suggestion that formal QA or manual functional or acceptance testing shouldn't be performed by qualified personnel. Developers are capable of testing, just as much as authors are capable of editing. But just as authors shouldn't be the editors of their own work, so too should software developers not be the sole gatekeepers of a product's quality. There needs to be an arm's-length relationship between who has the final say over quality and who creates the software.

This doesn't mean that software developers don't have a responsibility to provide the highest quality software to the people assuring the quality of the product. Software developers have a responsibility to provide bug-free software and ensure that their changes to existing software haven't caused regressions.

Having said that, I've never encountered a software developer that actually didn't do *any* testing. The typical example is a developer who's written a small test app, maybe a console application that runs some of the code that they are working on, and exercises it in a certain way so that he can verify postconditions by tracing through it in the debugger. Some developers I've talked to think this is the extent they need to go to for quality. These small applications provide value with regard to checking initial quality, but they do one thing and often developers spend their time writing them over and over again. They need to create the application and *bootstrap* it before they can actually exercise their code.

Once they exercise their code the application usually languishes, becomes out-of-date, or worst still, stops functioning. This is because it's never run again so it's not front-and-center in someone's mind to get the attention to fix problems as they occur. This is a shame because that tested code is valuable. It's likely to be applicable to the software for most of the life of that software.

If you're writing test applications or test harnesses such as this, just make a small change and use unit test projects or automated test runners to exercise the code, instead of writing many test harnesses.

Why automated?

In the previous section I touched on moving *test harness* code from an application to a unit test project or a unit test assembly that can be run in a test runner. The test runner becomes the testing application that executes the code. Once you do this you can simply run the tests any time you like.

For any particular defect, the cost of fixing that defect is cheaper the closer it's found to the creation of the code that contains the defect. This fact has been drilled into software developer's heads for years, but often software developers don't do enough to avoid those costs. There are all sorts of reasons for the avoidance, but we're going to concentrate on responding to that fact and not on ways to avoid the problem.

Regressions are probably reason number one why testing is automated. If we automate testing we automatically detect potential problems in software. We can still concentrate on creating, fixing, and modifying software. But with automated tests, we can be reasonably assured that the changes we make didn't break something that was working before.

Another reason for automated testing is complexity. We often work with a team of software developers on complex software systems that consist of many components, and each component consists of many classes. It's rare that one person works on an independent part of the code base that isn't influenced by any other part of the code base. We try to decouple systems as much as possible, but any software that works with any other software influences it at some degree. Automated testing makes sure that when I make a change to one part of the system it didn't cause any problems to that part of the system or cause a defect.

Benefits

Given the degree to which automated testing *isn't performed*, it seems useful to outline some of the benefits of automated testing.

Continuous verification

Tests provide a certain level of verification of *quality* of a code base. If that verification is only performed once (test applications or harnesses that are "thrown" away), then that verification is lost. Automated testing makes that important verification continuous. Every time automated testing is run, those tests reverify the code. Not only is the code constantly verified, but our view of *correctness* is also verified. It could very well be that a code change that fails a test could mean the test is now flawed. We may not have known about changes in verification until much later.

Continuous verification means that problems in code are noticed much, much closer to when the code was written. There are numerous studies showing how much more costly it is to fix problems in software the further in time the problem is found compared to when it was created. These statistics have been repeated so many times to have basically become an axiom. It's outside the scope of this book to re-prove axioms.

Documentation

The quintessential benefit of unit testing is documentation. Unit tests document how to use your API or how to use the classes in your code base. Integration tests document how modules in the system are intended to interact with each other, and at least one way of integrating the system.

But that's not the only documentation that unit tests provide. Unit tests can also provide a documentation of the acceptance tests of a system as well as *what* the system does and doesn't (that is, failed tests). This is one area that many teams fail to take advantage of. Tests can act as requirements and acceptance round-tripping. Tests act as verification that requirements have been implemented as well as acting as an interpretation of the requirements. Round-tripping can be the impetus for keeping requirements "alive" throughout the life of the project, rather than living only at the very start or even just at the elicitation stage of the project.

Caveats

I've worked on several projects that I wouldn't call "successful." They were failures for various reasons like applicability, competition, lack of focus, and so on. But they all had automated testing verifying the code being written.

Automated testing is not a panacea. It doesn't automatically provide implicit quality. It's prone to human error like almost everything in life. Automated testing requires skill, attention, consistency, and knowledge to get the most out of automated testing. Use it like any other tool, learn how to use it right, and learn when and when not to use it.

Aspects of good tests

A good test obviously verifies something important about the component (unit) or components (integration) that it is verifying. That's the basic definition of a **test**, so I'm not going to get into details like that. Given that we know we need tests and we know what we are going to test, what makes for good tests? Let's look at some aspects of good tests.

Repeatable

Any test that verifies anything in particular about a part of a system should be repeatable. If we can only run it once, there's not much value to it. Once we accept this as a basic truth we can begin to see the benefits of automating our tests. We'll get into the details of automating tests, but automatically running your tests takes the drudge work of running these tests to verify new or changed code. Tests cannot be automatically run if they are not repeatable.

Independent

Good tests should be independent of one another. Test runners typically can't be consistent in the order in which they run a test. With .NET, test runners normally reflect upon the provided assemblies to find classes or methods with specific attributes. There is no defined order in which classes and methods will be enumerated for any given test runner. Consequently, there is nothing guaranteeing that test A will be run before test B. If test B has a dependency on test A in any way, shape, or form, then test B will eventually cause failures.

Tests should stand on - their - own and verify criteria without the need for another test to be run before or after, nor require two tests to be running simultaneously.

Verifies one thing

It's a fairly common opinion that each test method should contain one `Assert` method call. This is what is meant by *verifies one thing*. The more things a test verifies, the more muddled what actually fails become. This makes it more work to find and fix bugs because you may only see **failed...Expected: <80> . Actual <81>** in a test report and you won't necessarily know which Assert failed. Of course, this must be taken with a grain of salt because multiple things can be verified by a single Assert.

Simple

Good tests are simple. We use things such as *Arrange, Act, Assert* to keep them simple. Each test shouldn't consist of many lines of code. We'll see in the following sections ways to help keep the tests simple in light of more complex arrangements. Keeping with *verifies one thing* helps to keep tests simple.

Readable

Simple doesn't imply readable, but good tests should also be readable. Most code should be readable, but tests act as documentation for the rest of the code, so it's important that the tests be as readable as possible. There are some frameworks and libraries that offer fluent interfaces. For example, instead of `Assert.AreEqual(42, actual)`, NUnit offers the ability to do things as follows:

```
[TestMethod]
public void TestMethod1()
{
  // Arrange
  var o = new Class1();

  // Act
  var actual = o.Method1();

  // Assert
  Assert.That(actual, Is.EqualTo(42));
}
```

Developers and fluent interfaces typically have a love/hate relationship. Either a developer *loves* fluency, or they *hate* it. I'll leave it as an exercise for the reader to decide whether they find using fluent interfaces more or less readable.

I do recommend though, in terms of readability, that consistent use of a fluent interface be used. Otherwise, switching back and forth between fluent and non-fluent as you go from test to test hurts readability.

Fast

The point of automating tests is so the automation can be run as often as needed. This could be as little as every nightly build, or every check-in with gated check-ins, or even every save of a source file with ContinuousTests. The longer tests take to run, the longer developers wait between writing code and finding potential bugs.

Reliable

Automated tests need to be reliable. They effectively need to be able to give you a constant *state of the union* of the code. If you can't rely on the tests doing that (they're not repeatable or not independent), then you won't feel you can rely on the tests. If you don't feel you can rely on the tests, you won't feel confident that refactoring code or fixing bugs won't introduce unexpected side effects that would cause the system to fail. In effect, you may think twice about making a change that would make the code better or make the system better.

Informative

Tests should tell you *the* problem, not be *a* problem. It is useful to know that there is a problem that is blocking you, but the quicker you find, fix, and retest the problem, the faster the project gets back on track. As long as automated testing is a perceived bottleneck to anyone in the organization there will be some sort of friction around it. Making sure test failures are as informative as possible when they occur means tests can be leveraged to their fullest potential.

Context: When writing good tests.

Practice: Ensure tests are repeatable, simple, readable, fast, reliable, informative, independent, and verify one thing.

Test naming

The actual test is important, but if a test fails and it's hard to figure out what to do to fix the code to pass the test or where the problem is, developers can waste precious time tracking down where the roots of failures are. The name of a test, its parent class, and (to a certain extent) the namespace and project name can go a long way to providing useful context in failure messages or automated testing reports. Let's take the following class, for example:

```
namespace UnitTests
{
  [TestClass]
  public class Class1Tests
  {
    [TestMethod]
    public void TestMethod1()
    {
      var o = new Class1();
```

```
            var actual = o.Method1();

            Assert.AreEqual(42, actual);
        }
    }
}
```

If the `TestMethod1` test failed in its assertion, we would see the following screenshot in the **Test Results** report:

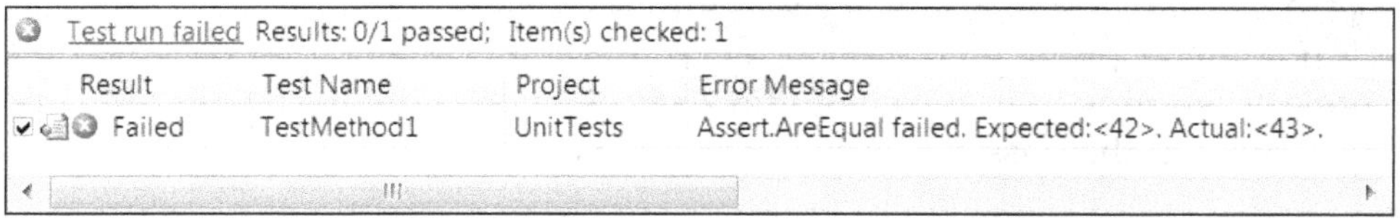

This report really doesn't tell us much. We know that `TestMethod1` had an assertion failed and that it expected `43` but got `42`. But, had I never worked on this method and I made a code change that caused this, how likely would this information be very actionable?

I'd need to resort to double-clicking on the line item in the report to go to the test to at least read it. If that didn't tell me much more, I may need to resort to tracing through the code in the test to figure out what code is involved, and how that relates to the changes I've made recently. And "recently" could be a long time if I'm not running tests that often.

We could fall back to continuous verification, checking-in often (if we use gated check-ins), readable tests, and so on, but the fact is sometimes we break tests that other people wrote and we don't really know much about them. The name of the test and the name of the class are basically unused in this report. It may just as well not be there as we'd have the same amount of information. The problem is this test isn't very *informative*.

This sometimes unused aspect of writing tests is easy to rectify. There are several easy strategies we can use to exploit the class and method names to provide a much better test report experience.

There is probably an equal number of test class/method naming strategies as there are books on unit testing. For the most part, I feel what naming strategy you pick depends on how you group tests.

Let's look at a couple of popular ways of "grouping" tests (a.k.a. naming tests and test fixtures). Naming standards or guidelines shouldn't exist simply to avoid needing to think of a name for a fixture or a test.

Context: When naming tests and test methods.

Guidance: Give them names that make finding and fixing the problem easier.

Separate test projects or not?

There's nothing stopping your test classes from being in any of your projects, even EXE projects (starting with Visual Studio 2005). So, you could have your tests in the same assembly as the classes that you are testing.

I haven't seen any particular arguments for or against separate test projects that are especially persuasive for every situation. For a "production" project (as opposed to "enterprise"), you can't redistribute a third-party testing framework. The easiest way to ensure this doesn't happen is to have a separate test project.

Context: Software under development is being delivered outside the organization.

Practice: Have separate test projects so that they do not need to be deployed into environments they are not needed.

Test styles

Testing styles go a long way to making tests readable. Tests help document how the code is used within the system, as well as document certain requirements and acceptance criteria. Test styles help give tests a consistent form and flow so that reading them "flows" and that they are more consistent with one another. Let's go over a couple of well-known testing styles.

Arrange, Act, Assert

Probably the most common test style is *Arrange, Act, Assert*. This is sometimes referred to as the AAA style. This style of writing separates the code that arranges the variables and state of the test, from the act of operating on the state, from the asserting that the expected state exists at the end of the test.

An example of a test that uses the *Arrange, Act, Assert* style:

```
namespace UnitTests
{
  [TestClass]
```

```
    public class Class1Tests
    {
      [TestMethod]
      public void TestMethod1()
      {
        // Arrange
        var o = new Class1();

        // Act
        var actual = o.Method1();

        // Assert
        Assert.AreEqual(42, actual);
      }
    }
}
```

But, don't put the Act, Arrange, and Assert comments in the code. Simply group the code that arranges together, group the code that acts together, and group the code asserts separately from the code that arranges and acts. In some circles, *Arrange, Act, Assert* is known as *Build, Operate, Check.*

Using this style consistently within a project helps make each test easier to read and understand because of the consistent flow. The top of a test method is the arrangement of variables and preconditions, the end is the call to `Assert`, and the middle is the logic whose side effects are being tested.

There are a couple of drawbacks to *Arrange, Act, Assert* that are worth being aware of. One is that it implies tests are only asserting success conditions. With many automated test frameworks, the act of verifying expected exceptions are thrown is signified by attributing the test method with an attribute such as `ExpectedExceptionAttribute`. The following is an example of a test that verifies an exception is thrown from a method:

```
[TestMethod]
[ExpectedException(typeof(ArgumentException))]
public void TestMethod2()
{
  // Arrange
  var o = new Class1();

  // Act
  o.Method2(double.NaN);
}
```

Notice the `ExpectedException` attribute signifying that the code in this test should throw `ArgumentException` (and only `ArgumentException`). This is a perfectly valid test, but there is no call to an `Assert` method to make an assertion. The assertion is effectively the attribute on the method.

I don't think this detracts from the *Arrange, Act, Assert* style, but it's something to keep in mind when reading tests.

Now, you could say that we could strictly abide by the *Arrange, Act, Assert* style and still verify that exceptions were thrown. We could write code to catch exceptions and assert the type is correct, for example:

```
[TestMethod]
public void TestMethod2b()
{
  // Arrange
  var o = new Class1();
  Exception exception = null;

  try
  {
    // Act
    o.Method2(double.NaN);
  }
  catch(Exception ex)
  {
    exception = ex;
  }
  // Assert
  Assert.IsInstanceOfType(exception,
    typeof(ArgumentException));
}
```

In this example, we catch any exceptions and then pass that off to the `Assert.IsInstanceOfType` method to validate our assertion that `Class1.Method2(double)` should throw an `ArgumentException`, when it is passed a value that is considered *not a number*.

But I find this to be less readable. We start including things in our Arrange section that are not preconditions. They're actually variables to track postconditions. Plus, we've increased the size of our code by nine lines. The amount of code is somewhat trivial, but it does add verbosity without any value other than to appease *Arrange, Act, Assert*.

This example segues into an important part of testing: don't test only successful conditions. It shows a test that tests, that a failure is handled as expected.

Context: When testing code with specific error conditions.

Practice: Also test successful error conditions.

Another drawback with *Arrange, Act, Assert* is that arrangement of preconditions, or test context, is done at the start of a test method. In almost all automated testing frameworks there are specific methods of a test fixture class than can be used for "setup" and "teardown" of test context. We've seen two test methods that have the same Arrange code, which is basically to create a `Class1` instance. **Don't Repeat Yourself** (**DRY**) applies to tests as well, and we may not want to repeat the creation of an instance of `Class1` over and over again in code. We could rewrite this test to create the `Setup` (attributing an instance method with the `TestInitialize` attribute) and `Teardown` (attributing an instance method with the `TestCleanup` attribute) methods to create and unroot instances of `Class1` in our case. An example of doing this could be:

```
[TestClass]
public class Class1TestsB
{
  private Class1 sut;

  [TestInitialize]
  public void Setup()
  {
    sut = new Class1();
  }

  [TestCleanup]
  public void Teardown()
  {
    // Dispose, if possible
    sut = null;
  }

  [TestMethod]
  public void TestMethod1()
  {
    // Act
    var actual = sut.Method1();

    // Assert
    Assert.AreEqual(42, actual);
  }
```

```
        [TestMethod]
        [ExpectedException(typeof(ArgumentException))]
        public void TestMethod2()
        {
          // Act
          sut.Method2(double.NaN);
        }
    }
```

We now have an instance field `sut` that contains the instance of `Class1`, which we wish to use to verify our assertions that this test fixture contains. Our new `Setup` method instantiates a `Class1` instance and assigns it to our `sut` field. The test methods now act on that field instead of a local variable. As we can see, each of our test methods now have no *Arrange* code in them, and in the case of `TestMethod2`, has neither an *Arrange* section nor an *Assert* section. Our `Teardown` method simply unroots the existing instance of `Class1` so that it cannot be used again and can be collected by the garbage collector.

So, clearly the *Arrange, Act, Assert* style can't be followed to the letter in every scenario.

Context: When applying any test style.

Practice: Don't force a test style for the sake of the style.

We'll see more about organizing tests to keep with the DRY principle shortly to keep tests easier to maintain and read.

Now that we've seen the `Setup` and `Teardown` methods, and that we've basically implied that the `Setup` method is called before each test method, and the `Teardown` method is called after each test method, let's have a closer look at what happens when test runners run tests.

Despite having multiple test methods in one class, each test is actually executed on a different instance of the test class. This makes tests completely independent of one another in terms of the instances fields and values of the class. For example, in our previous class, when it is run in a test runner, the following methods are invoked in this order: constructor, `Setup`, `TestMethod1`, `Teardown`, constructor, `Setup`, `TestMethod2`, and `Teardown`. Had our method implemented `IDisposable`, those method invocations would be: constructor, `Setup`, `TestMethod1`, `Teardown`, `Dispose`, constructor, `SetupTestMethod2`, `Teardown`, and `Dispose`.

Context: When working with test runners.

Practice: Remember that methods in test classes are executed independently of any other instances of the test class.

What we've basically shown is that our test grouping is effectively by class under test, in this case `Class1`. If all our tests in a test class share the same context, or the same *Arrange* code, then *Arrange, Act, Assert* may not be the best style to use as the *Arrange* section becomes disconnected from the *Act* and *Assert* sections.

Let's have a look at a different testing style.

Given, When, Then

Behavior-driven development (**BDD**) takes an approach of capturing acceptance criteria of a system by defining an initial context, an event that occurs within that context, and the expected outcome of that event for that context. This approach is intended to be easily understood by non-development or non-technical stakeholders. The idea is that the expected *behavior* is also considered when gathering requirements. This concept was introduced by Dan North and details expectations and acceptance criteria in prose. The following is one of Dan's examples:

```
Given the account is in credit
  And the card is valid
  And the dispenser contains cash
When the customer requests cash
Then ensure the account is debited
  And ensure cash is dispensed
  And ensure the card is returned
```

This is called a specification. It's how stakeholders can specify success (or failure) criteria. There's much more to BDD, but in the context of tests, *Given, When, Then* helps us decide what to assert and how to organize our tests.

Now, we could simply take on the same basic structure in our tests and say that we've used *Given, When, Then* style:

```
[TestClass]
public class GivenWhenThenTest
{
  [TestMethod]
  public void TestMethod1()
  {
    // Given
    var account = new Account(100.00);
    var card = new Card();
    var dispenser = new Dispener();

    // When
    dispenser.InsertCard(card);
```

```
        dispenser.SelectAccount(account);
        var cash = dispenser.RequestCash(20.00);

        // Then
        Assert.AreEqual(cash, 20.00);
        Assert.AreEqual(80.00, account.Balance);
        Assert.IsFalse(dispenser.HoldsCard);
    }
}
```

But this partially misses the point, and doesn't provide anything distinctly different from *Arrange, Act, Assert*. There's so much more information collected around BDD that gets lost if we do it this way.

We can use the information about context, requirements, and acceptance to name and organize our tests. If we look at our *Given*, *When*, and *Then* details for a particular scenario slightly differently, and look at the *Given* and *When* as our test setup and our *Thens* as our tests, we could name our test class and test methods much more clearly. For example:

```
[TestClass]
public class when_the_customer_requests_cash
{
    private double dispensedCash;
    private Account account;
    private Dispener dispenser;

    [TestInitialize]
    public void Setup()
    {
        account = new Account(100.00);
        var card = new Card();
        dispenser = new Dispener();

        dispenser.InsertCard(card);
        dispenser.SelectAccount(account);
        dispensedCash = dispenser.RequestCash(20.00);
    }

    [TestMethod]
    public void then_the_account_is_debited()
    {
        Assert.AreEqual(80.00, account.Balance);
    }

    [TestMethod]
    public void then_the_cash_is_dispensed()
```

```
    {
      Assert.AreEqual(dispensedCash, 20.00);
    }

    [TestMethod]
    public void then_the_card_is_returned()
    {
      Assert.IsFalse(dispenser.HoldsCard);
    }
  }
```

As we can see, we now have three tests instead of one. This gives us three things that have a name which we can use to be more descriptive. In this case, we've chosen the *Then* criteria from our original scenario: `Then ensure the account is debited`, `And ensure cash is dispensed`, and `And ensure the card is returned`. We now have three test methods that effectively match those conditions: `then_the_account_is_debited`, `then_the_cash_is_dispensed`, and `then_the_card_is_returned`. The class name is now the `When` clause: `when_the_customer_requests_cash`.

This is an example with a canonical BDD example scenario. It uses three classes `Account`, `Card`, and `Dispenser`. Depending on your view of *units*, and whether these classes exist in the same *module*, this particular example may better be called an *integration* test. I would tend to see `Account`, `Card`, and `Dispenser` as being within a single *domain* and view this more as a unit test than an integration test. Regardless this test clearly takes into account a particular usage scenario.

Now, if one of these test methods were to fail, and we rearranged our test report slightly to group by class, our test report might look like the following screenshot:

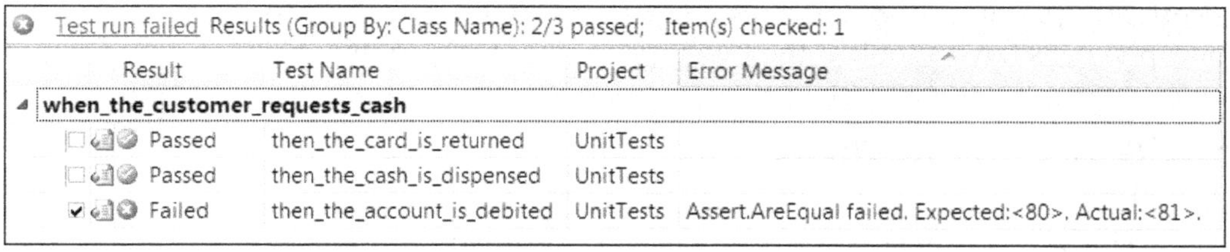

We can now see much more information about failures. In this case, we can see that when the customer requests cash, the account is not debited correctly.

This form of development (based on stakeholder specifications) is called **spec-driven development**.

The use of `when_` and `then_` in the example classes and methods is obviously going to occur every single time, which is tantamount to not being there at all. Depending on what you find readable, I feel it's perfectly acceptable to leave those out of the class and method names . You could name the class `customer_requests_cash`, and the methods `card_is_returned`, `cash_is_dispensed`, and `account_is_debited` respectively. I find this to be equally readable within code and test reports, but you may disagree. If you choose this way to organize and group your tests, then just be consistent with whether you choose to include `then` and `when` in names or not.

I've also chosen to use underscore characters to separate English words in the names of these tests. I do this only for tests. We only ever write tests once and we never call them manually within code (the test runner does), not like our other methods and classes where we wouldn't want to pay the "underscore tax" typing out *those* names. I find using the underscore in the name to be easier to read and action in test reports, but I'd never recommend using underscore in non-test classes and methods as a general style.

We'll shortly see another way underscores give us benefits.

Context: When organizing test code that doesn't share setup.

Practice: Physically group code that initializes (or arranges) from the code that causes side effects (acts), from the code that verifies (asserts).

Test types

There are really two types of tests. Tests that test side effects (state-based tests) or tests that test how classes are used (interaction tests). Both approach testing in different ways but both also test different things. Each type of test is better suited to certain types of testing scenarios and better suited for testing certain types of concepts. Let's have a look at the two types and see where they fit.

State-based testing

Most of the time, our tests are intended to verify that something had the correct result. This type of a test is verifying certain side effects or that a certain state exists after execution of a certain code within a certain context.

In terms of *unit* tests, this is probably the most common type of a test. This type of a test acts upon the public members of classes to perform certain actions, and then looks upon the public members of the classes to verify a certain state exists afterwards. It effectively ignores the internals or privates of classes, and leaves the encapsulation of the data to the class and looks only at their interfaces.

Clearly, these types of tests work well if we have public interfaces, and that those public interfaces contain everything we need to verify. There's an implication that verification criteria is finite and easily comparable.

Most of the tests we've seen so far have been state-based tests. They've tested the side effects of certain actions or the side effects of specific code based on specific or known inputs.

However, sometimes we don't want to verify the resulting state.

Context: When testing code with side effects.

Practice: Use state-based tests to verify only side effects to test.

Interaction testing

Another type of testing is interaction testing. This type of testing verifies how input is given to a class, or how that class outputs to another class, effectively testing how two or more classes interact with each other.

There are various reasons why you may need to choose interaction testing instead of state-based testing. I can't possibly go over every possible reason but I'll go over a few very common reasons.

There are times when you simply don't have access to a particular resource in order to verify side effects. You might also not know the entire initial state of something within a test. In these cases, you may simply want to test that something specific happened.

To a certain extent, interaction tests assume a leap of faith that certain things will occur. This is normal and we often *must* have this faith. We either don't have the resources (time, processing power, and so on) to verify everything that could be verified, or that what we can verify is outside of our control and know whether or not it works is entirely unactionable. For example, we may require that some of our data is persisted to a database. We could easily write a test to write data to a row in a table in a relational database, read it back, and verify that what we wrote to that row was indeed read back This really just tests the relational database. We didn't write the database and we're not changing its functionality as we write or maintain the system we're working on. So the fact that it "works" isn't going to change in our context. There's no reason to continuously test it through automated tests. There may be some criteria by which you need to evaluate third-party tools and systems such as relational databases, but you do that as a separate exercise before you "accept" that product for use within your system. You need to assume that functionality won't change for no reason at all and not write tests to verify that unchanging functionality. You've got enough work to add value to your system.

Interaction tests often come into play with third-party software, such as libraries or frameworks, because those libraries and frameworks may need to be used in a certain way. For example, a scheduling library may operate only in a specific way. It won't schedule something unless you ask it to. You can't really verify that what you ask it to do will be actioned, but you can test that you use it correctly.

Context: When writing tests that involve multiple classes that are required to interact in specific ways.

Practice: Use interaction testing to verify that interaction occurs correctly.

Object-orientation and tests

We've briefly covered the concept of object-orientation with regard to tests. We covered encapsulating context within a test class to be shared amongst test classes. But there's much more to object-oriented design that can be taken advantage of in automated tests.

Each test class is a test fixture. The name of the fixture can focus group a given set of tests. We've seen examples of test fixtures that share setup and how that setup would be extracted into a single method or into the constructor to stay DRY. This concept can be expanded to a subgroup related tests into multiple classes to gain extra clarity through the class name into a base fixture class. If we return to our `Class1TestsB` example, let's say moving `TestMethod1` and `TestMethod2` into separate classes gives us the ability to subgroup these tests into an individual class with a more clear class name. We could pull up the setup and teardown into a new base class shown as follows:

```
[TestClass]
public abstract class Class1Fixture
{
  protected Class1 sut;

  [TestInitialize]
  public void Setup()
  {
    sut = new Class1();
  }

  [TestCleanup]
  public void Teardown()
  {
    sut = null;
  }
}
```

And reorganize our previous class into two new classes both deriving from `Class1Fixture`:

```
[TestClass]
public class Class1TestsC : Class1Fixture
{
  [TestMethod]
  public void TestMethod1()
  {
    // Act
    var actual = sut.Method1();

    // Assert
    Assert.AreEqual(42, actual);
  }
}
[TestClass]
public class Class1TestsD : Class1Fixture
{
  [TestMethod]
  [ExpectedException(typeof(ArgumentException))]
  public void TestMethod2()
  {
    // Act
    sut.Method2(double.NaN);
  }
}
```

Assume for a moment that we have something more meaningful than `Class1TestC` and `Class1TestD`, we now have effectively subgrouped tests and given those subgroupings distinct and meaningful names, that is, the names of the classes.

Fluent interfaces revisited

One problem with test code is it often has many magic numbers strewn through it values such as `20` or `new TimeSpan(1, 30, 15)`. We want our tests, to be readable and easily maintained. Magic numbers such as this often don't tell us much about what's going on in the tests.

Fortunately, extension methods can be added to our test assemblies to make intention more explicit. For example, let's say we wanted to test a class that accepted a number of hours in the constructor and provide a method to add a time span to that original hours. We might think we'd write a test as follows:

```
[TestMethod]
public void TestAddTimespan()
{
  var sut = new TimeCalculator(20);
  sut.Add(new TimeSpan(1, 30, 15));

  Assert.AreEqual(sut.TotalSeconds, 77415);
}
```

Reading through this test long after you wrote it, or if you never wrote it, `20`, `new TimeSpan(1,30,15)`, and `77415` seem merely like magic numbers. They provide little value. You'd probably need to go look at the constructor for `TimeCalculator`, or look at the implementation of the `Add` method to find out what's really going on. Fortunately, we can write a few extension methods to get something more clear. For example:

```
[TestMethod]
public void TestAddTimespan()
{
  var sut = new TimeCalculator(20.Hours());
  sut.Add(new TimeSpan(1.Hours(),
    30.Minutes(), 15.Seconds()));

  Assert.AreEqual(sut.TotalSeconds, 77415.Seconds());
}
```

This provides much better meaning through specific intent. This can simply be done with simple extension methods shown as follows:

```
public static class IntegerExtensions
{
  public static int Seconds(this int value)
  {
    return value;
  }
  public static int Hours(this int value)
  {
    return value;
  }
  public static int Minutes(this int value)
  {
    return value;
  }
}
```

Simple methods, but they provide much more information. Methods such as these would never need to be used in production code (only in test code), because we rarely ever had to build up our types like this as they're usually loaded from some persistence store and constant values rarely come into play.

Context: When building up test data within test fixture.

Practice: Avoid *magic numbers* and use specific types or extension methods to provide information about intent.

Mocking

Mocking is a general term for objects that simulate other objects. These can be hand coded classes to simulate other objects, or they can use isolation frameworks to automate the creation of an object to simulate other objects.

I personally prefer to call objects like these "doubles," rather than mock objects. "Mock" implies a specific type of double. I generally follow the definitions from xUnit patterns. **Mock** is a double that facilitates in validating the correctness of results within a test via its behavior being called by the SUT, by acting in the same way as what it is doubling for. There are other types of "test doubles" that we can make use of when we're attempting to verify our code through tests. A **stub** acts in the same way as another object to provide inputs to a third object, so that inputs can be verified. A **dummy** is an object that "fills in the blanks" for something else that otherwise couldn't operate without "something," A **fake** object takes the place of something else to provide behavior that is otherwise ignored. A **spy** is effectively a mock, fake, or stub that records what happens to it for later verification.

Dummies and fakes can be used by any type of test. Dummies generally take the place of a parameter that, while ignored, is required to get the test code to run. Fakes are similar to dummies except they provide expected behavior to "appease" another object. The other types of test doubles are generally used in interaction tests to verify interactive behavior in some way.

Context: When interaction testing with classes that need to be isolated.

Practice: Use test doubles such as stubs, mocks, fakes, or spies to verify interaction between two or more other objects.

Isolation frameworks

Mocking frameworks, such as Rhino Mocks or Moq, help you isolate one layer from another or one class from another. This is why they're generally considered part of a larger category of frameworks called **isolation frameworks**.

Context: When hand-crafting test doubles would otherwise be overly time-consuming.

Practice: Use an isolation framework to make creation of test doubles easier and faster.

Methodologies

Automated testing involves writing tests in code that are automatically executed. As we've seen, there are some things we can do to focus our testing efforts and make those tests more effective. Testing methodologies provide holistic methods towards testing which attempt to address a common goal or theme. Let's look at the two most common methodologies.

TDD

We've already talked a bit about **test-driven design** (**TDD**). Technically, TDD doesn't facilitate automated testing. Rather, it facilitates better design through a test-first mentality. But, it does help us improve code coverage from tests, write more testable code, and hopefully make better APIs and better designed software.

When nothing else is really known about lower-level details of a system, TDD helps us focus on some of the interface-specific details that could otherwise cause "analysis paralysis." Getting into too much detail when there are so many other great books on TDD is somewhat pointless. But I'll give a short example of using TDD to flesh out an API or an interface for required implementation.

Let's look at Kent Beck's quintessential currency multiplication example. Let's say we need to multiply an amount of currency by a specific quantity. With TDD, we'd design the API to do this by first writing a test that makes sense. Beck's example supposes a `Dollar` class with a `Times` method and an `Amount` property. So we'd write a test shown as follows:

```
[TestMethod]
public void then_multiplying_dollars_results_in_correct_amount()
{
    Dollar five = new Dollar(5);
    five.Times(2);
    Assert.Equals(10, five.Amount);
}
```

Of course, we now see errors with `Dollar`, `Times`, and `Amount` because they don't exist. We can let Visual Studio generate a class, a constructor, a method, and a property to produce something shown as follows:

```
class Dollar
{
  private int p;

  public Dollar(int p)
  {
    // TODO: Complete member initialization
    this.p = p;
  }
  internal void Times(int p)
  {
    throw new NotImplementedException();
  }

  public object Amount { get; set; }
}
```

We don't really want to test throwing exceptions, so, we update the `Dollar` class to contain the minimum that will compile and run without throwing an exception (and better access modifiers):

```
class Dollar
{
  public Dollar(int p)
  {
  }

  public void Times(int p)
  {
  }

  public object Amount { get; set; }
}
```

Now, we can compile without error and run the tests without exception. But, because nothing is implemented we get a failing test. This gives us "Red." We can now implement only as much as we need to pass our test:

```
class Dollar
{
  public Dollar(int p)
  {
```

```
            Amount = 10;
        }

        public void Times(int p)
        {
        }

        public object Amount { get; set; }
    }
```

In this test, we're looking specifically for an `Amount` of `10`. So to pass the test we simply initialize `Amount` to `10` and our test passes. This gives us "Green." Of course, this is not a useful class as is, so the expectation is that we'd continue writing more tests to verify the other behaviors of `Dollar` until we have something complete.

Context: When designing interfaces with little or no stakeholder collaboration.

Practice: Use TDD when designing APIs that will be used extensively by other developers that require specific levels of decoupling and testability.

BDD

Behavior-driven design (**BDD**) centers around eliciting and documenting requirements and acceptance criteria, and using stakeholder language to aid collaboration.

BDD is an agile technique of documenting user stories. Stories center around detailing features and benefits for specific user roles. Scenarios are then written to detail the acceptance criteria of each scenario. Typically, these scenarios take the natural language form of "As a *role* I want *feature* so that *benefit*." For example, given our previous BDD example scenario of withdrawing cash from a dispenser, the user story around that scenario would be "*As a* customer, *I want* to withdraw cash from an ATM, *so that* I don't need to wait in line at the bank."

BDD is another form of testing that we can use in our tool belt. It doesn't assume we are only doing BDD, we may use BDD to automate our acceptance testing and continue to do more technical unit and integration testing.

Context: When engineering requirements with involved stakeholders willing to collaborate.

Practice: Use BDD to guide collaboration to elicit requirements and acceptance criteria using natural language within automated testing to closely model stakeholders' reality.

Test coverage

Code coverage and tests often go hand-in-hand. How do you know you're testing enough, or even if you're testing certain things too much? You can use code coverage tools to see the level to which code is tested. By running tests through a code coverage tool you can see what code was executed and what code wasn't executed by tests. To a certain extent, you can use certain static analysis tools to see what classes and methods would be executed by tests. However, code coverage tools show you what parts of those classes and methods were executed.

Context: When automating builds with techniques such as nightly builds.

Practice: Monitor code coverage percentage deltas to see if coverage is increasing or decreasing, rather than specific percentages.

Code coverage generally gives you a percentage metric that tells you what percentage of code is covered by tests. Having code coverage monitor during automated tests can lead to obsession about code coverage. Knee-jerk policies such as "never go below 75 percent coverage" can lead to irrational decisions to fail a build and to spend inordinate amount of times writing tests to ensure "quotas" are met. This is dangerous because the mandate becomes about quantity and not quality.

Context: When using test code coverage to manage project tasks.

Practice: Don't fixate on 100 percent coverage. It's usually takes much more work than is realistic to get the software done on time and budget.

Continuous testing

I've spoken earlier about continuous verification and how this involves running tests on a periodic basis to ensure all tests are passing. This could be during nightly builds, during check-ins using concepts such gated check-ins, or simply pressing *Ctrl + R, A* occasionally while coding.

There is another class of tools that performs continuous testing. This means these tools execute automated tests in the background, automatically. These tools, such as NCrunch, simply see if anything in your project changes and run all tests automatically (in the background) or, like ContinuousTests, they monitor what files are saved to disk, analyze what was changed since the last time tests were run, and only run tests that apply on the code that was changed.

These tools are great at taking the tedium out of running tests, especially when you or your team isn't using tools such as gated check-ins to make sure the code that breaks a test isn't checked-in. When you have continuous testing tools running, you're informed as quickly as possible when a code change causes a test to fail, and you avoid checking something in that potentially *breaks the build*.

Context: When working with any significant amount of automated tests.

Practice: Use a continuous testing tool to aid in finding failing tests as close to when the violating code was written.

Round-tripping requirements and acceptance

One of the benefits of writing in .NET is that its managed code "compilation" produces an abstract **intermediary language** (**IL**). The results of this compilation are code and meta-information that we can analyze very easily and directly with .NET, using reflection or other tools via inspection of the generated IL or bytecode.

As tests and test classes are generally attributed with information around tests and test methods, we're free to search for and specifically analyze our tests in very useful ways.

One analysis, of course, involves static analysis of test to check for specific rules. There are various tools out that perform such tasks, such as FxCop or Visual Studio Code Analysis. We won't look too closely at those (I'll leave that as an exercise to the user).

One thing we can do with our tests is perform round-trip requirements and acceptance documentation.

The typical "waterfall" type approach is that you are given requirements, you implement those requirements, and someone (maybe a tester) validates that those requirements are met. "Waterfall" or not, there are requirements that need to be met throughout the lifecycle of a software project, and those requirements often get forgotten about as an "asset" once the project is underway. The "engineering" of those requirements often falls to the wayside once development is fully underway because, for the most part, most requirements are known beforehand. Only occasionally will requirements need to change or be added. So the same zeal and effort that might occur in the beginning of the project wanes.

We can help keep those requirements, or the acceptance criteria, alive and closer to the forefront of consciousness through the constant "report" of what the project is verifying and what has been verified.

One way of doing this is to analyze the tests and produce a human-readable "report" of what certain tests are testing, their criteria, and the results. This can act as a living requirements document or living acceptance document.

Finding test classes within a specific assembly, by assembly name, can be found easily with a simple LINQ statement:

```
return Assembly.LoadFrom(assemblyName).GetTypes()
  .Where(t => t.ContainsAttribute("TestClassAttribute"));
```

Using this collection of types we can easily form prose-style text to document the context of the test, the acceptance criteria, and the current results of the test.

Remember the underscores I mentioned earlier? This is where they come in handy. We can simply replace all of the underscores in test class names and test class method names with spaces to quickly and easily generate English prose from our class and member names. Along with the *When/Then* convention, we can easily generate a document that lists all of the tests in our assembly in a document that details the current "state of the union" as it pertains to verifying acceptance.

Make this document available to stakeholders and not only can they see the status of "acceptance" (hopefully based on *their* criteria), but they can also provide feedback on existing tests or new tests because they can see what the automated tests are doing, all based on English prose that is easily understood by them.

With our previous BDD example test, this might result in documentation similar to the following:

```
Scenario: When the customer requests cash
  Then the account is debited
  And the cash is dispensed
  And the card is returned
```

We could further extend this type of documentation generation with a series of extensions to detect specific domain class usage, format, and detail the inputs for each test.

Context: When involved with a project of any significant domain complexity.

Practice: Make use of techniques that keep requirements and/or acceptance criteria front and center through the entire lifecycle of the project.

Summary

I hope this chapter opened your eyes about the possibilities of automated testing. We saw some practices around how to make tests easier to read and provide information facilitating faster finding and fixing of failures. We also detailed some practices on how to organize tests and help to make them easier to read, more concise, and more effective.

This chapter should give you more than a few practices that you can put in your tool belt to make automated testing work better for you, or provide more benefits, and to help improve the quality of your code base, while at the same time letting automated testing improve your software development experience.

The next chapter goes on to detail ways of making Visual Studio work in our favor. We'll look at ways of making Visual Studio operate more efficiently, work to our advantage, and ways to make working with Visual Studio friendlier.

7
Optimizing Visual Studio

Visual Studio (**VS**) is a tool. It is the **integrated development environment** (IDE) by which many .NET developers organize, maintain, analyze, design, compile, and document their product. Visual Studio supports language-specific projects to produce assemblies: executables, class libraries, native DLLs, native executables, and anything add-ins and extensions might add to available projects.

As with any tool, it's designed to be used in certain ways, but can be used in ways it wasn't designed to be used. This chapter attempts to detail some practices on using Visual Studio in the way it was designed, as well as some practices on not using Visual Studio in ways it wasn't designed, to avoid grief.

Visual Studio efficiency through configuration

As with any piece of software, Visual Studio uses resources on your computer. The use of those resources can be directly proportional to the complexity.

The recommended configuration for Visual Studio is a 1.6 GHz processor, 1–2 GB of RAM, 3 GB available hard drive space, 5400 RPM drive, and so on. While this setup will likely allow Visual Studio to run, it's not going to be running as fast as it can.

Recommended computer specifications

To start off, the lower the amount of RAM the greater the possibility that Windows will start swapping memory in and out to disk. This is *really expensive*. It's probably the slowest thing that can happen without accessing the network. It's recommended that you put as much RAM on the computer as you possibly can. For 32-bit processors, this limit is 4 GB. This effectively gives you 2 GB of RAM that can be physically committed per application. If you have a 32-bit processor, it's highly recommended to have 4 GB of RAM for Visual Studio.

Visual Studio is a 32-bit application (and probably will be for the most part of the next couple of versions). As such, it can only physically access 4 GB of RAM. But on 32-bit versions of Windows, applications can really only access 2 GB of RAM (anything above that gets swapped to disk and things get *really slow*). On 64-bit versions of Windows that limit rises to 4 GB which is the full 32-bit addressable space. The choice between 32-bit and 64-bit computers at present isn't much of a choice. There's likely to be only a 64-bit option for new computers. However, it's recommended to upgrade to 64-bit so you can have more available memory for each application. Also, since 64-bit Windows can access 192 GB (Professional and above, but all address at least 8 GB) each 32-bit process can be using their own 4 GB of RAM, further decreasing the possibility of swapping memory to disk.

Regardless of whether you have enough RAM, to avoid swapping memory to disk most of the time, Visual Studio makes use of the hard drive quite a lot. Every build means a huge amount of disk access. While 5400 RPM disks are reasonably fast, that speed can be noticeably increased with a 7200 RPM or 10000 RPM disk. But the speed increases that can be achieved with a **solid-state drive** (**SSD**) are drastically better. Of course, the maximum throughput any drive can achieve depends on the IO bus. Traditional ATA buses (parallel) could manage a top speed of 133 megabytes per second. The latest Serial ATA (version 3) reaches 600 megabytes per second, which is almost five times faster. The average drive can really only muster as much 10 megabytes per second due to technology, seek speed, and so on. This is why defragmentation is so important with traditional hard drives. SSD's can easily handle 40 – 50 megabytes per second. Using Visual Studio on a computer with SDD is noticeably much faster than with a traditional drive. The caveat for the near future is cost. They're more expensive than traditional drives, easily costing two to three (and more) times more expensive, depending on the size and speed.

Context: When considering a computer to install Visual Studio on.

Practice: Consider 64-bit computer with at least 8 GB of RAM and at least 250 GB SSD.

Multi-monitor

Visual Studio 2010 got rid of the **multiple document interface** (**MDI**) mode in favor of tabbed documents. In addition to this change they added the ability for child windows to be dragged outside of the top-level window. This means you can have the main Visual Studio window on one monitor and any documents windows can be on any other monitor (or monitors). For example, you could have one file on one monitor and Visual Studio (and another file) on another monitor, as shown in the following screenshot:

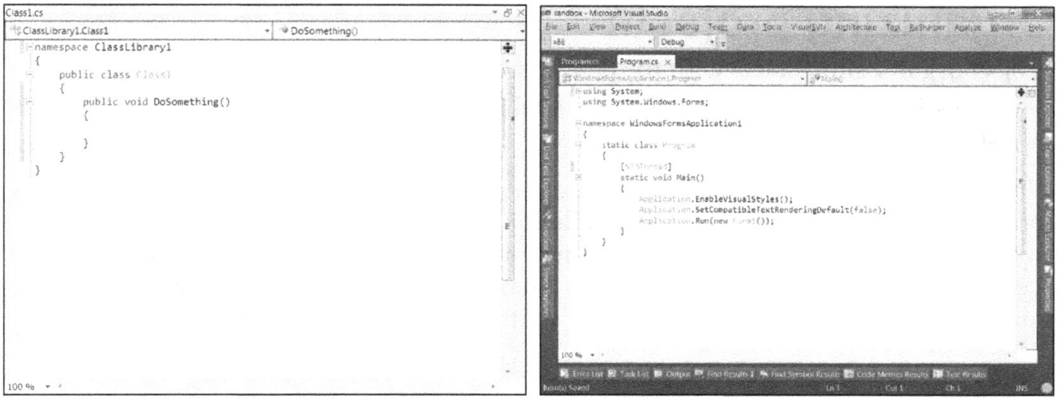

Or, while debugging, one monitor could contain the **Call Stack** and **Watch** windows, as shown in the following screenshot:

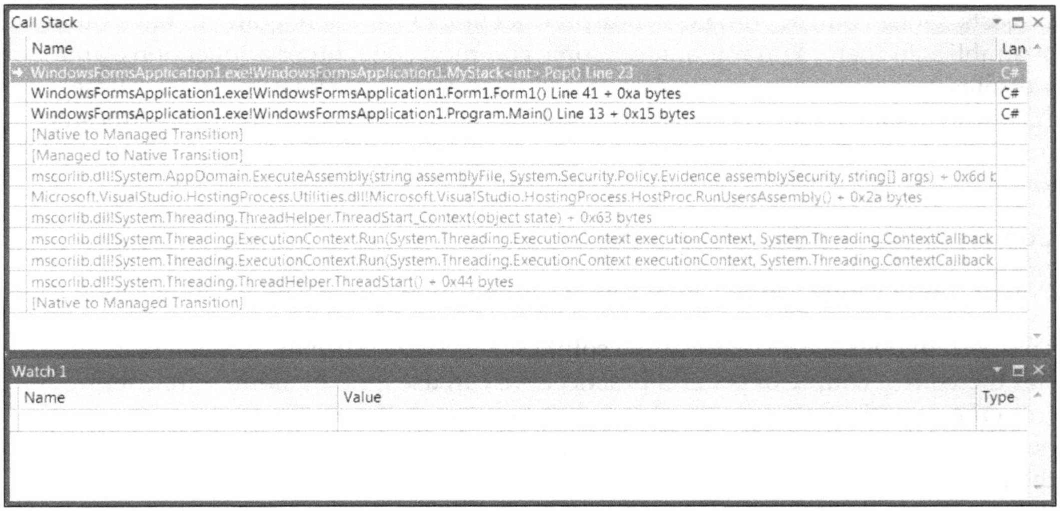

Placing a window onto another monitor is simple. You can simply drag the title/tab of the window to put the window in float mode and drag it to whatever monitor you want it on. Another option on Windows 7 is to right-click on the tab and select **Float** to get the window into float mode, and then press the *Windows* key + ← or the *Windows* key + → to put the window onto another monitor.

Organizing projects

Project organization starts with the creation of the solution. Visual Studio makes it easy to be disorganized right out of the gate by using the name of the new project you create as the name of the new solution.

When you create a project, Visual Studio automatically uses the name of the project for the name of the assembly. If you follow *Framework Design Guidelines* (available from *Addison-Wesley Professional,* or online in MSDN) and want your project to use accepted namespace style, then you'll want to use that in the name of the project. But, of course, you probably don't want that in the name of the solution.

Context: When creating a new project.

Practice: Use the namespace names in the project name.

I recommend always changing the name of the solution since the project name almost never makes sense as a solution name. A solution contains one or more projects. Once you get going on your product you're probably going to have other assemblies in there. You might have some common code, other applications, and websites, or at least one test project (if you've chosen to keep your tests separate). A solution name `WindowsFormsApplication1` with a project name `Tests` doesn't make much sense and offers no value. You might as well name your solution `asdffdsa` for the amount of value either provides.

Context: When creating a new project.

Practice: Pick a name that makes sense for the project.

To a certain degree, the name of the solution is product-specific, or even stylistic. But there are a couple of general practices we can use if no mandates are coming from the organization. If we decide to use *Framework Design Guidelines* and name our project something like `OrganizationName.ProductName.SubsystemName`, then the solution name could simply be `ProductName`. Adding types to the project will automatically take on the namespace that got created by the product name and subsystem name combination.

Of course, most of the things we just discussed are only true if you're creating a project and the **Create directory for solution** option is checked. When Visual Studio creates the solution/project pair when **Create directory for solution** is checked, it puts the project in its own subdirectory where the `.sln` file is created (which is really "Create directory for project," but don't pay attention to those details).

If you uncheck **Create directory for solution**, Visual Studio puts the `.sln` and the `.csproj` files in the same directory. This might seem like a viable way of creating a solution, but when you add projects to the solution at a later date, it puts those projects in the directory above the directory it put the `.sln` file (and also the first `.csproj`), so all of your `.csproj` files are not in the same place as the `.sln` file. It's much more consistent to simply let Visual Studio create the directory for the `.sln` file and have every project within a subdirectory of that.

Context: When creating projects.

Practice: Don't uncheck **Create directory for solution**.

Sometimes you don't want to *create* a directory for the solution as you might already have a place you want to put it. If you want your solution, and each project within the solution, to be in its own subdirectory, you should still check **Create directory for solution**. The caveat here is that the name of the solution must match the name of the directory where you want the `.sln` to go (Visual Studio won't *create* the directory, it will simply use the one that's already there).

For example, let's say you have a folder `c:\src\Project42`, and you want Visual Studio to create an `.sln` file within that directory when you create a test project named `Tests`, and you want the `Tests` project to be in its own subdirectory. For example, you want to end up with something like the following screenshot:

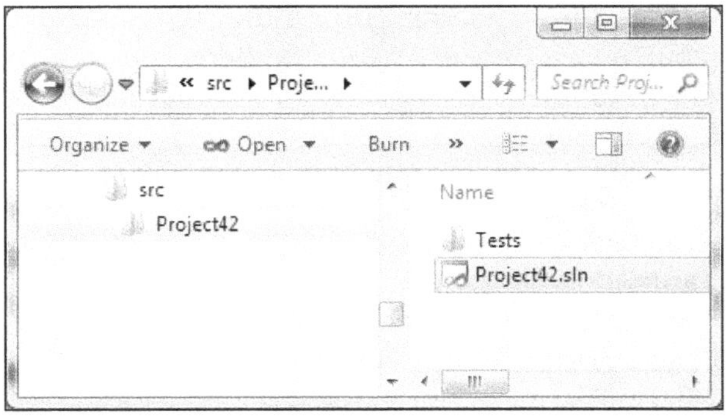

You can only accomplish this by checking **Create directory for solution**. You can simply set the **Location** textbox in the **New Project** dialog to the root of that directory (`C:\src`), set the name of the project to `Tests`, and set the name of the solution to `Project42` (setting the name of the solution after the name of the project means Visual Studio can't overwrite it when it synchronizes the solution name with the project name). This is shown in the following screenshot:

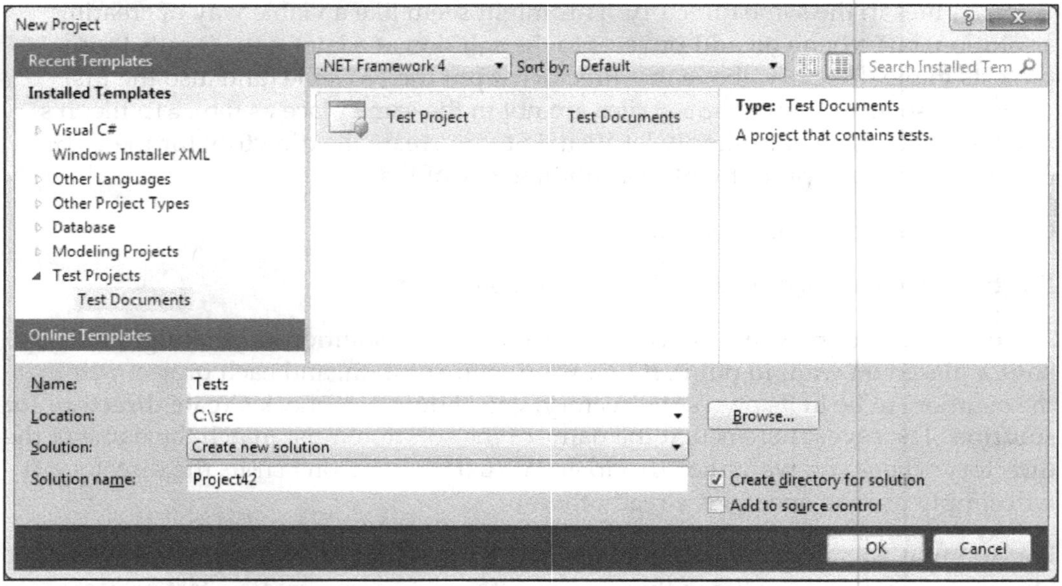

Organizing windows

Most of the tool windows don't do much good if they're not visible. But these windows can be in your way if they're on top of other windows. Fortunately, Visual Studio allows you to "dock" these windows so that they will organize themselves nicely with other windows, and don't overlap or cover up windows you want to view.

All tool windows can be docked to the left, right, bottom, or top. Dock windows to the top or bottom that tend to be "report" windows (such as lists, wide grids, and so on). Windows that have information organized vertically (such as tall lists or trees) can be docked on the left or right.

Context: Commonly used tool windows.

Practice: Should be docked.

Auto-hiding

Visual Studio allows you to dock most tool windows to the left, right, bottom, or top of the main area of the Visual Studio window. Once docked, these windows can then be put into **Auto Hide** mode (or unpinned) and will automatically shrink to a tab when they don't have focus. Coding likely means spending a lot of time in the text/code editor editing code, or in the designer designing visual elements, and not much time in tool windows such as **Solution Explorer** or **Team Explorer**. By auto-hiding these tool windows, this frees up much more space for text or design windows when you want to focus on code or visual design, as shown in the following screenshot:

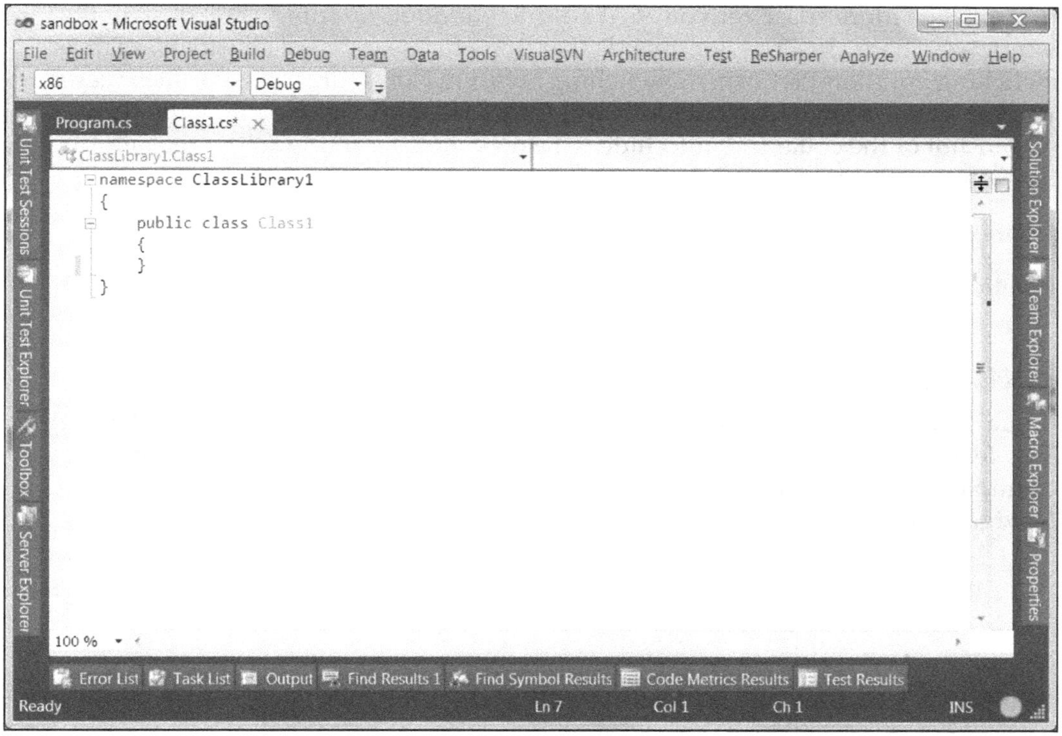

Showing these auto-hide windows is as easy as clicking on the tab or hovering the mouse over the tab and the window will reappear. When you're done with the window, and change focus to another window, the window will get out of your way and auto-hide.

Context: When you want to provide as much editor/designer space as possible.

Practice: Set tool windows to **Auto Hide**.

Toolbars

Once people know the keyboard commands for most of the commands they use, they can be far more productive. To copy selected text from one place and paste that text beside the copied text with the keyboard is a fast, *Ctrl* + *C*, ←, and *Ctrl* + *V*. With the toolbar it's: move the mouse to the **Copy** button and press it, move the mouse to where you want to paste the text, then move the mouse to **Paste** button and press it. Much slower.

Once you know many of the keystrokes (or chords in Visual Studio) to perform many of the tasks you normally need to perform, you can close many of the toolbars to gain even more space for your text editing windows or your visual designer windows. There are a few commands that don't have keyboard shortcuts, such as switching Solution Platform or switching Solution Configurations. For these cases, you can create a small custom toolbar that contains only those commands. The screenshot of the collapsed auto-hide windows shows a short toolbar that simply has Solution Platform and Solution Configuration drop-downs.

Context: When you want to provide as much editor/designer space as possible.

Practice: Close all toolbars and create a new small toolbar with a few buttons.

Exceptional features

Visual Studio 2010 added the **Navigate To** feature (press *Ctrl* + , in the C# layout). This feature allows you to quickly navigate to any type, file, or member. For example, if we wanted to quickly go to `Class1`, we could type `Class1` in the **Navigate To** window, as shown in the following screenshot:

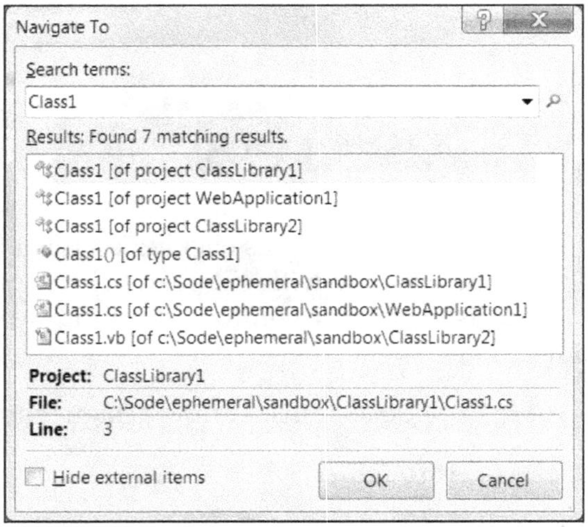

If we wanted to go to the `DoSomething` method, we could simply type enough of `DoSomething` to get it to show the `DoSomething` method in the list. For example, typing `DoSome` displays the following results:

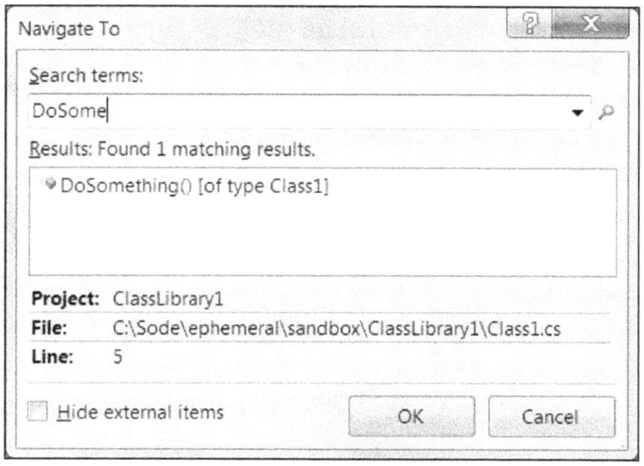

And just as we can navigate to types and members, we can also navigate to files simply by the filename (or part thereof) in the **Navigate To** window.

With this feature, we don't need to open up **Solution Explorer** and navigate to the folder/file that we want and double-click. Instead, we can simply press *Ctrl* + , and type `Class1` and we're there. Much faster and allows you to be much more productive.

Context: When navigating your projects.

Practice: Use **Navigate To** to navigate quickly and efficiently.

Exporting/backing up your custom look and feel

Now that you've configured Visual Studio how you like it, you have the option of exporting some or all of your settings. This is useful if you want to back up your settings to be restored later.

Another great use for this feature is to copy some or all of your settings from one place to another. Say you have a home computer and a work computer (or, you're like me and you have several home computers and several client computers), but you don't want to go through the process of configuring multiple installations of Visual Studio to get the look and feel that you're now used to. You can take the file that **Import and Export Settings** created and copy it to another computer, and then import the settings.

Another useful feature of **Import and Export Settings** is to be able to save multiple layouts. This is especially beneficial if you occasionally present code on a projector and you want to increase its font size to make Visual Studio more readable to the audience. Visual Studio allows you to change the font of the editor, the environment font (the font used for menus, and so on), as well as the font for almost all other windows. You can use **Import and Export Settings** to save your current font settings. Select **All Settings** | **Options** | **Environment** | **Fonts and Colors** in the **Which settings do you want to export?** step of the **Import and Export Settings Wizard**:

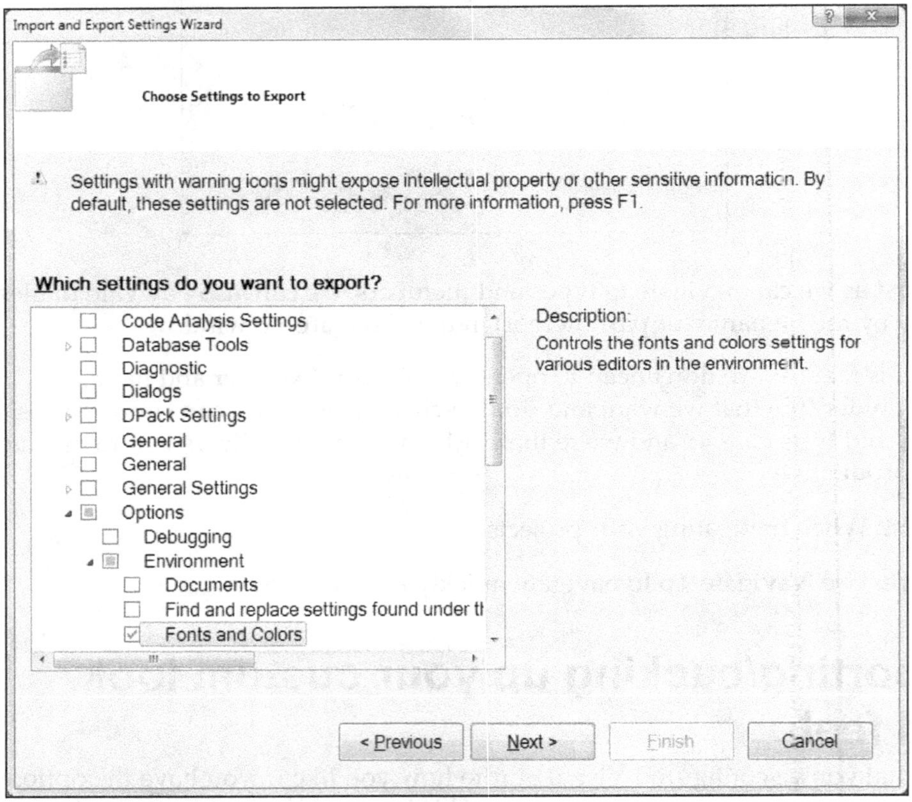

Then, modify whatever fonts you want to make larger. Once done, re-export the same settings (to a different file). Now you can reload the original settings to restore and load the larger font settings whenever you present code on a projector without having to continuously fiddle with font settings.

Context: When you periodically want to switch between a different look and feel.

Practice: Export each look and feel to independent settings files and load them when needed.

Add-ins and extensions

There are many add-ins and extensions available for Visual Studio. Each of these is useful in its own right, but I cannot possibly detail all of them. I've chosen a couple that I've found which have increased productivity in my own teams.

Productivity Power Tools

The Productivity Power Tools (the Tools) is a set of extensions produced for Visual Studio 2010 by Microsoft to improve developer productivity. The Tools contain numerous extensions to Visual Studio. A subset of these extensions are detailed next.

Searchable add references dialog

One area of Visual Studio that has consistent complaints is the **Add Reference** dialog. The most common complaint is usability and slowness. The Tools replaces the **Add Reference dialog,** which improves the performance of loading the assembly list and includes the ability to search assembly names by substring (in the top-right **Search Assembly** box). Following is a screenshot of the Tools' **Add Reference** dialog:

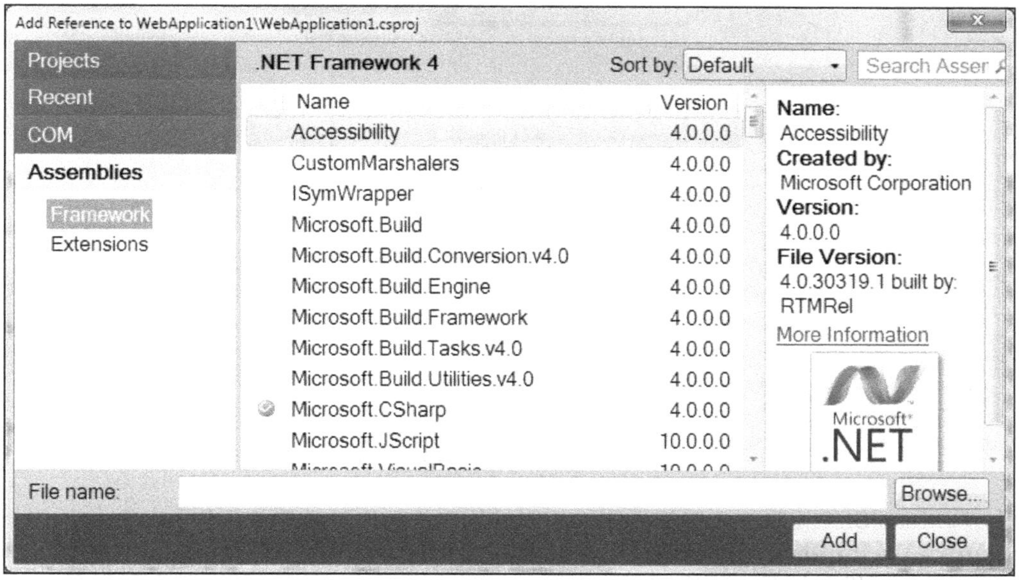

Quick Find

The Quick Find extension provides the various search functionality within a small control at the top-right of the text window being searched. This replaces the **Find** and **Incremental Search** dialogs that can obscure the code being searched. The Quick Find extension is context-sensitive and provides **Current Document**, **Selection**, **Current Project**, and **Entire Solution** search.

Solution Navigator

Solution Explorer gets an upgrade with Solution Navigator that provides modified navigation abilities for the solution. Solution Navigator provides similar functionality to Solution Explorer, but includes features such as method leaves (lowest-level tree item is not the file, but the methods within the file), solution search, filtering the tree-view, and preview of images. Solution Navigator is similar to merging Solution Explorer with Class View, Object Browser, and Find Symbol References.

Following is a screenshot of **Solution Navigator** that shows the **Search Solution** box, filtering (**All**, **Open**, **Unsaved**, and **Edited**), along with the familiar tree-view of the files/folders within the solution:

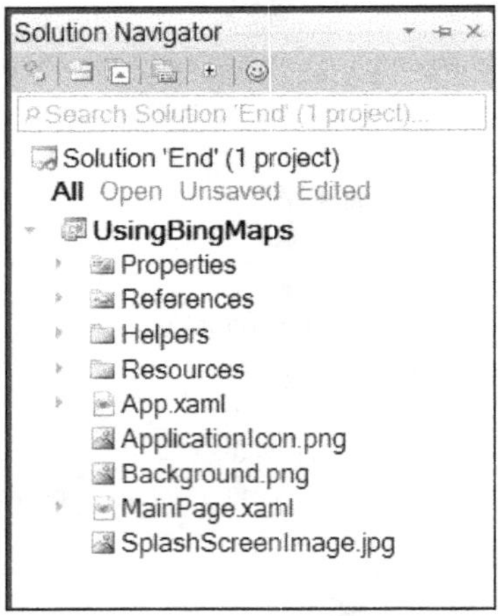

Other extensions in Tools include Enhanced Scroll bar, Middle-click Scrolling, Organize VB Imports, Tab Well UI, Quick Access, Auto Brace Completion, Highlight Current Line, Triple Click, Fix Mixed Tabs, Ctrl+Click Go To Definition, HTML Copy, Align Assignments, Move Line Up/Down Commands, Column Guides, and Colorized Parameter Help. Productivity Power Tools is available in the Visual Studio Gallery at http://`visualstudiogallery.msdn.microsoft.com`.

Some of the extensions such as Solution Navigator, Quick Find, and Quick Access have been included in Visual Studio 2012.

Resharper

Tools such as Resharper and CodeRush drastically expand the productivity potential of Visual Studio.

While Visual Studio 2010 includes Navigate To, tools such as Resharper include very similar navigation extensions that work in Visual Studio 2008 (and prior versions) as well. CodeRush has Quick Nav (which is very similar to Navigate to) and Resharper has Goto Type, Goto Symbol, and Goto File. Goto Type simply allows you to type any type name, or part thereof, to find a type:

Goto Type also recognizes camel case. So, if you wanted to find the type `UnitTests1`, you could simply type `UT` (all uppercase).

Goto Symbol works almost identically but lets you focus on just symbols (members and local variables):

You can also quickly go to a particular file with Goto File:

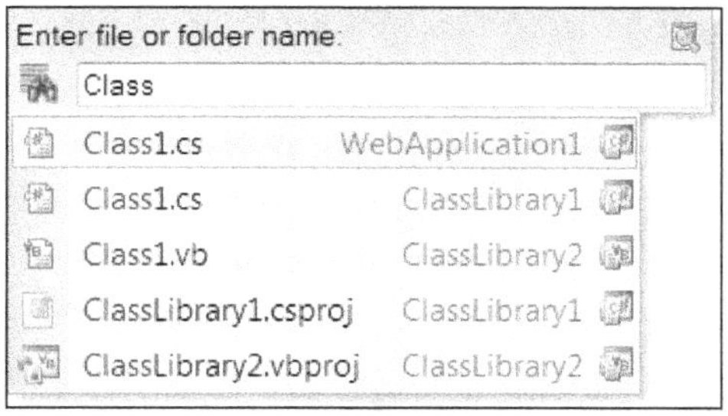

In addition to Goto File/Symbol/Type, Resharper also has Go To File Member (*Alt* + \) that is basically Goto Symbol but restricted to the current file, as well as Base Symbols (*Alt* + *Home*) that goes to the base class of the class of the current class (the class that owns the code where the caret is currently located).

Context: To make Visual Studio usage as efficient as possible.

Practice: Keep abreast of various add-ins and extensions and evaluate their usage for your team.

Visual Studio efficiency through usage

Visual Studio can be used in many different ways, and some ways are more efficient than others. This section attempts to detail some more efficient ways of using Visual Studio.

Using the keyboard over the mouse

As mentioned earlier, the time it takes to use mouse commands, such as right-clicking, menus, toolbars, Solution Explorer, and so on, is reasonably lengthy.

Visual Studio offers keyboard shortcuts for almost all of the possible commands that it offers. While it's probably not possible to remember them all, you can usually remember the shortcuts for some of the most common actions you want to perform. The following table highlights some common commands:

Command	Keyboard shortcut
New Project	*Ctrl* + *Shift* + *N*
Add New Item	*Ctrl* + *Shift* + *A*
Open File	*Ctrl* + *O*
Save	*Ctrl* + *S*
Save All	*Ctrl* +*Shift* + *S*
Cut	*Ctrl* + *X*
Copy	*Ctrl* + *C*
Paste	*Ctrl* + *V*
Undo	*Ctrl* + *Z*
Redo	*Ctrl* + *Y*
Navigate Backward	*Ctrl* + -
Navigate Forward	*Ctrl* + *Shift* + -
Find in Files	*Ctrl* + *Shift* + *F*

Command	Keyboard shortcut
Quick Find	*Ctrl* + *F*
Solution Explorer	*Ctrl* + *W*, *S*
Properties Window	*Ctrl* + *W*, *P*
Team Explorer	*Ctrl* + *W*, *M*
Object Browser	*Ctrl* + *W*, *J*
Toolbox	*Ctrl* + *W*, *X*
Start Page	*Alt* + *V* + *G*
Command Window	*Ctrl* + *W*, *A*

In addition to the list we just saw, the entire list of default keyboard shortcuts can be found at `http://bit.ly/MS12I3`. Additionally, the Visual Studio team provides a PDF poster that categorizes and shows many of the keyboard shortcuts in a handy poster format, which can be found at `http://bit.ly/Qftq7y`.

Dividing up solutions

Sometimes a product can be so complex that it constitutes several dozen projects (I've seen some as complex as hundreds). Visual Studio becomes more sluggish as the solution project count grows exceptionally high. There are certain actions where it makes sense to do them in a solution that contains all related projects, for example, refactoring. Refactoring tools only search code within the current solution and only within loaded projects.

Under certain circumstances, it may be reasonable to only be working with a subset of entire projects for a product. In this case multiple solutions can be created, each containing a subset of the projects, maybe related in some way. How you group these projects is largely up to you. If possible, keeping together any projects with direct references that are made from another project is a good idea.

In the absence of creating multiple projects, another method of alleviating the burden of large solutions is to selectively unload certain projects (right-click on a project in **Solution Explorer** and select **Unload Project**).

Macros

Visual Studio has the ability to write and execute macros. These macros make use of a variant of Visual Basic which lets you automate almost every feature of Visual Studio, as well as make use of Visual Basic for almost anything else.

Advanced search/replace

Macros let you expand the bounds of traditional "search and replace" by making replace a multi-step process (or search for that matter).

I encounter this most frequently with data. Let's say I have the following data:

```
2
3
5
7
11
13
17
19
23
```

Maybe I've copied the data from somewhere else (other than code), but I want to put that data in an array. However, I don't want the code to take up nine lines, I just want it all on one line. With nine lines, it's not much of a chore to simply edit it by hand, but imagine you have dozens or hundreds of values. This becomes tedious, time-consuming, and prone to error. You can easily "write a macro" to do this.

While we could write this macro from scratch, I find it much easier to get Visual Studio to do most of the heavy lifting for us and "record" most of what we want. In this case, we want to effectively replace line endings with " , " (a comma and a space). We can start by turning on Macro Record (**Tools | Macros | Record TemporaryMacro**). We can then do a regular expression search for end-of-line (`$`). This puts us at the first end-of-line. Now, we simply press *Del* , (comma), and space. We then stop macro recording (**Tools | Macro | Stop Recording**). Opening **Macro Explorer** and right-clicking on **TemporaryMacro | Edit** results in something similar to the following:

```
Sub TemporaryMacro()
  DTE.ExecuteCommand("Edit.Find")
  DTE.Find.FindWhat = "$"
  DTE.Find.Target = vsFindTarget.vsFindTargetCurrentDocument
  DTE.Find.MatchCase = False
  DTE.Find.MatchWholeWord = False
  DTE.Find.Backwards = False
  DTE.Find.MatchInHiddenText = False
  DTE.Find.PatternSyntax = _
   vsFindPatternSyntax.vsFindPatternSyntaxRegExpr
  DTE.Find.Action = vsFindAction.vsFindActionFind
  If (DTE.Find.Execute() = _
```

```
    vsFindResult.vsFindResultNotFound) Then
     ThrowNew System.Exception("vsFindResultNotFound")
   EndIf
   DTE.Windows.Item("{CF2DDC32-8CAD-11D2-9302-
    005345000000}").Close()
   DTE.ExecuteCommand("Edit.Delete")
   DTE.ActiveDocument.Selection.Text = ", "
EndSub
```

We don't need to open or close the find window, so we can remove those lines and we end up with a macro similar to the following:

```
Sub TemporaryMacro()
   DTE.Find.FindWhat = "$"
   DTE.Find.Target = vsFindTarget.vsFindTargetCurrentDocument
   DTE.Find.MatchCase = False
   DTE.Find.MatchWholeWord = False
   DTE.Find.Backwards = False
   DTE.Find.MatchInHiddenText = False
   DTE.Find.PatternSyntax = _
    vsFindPatternSyntax.vsFindPatternSyntaxRegExpr
   DTE.Find.Action = vsFindAction.vsFindActionFind
   If (DTE.Find.Execute() = _
    vsFindResult.vsFindResultNotFound) Then
     ThrowNew System.Exception("vsFindResultNotFound")
   EndIf
   DTE.ExecuteCommand("Edit.Delete")
   DTE.ActiveDocument.Selection.Text = ", "
EndSub
```

Now, to simply do the search and replace on the rest of the text, we simply press *Ctrl* + *Shift* + *P* until we have what we want.

Playing nice with source code control

Visual studio works with a variety of **source code control** (**SCC**) providers. There are add-ons and extensions to work with, such as Git, Subversion (SVN), Mercurial, and so on. There are also built-in support for Team Foundation Server (TFS) source code control. Visual Studio recognizes that solution and project files will be checked-out, edited, committed, and so on.

Visual Studio supports adding project and solution files automatically when you "check-in" or "commit" the solution. It also supports adding the solution to SCC via **Add Solution to Source Control**.

Tracked file in project/solution

In order for Visual Studio to know to add files to SCC, it must first know about them. In the general case you can simply add any file to a project and Visual Studio will then know about it. Next time you "check-in," the file will be added to SCC.

Simply adding a file to a project works fairly well in the general case, but it does have some issues sometimes. Project files are generally files that need some degree of processing during build. If you have a file that shouldn't be processed during build, but does have a default build action associated with it, you can run into some issues (building the file such as compiling and linking when you don't want to). A `.cs` file, for example, adding this file to a project means it will be compiled and included in the assembly on the next build. If you don't want these types of files included in the build process there are a couple of options.

Change build action

Fortunately, you can change the build action individually for any file in a managed project. To "exclude" a file from the build you can simply set **Build Action** to **None** as shown in the following screenshot:

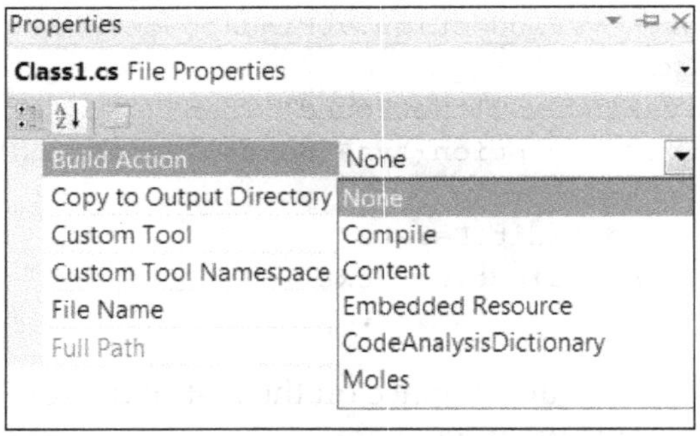

Solution items

A solution can also have files associated with it. These are called **solution items**. Some solution items are processed uniquely, but usually only those that are added automatically by certain actions in Visual Studio, such as test settings (MS Test).

When you add a file to the **Solution Items** folder, the file is not associated with any particular project and therefore won't, by default, have any processing associated with it during build. In fact, there is no **Build Action** in the properties for solution items (even file types that build by default, such as `.cs` files).

The caveat here is that "solution folders" don't map to physical folders, so dragging a file into a folder within the **Solution Items** folder, or adding a file through the right-click context menu puts it in the same directory as the `.sln` file. You'd need to manually read the file after moving it in Windows Explorer (that is, outside of Visual Studio).

Context: When you want a solution item file to be in a subfolder of the solution folder.

Practice: Create the folder and the file first, then add the file to the solution folder.

Context: When you want to include a file in SCC through Visual Studio.

Practice: Add the file to the solution as a solution Item.

Continuous integration

Continuous integration is the software development practice of integrating work frequently throughout the day, or at least once daily. Integration is verified by an automated build to detect integration errors.

Tests

I'm constantly surprised by the lack of tests, or the lack of coverage by tests, with some teams. It's not a rarity that I see teams make changes and cause regressions that they don't notice for days or sometimes weeks. Getting back to the code that broke and fixing it after a lengthy absence is usually time-consuming, and thus expensive.

Visual Studio (Professional and above with 2008 and 2010, and *all editions* in Visual Studio 2012) supports unit testing. You can easily run and create unit tests to test all aspects of your code.

Context: When developing software of any level of complexity.

Practice: Write unit tests to verify changes do not cause regressions.

Build

Working solely in VS can sometimes give you a false sense of reality. You can have files on your local drive that VS uses indirectly (or used by something else that VS uses). If you use VS solely for your interface to your SCC system, your check-ins might work on your local machine but won't work for anyone else. They might not be getting all of the files when they "check-out" and end up with errors.

Context: When working with SCC.

Practice: Add files that will be tracked in SCC to the solution.

One place that I see most often causes errors such as this is with the use of third-party libraries. Sometimes one person might perform the installation of this third-party library and reference the libraries (assemblies) that are in his `Users` directory. This works fine on his machine, but doesn't on anyone else's because they need to also install the library. Even if they do install the library, the reference in the project might be to a user-specific directory, which will still cause build errors.

When dealing with third-party libraries, even if there is an installation that places libraries/assemblies either in a `Users` directory or a `Program Files` directory, copy those files somewhere in your solution directory hierarchy. One common way of dealing with this is to add a `lib` directory in the root of the solution directory, then copy all dependent library files into this directory before referencing them in a project. These files can then be added to the solution so that "check-in" actions include all those files, and put them in SCC so that others will get the files and will not have build errors.

Context: When working with third-party libraries.

Practice: Copy dependent files into a directory within the source directory hierarchy and add them to the solution.

The packaging and deployment libraries and their dependencies have long been an issue in the software development community. Other communities have come up with various solutions to the problem. Microsoft, in kind, came up with a Visual Studio-specific solution with the NuGet extension. This extension provides the ability to add third-party libraries to a project from a registry of extensions by installing packages into the project. NuGet not only adds the necessary references to a project, but also includes the necessary files in the project or solution so that they will be checked-in and other team members will not need to install the same package.

Alas, not all library vendors support NuGet, but an organization can set up a local NuGet repository to keep track of dependencies not managed by the public NuGet repository.

Context: When working with third-party libraries.

Practice: Prefer integrating them with your solution and project through NuGet.

Summary

It's clear that Visual Studio can be used in good ways and it can be used in bad ways. This chapter outlined some of the ways it could be used *better*. You can configure Visual Studio in ways that make it work better for you in the usage patterns that you use it. That configuration can include the hardware on which it runs, or the hardware that it has access to use. Configuration can include optimizing the look and feel to better suit how you work or how your team works.

I invite you to take the practices in this chapter and try to make your work in Visual Studio more productive, and then build on these practices as a team. If you're interested in more details, or specific details on tips and tricks on using and living with Visual Studio (2008 - 2010), I highly recommend Sara Ford's books *Microsoft Visual Studio Tips: 251 Ways to Improve Your Productivity, Redmond, WA: Microsoft Press 2009* and *Coding Faster: Getting More Productive with Microsoft Visual Studio, Redmond, WA: Microsoft Press 2011*. The second book was co-authored by Sara Ford along with Zain Naboulsi.

In the next chapter we'll look at parallelization practices. We'll look at techniques such as threading, distributed architecture, and thread synchronization. We'll also look at technologies such as Task Parallel Library, Asynchronous CTP, and asynchronous additions to C# 5.0 and VB 10.

8
Parallelization Practices

In the early 1970's, Carver Mead coined the term "Moore's Law." This law has colloquially been detailed as "processor speed doubles every two years." Some people use the time span of 18 months.

The law stemmed from statements Intel co-founder Gordon Moore made close to 1965 describing minimizing cost by, "cramming more components onto integrated circuits." Moore detailed that, in 1965, the number of components in a given space, "has increased at a rate of roughly a factor of two per year." Of course, Moore goes on to suggest that, "over the longer term, the rate of increase is a bit more uncertain."

I'm sure Moore had not expected that the rate of increase would have continued for roughly another 40 years before reaching physical and atomic limitations, making the effort (and thus the cost) of putting more components into a given space extremely prohibitive.

The fact that processing speed, until very recently, had increased at expected amounts within a given timeframe really should not have impacted the ability or the applicability of parallelization of work within an application to gain scalability. However, I think it turned out to be a crutch used by many people in the industry.

This chapter will detail some practices for parallelization of code, including:

- Principles
- Threads
- Thread synchronization
- Asynchronous operations
- Division of labor
- Task Parallel Library
- Visual Studio 2012 asynchronous programming
- Reactive Extensions

For the uninitiated, it's important that we cover a few basics before we jump right into parallelization.

Principles

It's important to be clear about what we mean by **parallelization**: what it is *and* what it *isn't*. The minimum definition of parallelization is performing calculations simultaneously. Generally, I use multithreading and parallelization interchangeably, but as we'll see, this "simultaneously" becomes somewhat gray with respect to modern processors and operating systems.

An application's ability to take advantage of processing resources is termed **scalability**. When we talk about the resources within a given computer, we generally categorize that scalability as **vertical scalability** which is the ability to scale up within the physical confines of a single node. This type of scalability is easier to achieve in some circumstances compared to the converse: **horizontal scalability**. Horizontal scalability is the ability of an application or system to scale out to take advantage of other nodes in a network. This generally means the system needs to be architected to be distributable. Attaining this level of scalability at the application level is much more complex.

Modern operating systems don't really give software direct access to almost anything on the system. Processors are one of those components that operating systems effectively virtualize for us. We can actually run an OS in a virtual environment to get true virtualization of processors. But in an OS not running virtualized in a host the OS controls which processor is given to our software to run our code.

The OS abstraction that is used is a **thread**. A process is given one thread in order to execute, and then that process can request more threads to perform work. Each thread executes effectively independently of another thread and gets its own **thread context**: registers, stacks, stack pointers, and so on.

We don't always use multithreading for parallelization of calculations. We often use multiple threads to maintain responsiveness of our application. The way graphical user interfaces work is that they have a message queue of user interface actions that are processed one at a time. These actions may be things such as a mouse click, drawing of controls, timers, and so on. It's important to remember that each of these actions is performed independently and one at a time. This means for any given UI action, if we do too much work in response to that action, the user interface can become unresponsive. For example, let's say we want to update how a control looks based on the click of a mouse.

Theoretically, we'd process that mouse click message, perform some calculations, and then put a message in the queue to redraw or repaint that control. While we're performing those calculations the user is free to interact with our user interface and perform other actions, such as click on other controls that require similar calculations and repaints, or resizing of the window, selection of items, and so on. The OS places all of these as messages in the message queue after the click we are currently processing. The longer we take to perform the calculations that the control needs, the longer those messages take to get processed and the more the messages pile up in the queue to be performed farther away in time from the user's action that caused it.

In the UI responsiveness scenario, we use another thread to perform lengthy operations such as calculations in the **background**, in other words, *not* on the main application thread. In a graphical user interface application, we sometimes refer to the main thread as the **UI thread**. As we'll see, to keep an application responsive by using background threads doesn't come for free, but this frees up the message queue to process messages at a responsive rate.

Threading primitives

There are a few threading primitives that are useful to know about when we start talking about threading. They are as follows:

- **Fork**: A term meaning to launch work (usually a thread) asynchronously. This can be seen in .NET with things such as `Thread.Start`, `Task.Factory.StartNew`, `ThreadPool.QueueUserWorkItem`, and so on.
- **Join**: A term meaning to wait for one or more asynchronous operations (usually threads) to complete. This can bee seen in .NET with things such as the `WaitHandle.Wait` methods, `Task.Wait`, and so on.
- **Fork/join**: A pattern by which work is parallelized and the completion of all asynchronous work is waited on by blocking the current thread.

Threading caveats

Many have said this over time: "threading is hard." It's true, it's hard to cogitate on designing something to facilitate the interaction of multiple operations, the information they require, and that they produce at the same time.

Throwing more threads at a problem also is rarely a solution. With a modern computer, we have multiple processors, multiple cores, and virtual cores with technologies such as hyper-threading. But these are still limited resources, and trying to do more work than a resource is capable of doing has adverse side effects.

Operating systems have a concept called a "scheduler." It basically abstracts the fact that there are multiple processors that all other processes in the system need to share. From a process's stand point, it has complete control of all of the processors. (That is, it doesn't need to do anything specifically to "share" processors with other processes. This is called **preemptive multitasking**.) When another process requires some processor time, the scheduler (at specific timeframes called **quantums**) steps in and switches contexts from one process to another. This happens at the thread level. If there are enough processors available for each process, then the scheduler doesn't need to do anything. When there isn't enough processors to go around, the scheduler starts "pausing" threads and "unpausing" others so they have processor time. When one thread is paused so that the processor it was using can be given to another thread, it is called **context switching**.

Context switching is really expensive. It has been detailed that context switching can cost in the range of 2,000–8,000 cycles on various versions of Windows. With modern processors, that's tantamount to 2,000–8,000 instructions! You can imagine that if a quantum was 20 milliseconds, and you had to share a processor between two threads, that up to 8,000 cycles would be used every 20 milliseconds just for "housekeeping" like context switching before your code even gets to execute. Not overly effective use of a processor time. Although mostly undocumented, these metrics have been detailed by a former member of the CLR team and an authority on parallelization and multithreading in .NET and Windows. These metrics have been detailed on his blog at `http://www.bluebytesoftware.com/blog/default.aspx` and in his book *Concurrent Programming on Windows, Addison-Wesley Professional*.

It's important that we design our applications to make effective use of processors in order to improve performance rather than run slower by spending too much time context switching. This means not creating more than one **CPU-bound** thread per available core. A CPU-bound thread is one that is effectively using 100% of its assigned core for an extended period of time. The main UI thread is generally not considered a CPU-bound thread because it is designed to spend almost all of its time waiting for another message to appear in the message queue. So, if you only had one processor with one core and no hyper-threading, then spawning another thread in a UI application would not cause and undue amount of context switching.

The criteria by which the scheduler context switches is very complex and takes into account priorities, current load, and so on. Outside of the priority of our own thread, we have no control over the scheduler.

Other terminologies

Threads can be in one of two realistic execution states: waiting or executing. A **waiting thread** doesn't take up CPU time, but it is ready to be executed once whatever it is waiting on is done or times-out. The UI thread spends most of its time in this "wait" state. You can have many more threads than cores without incurring huge context switching issues by putting threads into a wait state, but this often involves much work usually outside the purpose of the application.

When dealing with multithreading design, **thread safety** is important for maintaining correctness and reliability. Thread safety is the ability of an application to maintain consistent shared data without causing deadlocks. A **deadlock** is when two threads are waiting on each other to complete some action, either directly or indirectly.

Shared data is data that is shared between two or more threads. Access to memory by multiple threads can be interleaved if thread safety isn't taken into account. That is, one thread could be changing parts of the data while another thread is reading that data.

There is some access to memory that cannot be interleaved or interrupted by another thread. This type of memory access is called **atomic**. Reading or writing fundamental 32-bit data types are examples of atomic memory access.

Shared memory that can't technically be accessed atomically on its own are generally called invariants. **Invariants** are application-specific structures, or data groupings, that have certain consistency or validity requirements, that is, the validity of the data is predicated on certain conditions. This type of data usually has interrelated information. For example, a data grouping to encapsulate sales figures may include east coast sales, west coast sales, and total sales. The invariant here is that east coast sales + west coast sales = total sales. If this is modeled with three variables, it is possible to update east coast sales, for example, before updating total sales (and vice versa).

Invariants can be protected through thread synchronization. **Thread synchronization**, at the lowest common denominator, is ensuring two threads don't execute the same piece of code at the same time. I tend to expand this definition to the invariant level and say that thread synchronization is ensuring one thread isn't accessing an invariant that another is affecting at the same time. But, one way of protecting invariants is to have only one piece of code that affects the invariant, and then synchronizing execution of that code.

There are various techniques to thread synchronization, each with specific applications and drawbacks. Much of this chapter details these techniques.

Threads

There are two important types of threads in .NET: **thread pool threads** and **non-thread pool threads**. Thread pool threads are generally threads that are implicitly created or revived (or otherwise implicitly "re-used"). Non-thread pool threads are created and terminated manually and not re-used.

Creating a thread is an expensive proposition. Each thread has its own stack that defaults to 1 MB of memory. That memory needs to be allocated and committed. It is said that starting a thread can cost upwards of 200,000 cycles, and terminating a thread can cost upwards of 100,000 cycles (for a total cost of 300,000 cycles). Taking on that cost shouldn't be a trivial decision. Thread pool threads are managed by the .NET Framework and the operating system for your use, but their use also has caveats.

So, when should you decide to create your own thread or use the thread pool? Generally, if you need a CPU-intensive operation to be performed that could take upwards of several seconds, creating your own thread might be the best bet. If you need a thread for a very short amount of time, or need many threads over time for very short amount of time, the thread pool is likely a better choice.

Context: When deciding how to multithread.

Practice: Avoid manually creating threads.

Context: When needing to run short, independent tasks in parallel.

Practice: Prefer using thread pool threads.

Creating a thread is really easy. You basically create a `Thread` object, telling it some method to use as the thread's entry point. That method can either take no parameters and return `void`, or take a single `Object` parameter and also return `void`. The following is an example of creating a thread with a parameter-less method:

```
var thread1 = new Thread(Start);
thread1.Start();
```

The following is an example with a method that takes an `Object` parameter:

```
var thread2 = new Thread(ParameterizedStart);
thread2.Start(42);
```

The parameter-less method is easy. With the parameterized method, since we don't have the luxury of type safety and generics with the `Thread` class, you need to convert the parameter from `Object` to whatever you are expecting, for example:

```
public void ParameterizedStart(Object arg)
{
  int number = (int) arg;
  Console.WriteLine(number);
}
```

It's important to notice that both forms of starting a thread use an entry point that returns `void`. Conceptually, there's no way to simply "return" information back to your program. The code that started the thread has long since executed. It is up to you to communicate data from this thread to other threads in the system. Communicating information to other threads in the system is a form of thread synchronization.

But creating threads isn't the hard part of multithreading. As we've seen, it's pretty easy to create a thread.

Thread synchronization

Trying to reason about the asynchronicity of interactions of threads that occur with multithreading is the hard part of multithreading. If you spin up a bunch of threads that work entirely independently and have no results to deal with, there isn't much thinking you need to do. But that's almost never the case.

There are two basic reasons for using multithreading. One is to simply keep a user interface responsive by doing lengthy operations on a background thread. The other is to make use of multiple CPUs to scale an application, or make it take less time processing. There's kind of a third scenario when it comes to multithreading, that is the recognition of asynchronous operations and the avoidance of blocking a thread to wait for an asynchronous operation.

Each scenario has some slightly different synchronization subtleties, but let's first take a look at some fundamental ways of synchronizing data access across threads.

Thread safety

There are many ways of ensuring your shared data doesn't get corrupted (thread safety). The challenge to knowing how to ensure consistent data is understanding how that data can be modified by multiple threads, its atomicity, and what rules (invariant) govern its consistency.

Whether or not you need to guard against corruption of data depends on whether you can read or write the data atomically. If the data you need to keep consistent cannot be accessed atomically inherently, you need to manually ensure that the access acts atomically.

Minding your invariants

Let's return to our simple example of an invariant: east coast sales, west coast sales, and total sales. As we stated earlier, our invariant is that total = west + east. If that predicate is not met, our data is corrupt.

From a programming stand point, we really only need to make sure that a thread modifies east or west, and that total locks out any other threads from performing these same actions.

We can do this in C# using the `lock` keyword. The `lock` keyword uses a reference object to represent a padlock for one or more blocks of code. The `lock` keyword effectively acts as a critical section. In the case of our east/west/total sales invariant, we may have code to update these values as follows:

```
public void UpdateSales(double east, double west)
{
  eastCoastSales = east;
  westCoastSales = west;
  totalSales = eastCoastSales
    + westCoastSales ;
}
```

Given this block of code, two threads, and that we assume that each thread will execute the instructions in the order they are written, there's about 16 combinations these instructions can interleaved (it's much more complicated than that). One combination is shown in the following table:

Thread one	Thread two
`eastCoastSales = east;`	
`westCoastSales = west;`	
	`eastCoastSales = east;`
`totalSales = eastCoastSales + westCoastSales;`	
	`westCoastSales = west;`
	`totalSales = eastCoastSales + westCoastSales;`

If the two threads had `east` values of `10, 20` and `west` values of `30, 40,` then thread one would calculate `totalSales` to be `50` instead of `40`! We've allowed our data to become corrupt.

Thread synchronization and locking

Multiple threads that access the same data need to access that data independently (atomically), so that the data does not become corrupt. This form of avoiding data corruption is called *thread synchronization and locking*. This section will detail some techniques for thread synchronization, including locking and non-locking techniques.

Locking

Luckily we can use the C# `lock` keyword to protect against this. We can create a private `Object` field to represent our invariant and use that `object` so that only one thread at a time can be modifying our values:

```
private readonly object salesLock = new object();
public void UpdateSales(double east, double west)
{
  lock (salesLock)
  {
    eastCoastSales = east;
    westCoastSales = west;
    totalSales = westCoastSales
      + eastCoastSales;
  }
}
```

With this code, whichever thread code locked, `salesLock` would be guaranteed to execute all of the instructions within that code block without any other threads being able to modify any of our fields.

In our example, we choose a private field of type `Object` to represent this invariant and to be used by the `lock` statement. We do this because if the reference we used for `lock` was publically available, any other code could lock on it and cause a race condition called a deadlock because both the locker could be waiting for the other to unlock.

Context: When locking an object to protect invariants or shared data.

Practice: Use an object that is not publically available.

Lock-free synchronization

Synchronization of data shared between threads doesn't always need to resort to locking. Lock is the slowest of the inter-process synchronization methods (kernel handle-based synchronization methods are slower). You may have invariants that don't involve multiple variables. For example, let's say we have a field in our class that signifies an age. If we were to perform some multithreaded operations that modify this value, we wouldn't necessarily need to use lock.

If the value were an `int`; `int`, along with `bool`, `char`, `byte`, `sbyte`, `short`, `ushort`, `unit`, and `float` reads and writes are considered atomic. This means no other thread can interrupt a read from, or a write to, a variable of this type since all of the data is retrieved or written before allowing another thread to continue. This is more a feature of the instruction set of the processor, but the guarantee is also at the language level.

Despite values of this type being atomic, that doesn't mean that reads and writes to the type alone are "thread-safe." Both the compiler and the processor are free to reorder instructions, so a read to a variable may not occur in the order in which it was written in the code. Also, processors cache values to improve performance. Just because an instruction wrote a value to a memory location on one core, doesn't mean the result of that write was visible to all other cores.

Volatile

One way to deal with this issue is to modify field declarations that are involved in operations like this with the `volatile` keyword. This tells the compiler that the field reads/writes should not occur from the cache. It also tells the compiler that the read/write operation should not be reordered.

The problem with the `volatile` modifier is that it's the actual operations on the field that require specific treatment by the compiler or processor, not the field in general.

The `volatile` modifier gives all accesses to a field both **acquire semantics** and **release semantics**. Acquire semantics means access is "guaranteed to occur prior to any references to memory that occur after it in the instruction sequence." Release semantics means access is "guaranteed to happen after any memory references prior to the write instruction in the instruction sequence." These also affect memory accesses prior to, and following, our "volatile" access. Given the modification of the following two fields:

```
value = 5;
flag = 1;
```

If `flag` were `volatile`, the write to `value` would also be flushed from the cache. The flushing from cache is done due to a **memory barrier**, which means all cached writes prior to a memory barrier are guaranteed to be visible. So, if that were the only way the two variables were modified, only `flag` would really need the `volatile` modifier. The problem with `volatile` is that you don't know if the order is going to be different, so your reaction is to make both `volatile`.

Fortunately, you can get the same side effect in a better way. You can use `Thread.VolatileWrite` and `Thread.VolatileRead`. In our previous example, if we avoid the `volatile` modifier, we could get the same result with the following lines of code:

```
value = 5;
Thread.VolatileWrite(ref value, 1);
```

Volatile reads and writes are more expensive, if we don't need to incur an expensive operation the better off we'll be.

Context: When guaranteeing field access is not reordered or cached.

Practice: Avoid the `volatile` keyword and prefer thoughtful use of `Thread.VolatileWrite` and `Thread.VolatileRead`.

Unfortunately, not all our accesses to atomic variables are single operations.

Context: When writing multithreaded code.

Practice: Understand what are and are not atomic operations.

Interlocked

We often want to modify an atomic field with two-part operations, such as increment and decrement. For example:

```
flag++;
```

This is equivalent to:

```
var t = flag;
flag = t+1;
```

Another thread is free to come in the middle of these two instructions and modify `flag`. If `flag` was `5` when we assigned it to `t`, and another thread changed it to `12` before assigning `5+1` to `flag`, the result would not be `13` — not necessarily what you want.

Fortunately, the `Interlocked` class includes some useful methods to make these operations thread-safe. For example, to make the increment thread-safe, we'd use `Interlocked` in the following way:

```
Interlocked.Increment(ref flag);
```

There is a complimentary method `Interlocked.Decrement` to do the opposite.

Context: When unsure of how to synchronize access to data.

Practice: Prefer controlling access to data by locking a representation of that data.

Context: When understanding your variants and atomicity.

Practice: Prefer `VolatileRead`/`VolatileWrite` or `Interlocked` access to variables.

Advanced synchronization

There are two types of synchronization primitives. Both primitives deal with synchronization between threads, but one type deals with synchronization between threads in different processes. In order to deal with shared data between processes, synchronization primitives based on kernel handles are required. You can tell kernel handle-based synchronization primitives from other synchronization primitives by the fact that they can be named. This allows two processes that could otherwise not be able to share memory can access the same kernel handle.

Kernel handle-based primitives require kernel-level resources, consistency, and registration, so they are very costly to use. They should only be used when you need to synchronize resources shared between two or more processes, not just within the same process.

Context: When deciding which thread synchronization primitives to use.

Practice: Choose kernel handle-based synchronization primitives to protect resources shared across processes.

We've looked at fairly simple thread safety: independent invariants. There are more complex invariants that become much harder to make thread-safe. There are many threading primitives in the .NET Framework which allow us to maintain thread safety in these circumstances, which I'll briefly cover.

Mutex

Mutex is short form for **mutual exclusion** . It alludes to the fact it is intended that two or more processes mutually exclude one another, as a means of protecting shared resources. Mutexes are a kernel handle-based synchronization primitive. A mutex is semantically identical to `lock` or the `Monitor` class. It has thread affinity, so the thread that acquired the mutex must also be the thread that releases the mutex. A mutex models the synchronization of a single resource.

Semaphore

A semaphore is a kernel handle-based synchronization primitive. The semaphore works the same way as mutex, but rather than allowing access to shared data by one thread at a time, it allows access to one or more threads at a time. A semaphore is intended to model synchronization amongst a pool of resources.

WaitHandle

The WaitHandle is a lower-level abstraction to kernel handle-based synchronization primitives. I've mentioned it here because they are used in the same way.

Reset events

Most of the synchronization primitives we've seen so far are about blocking threads from accessing shared data. Reset events model the converse of this: reset events awaken threads to execute. This concept is typically called **signaling**. they model, as the name suggests, events that occur. Reset Events are WaitHandle-based. Until .NET 4.0, there were two types of reset events: auto and manual reset events. **Auto-reset events** automatically return to a non-signaled state as the system releases a single thread in response to the signal. **Manual-reset events** require the application to manually return the event to a non-signaled state by calling `Reset`. Manual resets are useful when multiple threads processing a single event need to run one at a time.

In .NET 4.0, two other reset event types were introduced: `ManualResetEventSlim` and `CountdownEvent`. `ManualResetEventSlim` is a "slimmed" down version of `ManualResetEvent`, but for intraprocess synchronization only. If you need to model manual signaling within a process, prefer `ManualResetEventSlim`. `CountdownEvent` is a manual-reset event that signals only after a predefined number of `Set` calls (as opposed to always when `Set` is called).

Asynchronous operations

You'll sometimes need to perform actions that are technically "multithreaded" in that they use thread pool threads, but that fact is effectively transparent to you. Network communications, for example, is a series of asynchronous operations. You pass work onto your **network interface card** (**NIC**) and it does the work "in the background," and then informs you when the operation is completed.

Unfortunately in .NET, until Silverlight in 2007, operations in .NET that were inherently asynchronous had the option of being invoked entirely synchronously. For example, with an active `TcpClient` object, we could send data to the host synchronously as follows:

```
public void Write(TcpClient tcpClient, byte[] data)
{
  var networkStream = tcpClient.GetStream();
  networkStream.Write(data, 0, data.Length);
  // TODO: more, like invoke Read...
}
```

The call to `Write` basically just tells the NIC to send the data, then blocks (doing nothing and not allowing the thread to be used for anything else) until the communication is complete. In an ideal situation, this communication may take several dozen milliseconds, which is seemingly instantaneous. But in adverse conditions, our thread could be blocked for several seconds. If we performed this operation on our UI thread, the UI would be blocked until this operation completed or failed. Users never appreciate that.

The Silverlight designers recognized this inherent lack of usefulness to performing asynchronous operations synchronously, and simply don't provide the synchronous methods in Silverlight. While we can't hope to see the removal of these synchronous methods in the rest of .NET (because technically you could still use the synchronous methods and have a responsive UI), the trend of only having asynchronous version of these methods is continuing with Metro-style applications in Windows 8.

Context: When designing code to be asynchronous.

Practice: Prefer asynchronous APIs for asynchronous operations.

In .NET 4.0 and prior, there are generally two APIs for dealing with inherently asynchronous operations. They generally take on one of two patterns. One is the **Asynchronous Design Pattern** and the other is the **Event-based Asynchronous Pattern**.

Asynchronous Design Pattern

The Asynchronous Design Pattern, or the **Asynchronous Programming Model (APM)** as it has come to be known, involves two methods: a delegate (to a callback), and an interface. The first method starts the asynchronous operation and generally has the form `BeginXXX`. It takes the callback delegate that starts the operation in the background, and returns a "state" in the form of an instance of an `IAsyncResult` implementation reference. The second method has the form `EndXXX` and signals acceptance that the operation has completed within the callback. The callback would then be free to process the results, if any, of the operation. You can see many examples of this pattern within the .NET Framework as it's the oldest asynchronous pattern in .NET. For example, `TcpClient` and `NetworkStream`:

```
NetworkStream networkStream = tcpClient.GetStream();

networkStream.BeginWrite(data, 0, data.Length,
  OnWriteCompleted, networkStream);
```

This code takes the byte array data and sends it to the socket connected via the `tcpClient` object asynchronously. It tells `BeginWrite` that it should call the `OnWriteCompleted` method (callback), when the operation is done executing asynchronously. `OnWriteCompleted` may look similar to the following lines of code:

```
private static void OnWriteCompleted(IAsyncResult ar)
{
  NetworkStream myNetworkStream =
    (NetworkStream)ar.AsyncState;
  myNetworkStream.EndWrite(ar);
  // TODO: more, like invoke BeginRead...
}
```

`OnWriteCompleted` takes the state, which in our case is the `NetworkStream` object, and calls the corresponding `EndWrite` method. Theoretically, this could be chained on to perform the next logical operation, which could be something involving `BeginRead`.

In this example, the actual operation is passed on to the NIC, and the management of asynchronous operation is performed by I/O completion ports and OS-specific thread pool threads. For example, the thread used to call `OnWriteCompleted` is a special thread pool that the .NET Framework recognizes, but doesn't manage within its thread pool.

The act of beginning and ending the operation is independent of how the operation is performed asynchronously. We could, for example, model our own operation to use this pattern that doesn't use an I/O completion port and uses the .NET Framework thread pool:

```
public void DoSomething()
{
  BeginWork(OnWorkCompleted, null);
}

private class AlwaysAsynchonousAsyncResult : IAsyncResult
{
  public AlwaysAsynchonousAsyncResult(object asyncState,
    AsyncCallback asyncCallback)
  {
    Callback = asyncCallback;
    AsyncState = asyncState;
    ManualResetEvent = new ManualResetEvent(false);
  }

  public ManualResetEvent ManualResetEvent
  {
    get; set;
  }

  public bool IsCompleted { get; private set; }

  public WaitHandle AsyncWaitHandle
  {
    get { return ManualResetEvent; }
  }

  public object AsyncState { get; private set; }

  public bool CompletedSynchronously
  {
    get {  return true; }
  }

  public AsyncCallback Callback { get; private set; }
}

private void OnWorkCompleted(IAsyncResult ar)
{
  EndWork(ar);
}
```

```
public IAsyncResult BeginWork(AsyncCallback callback,
  object state)
{
  AlwaysAsynchonousAsyncResult result =
    new AlwaysAsynchonousAsyncResult(state, callback);
  ThreadPool.QueueUserWorkItem(DoWork, result);
  return result;
}

private void DoWork(object state)
{
  AlwaysAsynchonousAsyncResult result =
    (AlwaysAsynchonousAsyncResult)state;
  int x = 2 + 2; // THE WORK
  // signal done.  If result needed to be stored
  // some how, it should be done prior to this.
  result.ManualResetEvent.Set();
  result.Callback(result);
}

public void EndWork(IAsyncResult asyncResult)
{
  AlwaysAsynchonousAsyncResult result =
    (AlwaysAsynchonousAsyncResult)asyncResult;

  ManualResetEvent manualResetEvent =
    result.ManualResetEvent;
  if (manualResetEvent == null)
  {
    return;
  }
  try
  {
    manualResetEvent.WaitOne(Timeout.Infinite, false);
    manualResetEvent.Close();
  }
  catch (ObjectDisposedException)
  {
  }
  finally
  {
    result.ManualResetEvent = null;
  }
}
```

As you can see, it's fairly complex implementing this pattern. We need to first create an `IAsyncResult` implementation. This implementation implements `IAsyncResult` (creates a `WaitHandle`, keeps track of the completed state, stores the state, and always completes asynchronously) as well as keeps track of the callback. `BeginWork` simply instantiates our `IAsyncResult` implementation, and asks the thread pool to invoke our `DoWork` method. `DoWork` does the work, sets the completed state, sets the `WaitHandle`, and then invokes the callback. We simply re-use the thread pool thread we've been given to invoke the callback, passing along our `IAsyncResult` implementation instance. The `EndWork` method makes sure `EndWork` wasn't called before completion of the work by waiting on the `WaitHandle`, and then cleans up by closing the handle and setting handle to `null` so it can't be used again.

This is a fairly industry-wide design pattern for supporting asynchronicity, where there is a "Begin" or "Start" method and an "End" method, and clients of the API are technically required to call both of the methods.

Event-based Asynchronous Pattern

Just as you can recognize implementations of the Asynchronous Design Pattern through its tell-tale "Begin" and "End" prefixes, you can also recognize implementations of the **Event-based Asynchronous Pattern** (**EAP**) through the suffix `Async` and `XXXCompleted` events.

It's somewhat unknown the exact impetus of creating the Event-based Asynchronous Pattern in .NET when the Asynchronous Design Pattern already existed. We can detail some of the benefits and surmise that these, maybe, in part, were the impetus.

With using an API implementing the Asynchronous Design Pattern, you had to have at least one method to handle the callback when the operation completed. This could have been an anonymous method, but it was still required. With the EAP, informing the client of completed status was done through an event. With events, subscription is optional, so to use an API implementing the EAP, writing code to handle completion of the operation is no longer required.

The two patterns are not currently implemented in the same regions of the framework, so the following example will be more like comparing apples and oranges in relation to the Asynchronous Design Pattern that I previously detailed:

```
public void UploadData(Uri uri, byte[] data)
{
  WebClient webClient = new WebClient();
  webClient.UploadDataCompleted += UploadDataCompleted;
  webClient.UploadDataAsync(uri, data);
```

```
    }

    private static void UploadDataCompleted(object sender,
      UploadDataCompletedEventArgs e)
    {
      Console.WriteLine(Encoding.UTF8.GetString(e.Result));
    }
```

We can see here that we've created a new `WebClient` object that we're invoking the `UploadDataAsync` method upon. Prior to that, we subscribed to the `UploadDataCompleted` event. We know the two members are associated because of the `XXXAsync` and `XXXCompleted` pattern. When the upload of the data is complete, our `UploadeCompleted` method will be called which and we simply get the result of the POST operation to the URI supplied, which may simply be a bunch of HTML.

I'm not going to get too deep into this pattern. Despite being the newer of the two asynchronous patterns, it's actually going to be replaced by a newer pattern that will be used within new language-based asynchronicity support in Visual C# 2012 and Visual Basic 2012. See the *Visual Studio 2012 asynchronous programming* section. In effect, the EAP will become deprecated.

Division of labor

Of course, we really haven't shown truly parallel processing. We've shown how to make use of completion ports and not cause the main thread to be unresponsive. This really isn't doing two things at once when it comes to the cores in our system. We have multiple cores and we can use all of them to their full potential!

The real trick to making use of all your processors is your ability to divide up the work to be done, so that it can be offloaded, in parts, to each core. If you have an existing application and you're not already dividing up the work, this may be hard to do. You may already be dividing up the work within your application that we could possibly change to make use of multiple cores.

This book isn't a tome on parallelization of work, how to divide work by separating data involved in to units of work, and so on. The parallelization examples we'll detail here fall under the pattern of "embarrassingly parallel," which is code that is so obviously parallelizable as to be embarrassing.

Loops are a natural division of work. Each iteration through the loop is, in fact, a unit of work. We could pull apart some of those loops and explicitly spawn a thread for each iteration. But first, we need to make sure each iteration is independent. Take the following loop for example:

```
for(int i = 0; i < 10; ++i)
{
  Console.Write(i);
}
```

Each iteration of this loop is dependent on the previous iteration. We expect to see **0123456789** displayed to the console. Although we could invoke `Console.Write` on many threads at a time, the result will not be what we are looking for.

On the other hand, if we had the following code:

```
const int count = 10;
var results =
  new Dictionary<int, double>(count);
var source = Enumerable.Range(2, count);

foreach(var item in source)
{
  results.Add(item, Math.Sqrt(item));
}
```

This calculates the square root of `2` through `11` and stores the results in a dictionary. There is no implied ordering here, only that we have a dictionary of values and their square roots. Each iteration of this loop could easily be executed independently of one another, and executed on independent threads. You might think it would be just a matter of throwing each iteration into a thread from the thread pool, shown as follows:

```
foreach(var item in source)
{
  ThreadPool.QueueUserWorkItem(_ =>
    results.Add(item, Math.Sqrt(item)));
}
```

This, of course, will spawn off ten threads, each one attempting to add a value to our dictionary. But because we've used an anonymous method (as a lambda), we are actually using a closure here, one that captures the `item` value. So, what really happens is that we throw an `ArgumentException` because we tried to add the key `11` twice to the dictionary.

Closures are the capturing of the referenced local variables used in an anonymous method. This is necessary because there is no direct support in the CLR for anonymous methods (only actual methods) and the compiler needs to generate actual methods. These generated methods need the non-local variables in order to run. So they are *captured* as members of the class that contains the generated method. In a method used asynchronously, these captured variables can change between when they are captured and when this generated method is executed, often causing logic errors.

To rectify this we can easily pull the value out of the closure, shown as follows:

```
foreach (var item in source)
{
  var uncapturedItem = item;
  ThreadPool.QueueUserWorkItem(_ =>
    results.Add(uncapturedItem,
    Math.Sqrt(uncapturedItem)));
}
```

This fixes our closure problem and might actually work, at least occasionally. However, the problem now is that `Dictionary<TKey,TValue>.Add` isn't thread-safe. Every once in a while the previous code won't end up with a dictionary with ten items in it. `Dictionary<TKey,TValue>` has its own invariants that we need to protect for it, given *our* context. This can easily be done by wrapping the call to `Add` within a `lock` block:

```
foreach (var item in source)
{
  var uncapturedItem = item;
  ThreadPool.QueueUserWorkItem(_ =>
    {
    double result = Math.Sqrt(uncapturedItem);
    lock (locker)
    {
      results.Add(uncapturedItem,
                 result);
    }
    });
}
```

Notice that I've extracted the actual work we want to parallelize (calculation of the root) to outside the lock. If we did all of the work within a `lock` block, only one thread could be executing within the block at a time, and we would have effectively written a really slow synchronous loop.

The C# language designers recognized this capturing of local variables in an asynchronous context and the resulting potential logic errors as being unexpected. So, in Visual Studio 2012 and .NET 4.5, closures will close over a fresh copy of captured variables. This is actually a breaking change. But, from many points of view, this "breaking" change fixes broken code. More information about the caveats that prompted this change can be found at `http://bit.ly/MBw2K6`.

This is now a thread-safe version of splitting up work onto multiple threads. This means we can make use of more cores, but how often are we going to have exactly ten processors? If we didn't have ten processors and had, say, four processors, we'd likely end up with ten CPU-bound threads vying for four processors. Remember when I talked about context switching and how expensive it is? The OS would end up context switching these ten threads amongst the four processors, likely killing any performance increase we were hoping to achieve. We would need to know there are four processors, limit the number of threads to four, and start new threads as others complete. Much more work. You could actually limit the number of threads in the thread pool to get it to do the work, but that pool is shared amongst the rest of the framework, so you'd have a huge impact on the rest of your application.

Suffice it to say that division of work is actually much harder than we'd like when dealing with threads in this way. Due to space and the usefulness of an example that does everything we could want, I'm not going to get into that much detail. Instead, I'll detail how you'd do that with the **Task Parallel Library** (**TPL**).

Task Parallel Library

In .NET 4.0, the TPL was introduced into the .NET class library. .NET provides a lot of threading and thread safety capabilities. The TPL makes parallelization in .NET applications easier. Before we get into too much detail about using it for parallelization and asynchrony, let's cover some TPL fundamentals first.

The TPL introduces a high-level threading abstraction called a `Task`. Tasks are used to model individual operations that can be executed, including asynchronously or in parallel. Prior to the TPL, the work involved in an operation was modeled as a single delegate, and didn't provide an object-oriented interface for dealing with asynchronous operations as abstractions, encapsulating state and other properties such as exception, status, and optional result.

Tasks

Tasks effectively wrap a delegate in a similar way as threading was done before TPL.

Creating tasks are easy. They can be created from a member method or an anonymous method. For example, we can create a task with a lambda as follows:

```
var task = new Task<string>(() =>
                    {
                        var x = new BigNumber(100);
                        var y = new BigNumber(100);
                        x.ArcTan(16, 5);
                        y.ArcTan(4, 239);
                        x.Subtract(y);
                        return x.ToString();
                    });
```

This example creates a task by passing in an `Action<string>` delegate into the constructor. The `Action<string>` delegate is a lambda statement that calculates pi to 100 digits using John Machin's formula for calculating pi.

A task on its own, of course, doesn't execute anything.

Execution

In order to execute a task asynchronously, it needs to be scheduled for execution. Intuitively, to schedule and execute a `Task` instance, the `Start` method can be called:

```
task.Start();
```

Calling `Start` schedules the task for execution using a default scheduler. You can do the same thing manually by getting the default (or current if the task has a non-default scheduler associated with it) task scheduler via `TaskScheduler.Current`:

```
task.Start(TaskScheduler.Current);
```

This, of course, is a bit pointless considering there's a `Start` overload that does the same thing. Normally, you'll probably just want to use the default, but there are times when you may need application-specific scheduling. You may need to limit the number of concurrent threads, create your own threads instead of using the thread pool, or make use of fibers. In such cases, you would need to create your own `TaskScheduler`. There are good references on creating custom `TaskScheduler` classes which is outside the scope of this book.

Although `Task` and `Task<T>` are meant to model asynchronous actions and functions, they can, in fact, be executed synchronously, for example:

```
task.RunSynchronously();
```

This particular use of the `Task` object is extremely rare. When dealing with a single task that is required to be executed asynchronously, creating a `Task` instance manually is usually more work than necessary. In such cases, `TaskFactory` comes to our rescue with its `StartNew` method. For example:

```
Task<string> task = Task.Factory.StartNew(() =>
                        {
                          var x = new BigNumber(100);
                          var y = new BigNumber(100);
                          x.ArcTan(16, 5);
                          y.ArcTan(4, 239);
                          x.Subtract(y);
                          return x.ToString();
                        });
```

Note that we used `Task.Factory` here. `Factory` is a property that contains the default `TaskFactory`. You can instantiate new `TaskFactory` objects with specific parameters, but I'll leave those details as an exercise for the reader. As with our previous example of instantiating a `Task<T>` object and calling `Start`, this method calculates pi to 100 digits asynchronously.

Context: When writing code to queue work to the thread pool.

Practice: Prefer using task-based TPL functionality.

Parallelization

There are many avenues for parallelization in the TPL. The first I'd like to look at continues the theme of parallelizing a loop. The TPL has a class called `Parallel`. This class is a static class with a few helper methods dealing with invoking many actions and functions at the same time. One method is `ForEach`, which "Executes an… operation on an `IEnumerable<TSource>` in which iterations may run in parallel." The degree to which the operations on a loop are parallelized depends on the number of cores in the system.

We now have a way of efficiently parallelizing work on a loop. With our previous example, we could replace the `foreach` with `Paralell.ForEach`, and remove the need to uncapture the closure variable because we no longer are bound to an outside variable as `ForEach` provides the variable:

```
Parallel.ForEach(source, item =>
{
  double result = Math.Sqrt(item);
  lock (locker)
  {
    results.Add(item, result);
  }
});
```

It actually looks more readable.

`Parallel.ForEach` actually creates a `Task` to encapsulate the action given to `ForEach`, but doesn't create individual tasks for each iteration. The call to `ForEach` is synchronous (it blocks until all operations are completed). It's as if we created a `Task` whose action was to fork a bunch of threads, join them, and the framework called `RunSynchronously` on that task. You can also model collections of data that don't implement `IEnumerable` with `Parallel.For`, which is semantically similar to a `for` loop in C#.

Not every parallelization scenario revolves around iterating a loop or performing independent logic on each member of a collection. You may simply have several independent things you want to do at the same time. If they can be abstracted into a method (anonymous or otherwise), then you can simply group them in an array and pass them along to `Parallel`. `Parallel.Invoke` invokes several actions "... possibly in parallel." This gives us the same way of taking several methods and making an efficient use of all of the cores in our system.

Let's say that we have several dates in our system from sales, administration, and marketing. For each of these groupings, if we wanted to calculate the average age of whatever these dates represent, we could represent each calculation as an action, and pass each of those actions to the `Invoke` method, for example:

```
var now = DateTime.Now;
Parallel.Invoke(
  () => GetSalesDates()
    .Select(a => (now - a).TotalDays / 365)
    .Average(),
  () => GetAdministrationDates()
    .Select(a => (now - a).TotalDays / 365)
    .Average(),
```

```
() => GetMarketingDates()
  .Select(a => (now - a).TotalDays / 365)
  .Average());
```

Each one of our actions is taking each date/time, projecting it (`Select`) into the number of years between now and that date/time (`(now-a).TotalDays / 365`), and takes the average (`Average()`). `Invoke` then distributes execution of those actions on however many cores it deems necessary, hopefully most are in parallel.

Context: When you need to parallelize independent operations based on collections of data.

Practice: Prefer using TPL's `Parallel.ForEach` or `Parallel.For`.

Context: When you have a finite set of discrete operations that can be modeled as a method.

Practice: Prefer using TPL's `Parallel.Invoke`.

Working with Asynchronous Design Pattern

Of course, we already have lots of asynchronous APIs in the .NET Framework to work with. What if we wanted to work with those, and with the TPL at the same time?

If we take our previous `NetworkStream.BeginWrite/EndWrite` example from earlier in the chapter, in order to incorporate those methods into a single task, we would make use of the `TaskFactoryFromAsync` method. For example:

```
NetworkStream networkStream = tcpClient.GetStream();
var task = Task.Factory.FromAsync(networkStream.BeginWrite,
                                  networkStream.EndWrite,
                                  data, 0, data.Length,
                                  networkStream);
```

With the TPL we'd wrap our `NetworkStream.BeginWrite` and `EndWrite` in a `Task` object via the `FromAsync` static method on `TaskFactory`. That `Task` (which is really something that invokes `BeginWrite`, giving it a delegate that in turn calls `EndWrite`) immediately gets scheduled to execute.

When using the `FromAsync` overload that accepts the Begin method and the End method, TPL does not use any extra threads, and therefore does not introduce any extra blocking.

Context: When using APM APIs `BeginXXX` and `EndXXX` with TPL.

Practice: Prefer wrapping APM APIs with `TaskFractory.FromAsync` to preserve use of I/O completion ports and avoid overloading thread pools.

Continuations

When we're dealing with asynchronous tasks, we often need these asynchronous tasks to complete in a specific order. In the Asynchronous Design Pattern, we'd be forced to do this in our completion callback shortly after calling the End method. The fact that one operation continued after another was essentially lost in the multitude of methods and differing responsibilities within those methods.

One of the particularly powerful aspects of the TPL is the ability to chain operations together. Let's say we want to calculate a standard deviation. The first part of the standard deviation calculation is to calculate the mean average of a series of numbers. If we wanted to create that list on a background thread asynchronously, and then use the calculated mean in a standard deviation calculation also in the background, we could use continuations for that. For example:

```
Task.Factory.StartNew(() => CalculateMean(list))
  .ContinueWith((meanTask) =>
    CalculateStandardDeviation(meanTask.Result, list))
  .ContinueWith((standardDeviationTask) =>
    Console.WriteLine(standardDeviationTask.Result));
```

In this code we start a task to calculate the mean. Then, we call `Task<int>.ContinueWith` to create a new task that will take the result of the first task, along with the series of numbers, and calculate the standard deviation. We complete our series of operations with another `ContinueWith` taking the result of the standard deviation and outputting it to the console.

`ContinueWith` creates a task that is passed to the previous task as a parameter. The `Task<T>` object has a `Result` property that is populated with the result of the first task (in our case, the return value from `CalculateMean`).

We can do the same thing with APM APIs wrapped with `FromAsync`. In our previous `FromAsync` example we created one task to write data. If we wanted to continue our theme of reading data after we've written data, we could do the same with `FromAsync` and continuations. For example:

```
NetworkStream networkStream = tcpClient.GetStream();
var task = Task.Factory.FromAsync(networkStream.BeginWrite,
                                  networkStream.EndWrite,
                                  data, 0, data.Length,
                                  networkStream);
```

```
task = task.ContinueWith(_ => Task<int>.Factory.FromAsync(
  networkStream.BeginRead,
  networkStream.EndRead,
  incomingData, 0,
  incomingData.Length,
  networkStream));
task.Wait();
```

We now call `task.ContinueWith`, which tells the scheduler to schedule a task wrapping `NetworkStream.BeginRead` and `EndRead` once the first task is completed.

Of course, at this point we'd need to either continue with another task when that second task is complete and do something with `incomingData`, or otherwise detect when the second task completes and do something with the data. But, you get the point.

Visual Studio 2012 asynchronous programming

With the next release of the .NET Framework (.NET 4.5) and Visual Studio (2012) comes some language additions to C# and Visual Basic to support asynchronous operations. From a programmer's point of view, the language additions revolve around the introduction of two new keywords: `async` and `await`.

From a more holistic point of view, `async` and `await` (more so `await`) could do nothing without a great amount of work put into the .NET class libraries, but I'll get more into that soon.

With `async/await` you can write methods that are sequential in nature, but asynchronous when compiled and executed. The `async` decorator on a method causes the compiler to implement the method as a state machine. As the compiler runs into `await` statements it translates them into invoking asynchronous actions. The compiler basically creates a closure in response to one of the `await` statements to keep track of the local state of the method while it invokes the various `async` operations. This allows it to weave together the results of each operation back into a sequential series of events as you've described them in your `async` method.

We can invoke asynchronous methods in much the same way as we did before, but we don't need to directly deal with "callbacks," since the subsequent lines of code are the callback. We could cheat before and use anonymous methods instead of real methods, but we'd still need to pass in callbacks to certain asynchronous operations.

The Task-based Asynchronous Pattern

With .NET 4.5 there is a new asynchronous pattern. This pattern is called the **Task-based Asynchronous Pattern (TAP)**. This pattern is most similar to the Asynchronous Design Pattern, but bears some resemblance to the Event-based Asynchronous Pattern. TAP is similar to APM in that you invoke it asynchronously, and needs to deal with completion through methods. It's similar to EAP in that the methods in the framework end with "Async" and you don't need to call an `EndXXX` method, but there are no events.

The pattern is basically that asynchronous methods use the TPL and return a `Task`-derived object to signify the asynchronous operation, its state, any result it may produce, and so on, *and* is prefixed with "Async." So, with our `NetworkStream` class that has `BeginWrite` and `EndWrite`, we now have a `WriteAsync` method.

`await` works with methods that implement TAP. Let's return to our `NetworkStream` example to see how we might do the same thing with `async/await`:

```
public async void Write(TcpClient tcpClient, byte[] data)
{
  var networkStream = tcpClient.GetStream();
  await networkStream.WriteAsync(data, 0, data.Length);
  byte[] buffer = new byte[1024];
  await networkStream.ReadAsync(buffer, 0, buffer.Length);
}
```

In our modified `Write` method, we have now decorated it with the `async` keyword. This tells the compiler to prepare to manage the state in the method as if it could change asynchronously. This also makes using `await` syntactically correct within the method. Also, instead of calling a method such as `BeginWrite`, we now call `WriteAsync`, but we prefix the call with `await` to tell the compiler that this method executes asynchronously.

Although named "await," the compiler doesn't actually generate code that waits, that is,it doesn't block the thread. It actually builds up the equivalent of several continuations of each `await` call. The asynchronous methods are then chained together through these continuations on whatever thread the system responds with for completion. A thread wouldn't be blocked unless we asked the thread we invoked `Write` with to block. For example, if we wanted to not return from `Write` until both the write and the read completed, we would do something shown as follows:

```
public async void Write(TcpClient tcpClient, byte[] data)
{
  var networkStream = tcpClient.GetStream();
  await networkStream.WriteAsync(data, 0, data.Length);
```

```
    byte[] buffer = new byte[1024];
    networkStream.ReadAsync(buffer, 0, buffer.Length)
      .Wait();
  }
```

This would block the thread until the asynchronous read completed. In the previous method, we simply wrote some data then read some data, and threw the read data away. But that went and happened in the background, and the thread that called `Write` continued on to do something else. Neither of which you're likely to do.

Reactive Extensions

Reactive Extensions (Rx) is a library to compose asynchronous and event-based applications. The results of certain asynchronous operations can be communicated through events by "observable" objects. Results in Rx are generally a sequence of values.

Rx provides a push-based model that more closely models asynchronous operation than a pull model. "Reactive" is used because something that observes push notifications is "reacting" to notifications. This is done through subscription to notifications.

Rx builds its push model on `IObservable<T>` and `IObserver<T>`. An `IObservable<T>` is something that can be observed by an `IObserver<T>`. The sequence of values is observed through `IObserver<T>.OnNext()`. An optional signaling of completion is observed through `IObserver<T>.OnCompleted()`. `IObservable<T>` is often compared to `IEnumerable<T>` because they both deal with a sequence of values.

`IObservable<T>` and `IObserver<T>` are BCL types, independent of Rx. Rx adds to these by providing some static class and extension methods which make use of these two interfaces in a LINQ-like manner, in much the same way "LINQ to Objects" extends `IEnumerable`. You can generally operate on an `IObservable<T>` with Rx, in much the same way you can operate on `IEnumbable<T>` with LINQ. You get methods such as `First`, `Single`, `Range`, `Select`, `Where`, `GroupBy`, and so on. For example, an enumerable can be observed synchronously through the use of the `ToObservable` extension method:

```
var collection = new[] {1, 2, 3, 4, 5};
IObservable<int> source = collection.ToObservable();
```

Subscribing to, and processing, the observable (source) is as follows:

```
var subscriber = source.Subscribe(
  x => Console.WriteLine("OnNext:  {0}", x),
```

```
        ex => Console.WriteLine("OnError: {0}", ex.Message),
        () => Console.WriteLine("OnCompleted")
        );
```

Subscribing to, and processing, an asynchronous observable would be the same. When the subscriber no longer wants to be subscribed, simply dispose the value returned from `Subscribe`. Rx allows us to wrap Asynchronous Programming Model implementations in much the same way as the Task Parallel Library does. For example:

```
var read =
  Observable.FromAsyncPattern<byte[], int, int, int>(
    networkStream.BeginRead,
    networkStream.EndRead);
IObservable<int> readObservable =
  read(bytes, 0, bytes.Length);
readObservable.Subscribe(bytesRead =>
                      Trace.WriteLine(
              string.Format("read {0} bytes into inputbuffer",
              bytesRead)));
```

Similar to our `Task<T>` example, this example wraps the `NetworkStream.BeginRead` and `NetworkStream.EndRead` in an `IObservable` object. This object, when invoked with the required parameters (`byte[]`, initial offset into the byte array, and the size of the byte array) provides the result to the subscriber's `OnNext` method. The `OnNext` method is provided via the `Subscribe` method call as an anonymous method (lambda).

Rx is very complex and its complexities could take an entire book on its own. For more information on Rx, see `http://msdn.microsoft.com/data/gg577609`.

Rx may seem very similar to the EAP, but the EAP is designed to model a single result from an asynchronous operation (`Completed` event). The EAP is a pattern because it doesn't build on specific types or interfaces, it follows a style: an invoking asynchronous method that ends with "Async."

Rx can be very similar to some of the patterns dealing with UI view/model patterns. View/model patterns deal with decoupling views from models, and often decouple through the use of abstractions like interfaces to "observe" changes. WPF and Silverlight make use of types such as `INotifyPropertyChanged` and `ObservableCollection<T>` (that implements `INotifyPropertyChanged`) to decouple the view from the model and focus on the values that the view requires (and potentially needs to know change asynchronously).

Rx provides a way of dealing with sequences of values that change asynchronously and independently (or are observed independently). Rx is a good way of implementing an in-process pub/sub model (more on pub/sub in the next chapter). Any sequence can be a single value, and Rx can be used as a way of implementing asynchronous operations that result in a single value. Rx might not be the best framework for implementing these types of asynchronous operations. Rx takes a bit of work to implement, and if your asynchronous operations could be modeled with TAP and consumed with `async/await`, this is likely a better option. For example, to publish a value to an observer, you'd need to invoke both `OnNext` and `OnCompleted`, which is heavy-weight for a single value.

Summary

As we can see, threading has the potential to be very difficult. We not only need to decide how our code can operate on multiple threads, or how we can make use of asynchronous operations, we also need to guarantee our data doesn't get corrupted.

With some easy-to-follow practices, we can decide when and how we can parallelize work in our applications. We now know which APIs are best to use when we want to use asynchronous operations, but we also know how we can go about ensuring our invariants.

There are many ways of making our code thread-safe and protecting our invariants. With a few useful practices, we can not only make our code thread-safe, but we don't need to make it really slow either.

In the next chapter, we'll look at similar parallelization topics, except spanning process boundaries: distributed applications. We'll look at ways of architecting distributed applications, as well as specific technologies that help communication of nodes within a distributed application. In addition, we'll look at ways of debugging, monitoring, and maintaining distributed applications.

9
Distributed Applications

It's hard to write anything but a very simple application without needing to deal with distributed computing in some form. While many people have some fairly distinct views of what **distributed computing** is, it's a unobtuse concept. Google Code University defines a distributed system as:

> *A **distributed*** **system** *is an application that executes a collection of protocols to coordinate the actions of multiple processes on a network, such that all components cooperate together to perform a single or small set of related tasks.*

Wikipedia defines a distributed system as:

> *A* **distributed system** *consists of multiple autonomous computers that communicate through a computer network.*

The purpose of most distributed systems is to operate on multiple computers. Most distributed system can scale vertically, that is, on a single computer. I think pigeonholing distributed systems as systems running on separate computers is a bit narrow-minded. The important aspect is *multiple processes communicating with one another over the network*. Where the processes are executing is a deployment issue which is independent of the *distributed nature* of the system.

Knowing what is, and is not, a distributed system allows us to better plan and design our system using established practices and patterns.

This chapter covers various topics and practices with regard to implementing and maintaining distributed systems in .NET.

Seeking scalability

One major impetus of distributed systems is scalability. At some point, one component is offloading work to another component in a different process. The reason for offloading that work can be one or more of the following reasons:

- Finer granularity of work
- Distribution of load
- Reduction in duplication of work
- Abstraction of responsibility

Implementing a system that is distributed without planning for or utilizing the scalability abilities of the system is often an indication that there are miscommunications.

Design options

There are several design options for distributing components in a system. Obviously, some are better than others. This section will detail some of the bad and some of the good design options.

Communicating via a database

I do not recommend this design option in general. It is included here because I have encountered it in the wild more than once, and it deserves some detail.

Using a database as a communication medium generally leads to an architecture that is not optimal for storing and retrieving communication information. The more common databases are relational databases. Choosing to implement communication between distributed components through a shared database will generally mean choosing a known database, or a database that makes the development team most comfortable. Communicating information from point A to point B does not make much use of RDBMS's distinct features. Communicating information is a LIFO queue, the oldest data written is the first data read. The following RDBMS features are not used when we use a relational table in this way:

- Relations
- Relational operations
- Relational algebra/set theory
- Transactions
- Indexes

We do get data integrity without manually creating transactions.

Sure, we can index on the date/time field of a record to get faster LIFO retrieval, but using this 400 lb Gorilla just for that is a bit overkill.

For comparison, this is like taking a commercial airline to fly 100 km. The time it takes to get to the airport, check in, go through security, board the plane, fly to the other terminal, disembark the plane, leave the terminal, and take ground transportation to your final destination is usually noticeably longer than just taking *only* ground transportation from one place to the other.

What is the harm? I am sure there are a few readers wondering this. After all, this *is* a functional design option. It will "work," but it does not come without consequences. The overhead to get all of the relational functionality generally means we take a hit on performance. On a reasonably fast computer, I have clocked SQL Server at about 200–500 transactions per second, writing one kilobyte worth of data into a table at a time. If the granularity of your communications means you need to go faster than this, you might run into some roadblocks with a design that uses SQL Server as a communications medium.

Context: When designing distributed systems.

Pattern: Avoid using a database as the messaging channel.

Messaging pattern

Even if you use a database as the communication bridge between two components, you are effectively using the **messaging pattern**. The messaging pattern is when two or more components communicate via messages through some sort of messaging channel. In the case of the database design, the database (and whatever table you have chosen) is the channel. Messages are coherent blocks of structured data.

Many messaging patterns rely on messages to be of a "known" complex type. This is not necessary in the general case with many modern languages. Concepts such as **duck typing** can be used in some cases, as long as a message "looks" close enough to something else.

Acknowledging that messaging (and the message passing) is occurring allows design and thought about the system to utilize existing practices, patterns, and terminology.

Context: When communicating between different processes.

Practice: Acknowledge use of the messaging pattern.

Message queues

A **message queue** is for the independent communication of messages from one component to another independently. The act of sending a message should not be hindered or dependent on the act of receiving the message. Clearly, the act of communicating between two components requires that one side send and the other side receive a message, but how those messages are sent should not hinder the sender.

Most applications are not message queues. Work involved in creating and managing a proprietary message queue is not the intended value-add of the system. Any work involved in areas such as this takes away from the effort of the "purpose" of the system. This includes using a database as a message queue, which requires a lot of effort to design, implement, and maintain.

Context: When two or more processes require independent communications.

Practice: Consider making use of an off-the-shelf message queue.

Message queues allow asynchronous communication of messages. Not all components require that communication with another component be asynchronous. Synchronization of a message's send/receive can be implemented with various features of message queues such as acknowledgment. That is, the sender does not proceed to the next message until the receiver acknowledges receipt of the current message. Some communications between components are not as finely grained, as in one sender may need acknowledgement of a group of messages. Scenarios like this are best implemented within application-specific protocols.

Context: When dealing with message groups that seems to require being sequential.

Practice: Consider an application-specific protocol to enforce this sequence.

For example, we might want to tell one component to update a customer record and we need to know if that succeeded, so we do not lose the changed data. Rather than send a message to the other component and block, a command would be sent to the component asynchronously, and the receiving component can broadcast an event telling subscribers that it has updated a customer record. The component that sent the command could listen for the event and know that the sequence of updating that customer record is now complete. State within that component would be updated to reflect that. For example, a processing progress bar could be stopped and an update button could be re-enabled.

Command-query separation

Once you start to gain experience with messaging, you quickly start to understand the fundamental asynchronous behavior of communication over the wire. A message, based on data in the system, travels over the network, which inherently has a latency and is effectively "read only" once it has been sent. You start to understand you cannot change the data in transit, and it is asynchronously traveling to its destination, and you can no longer view it as data in the system. You can view the data sent as "parameters" in the message.

When you are dealing with messages that request change of state, those "parameters" are part of a *command*. When you are dealing with messages that request current state, they are part of a *query*. It is valuable to differentiate application state from the "parameters" in messages. Realizing the inherent asynchronousness of sending and receiving messages, you start to recognize the inherent separation of commands and queries.

You can begin to expand on the nature of this separation and make it first class in much of the system's design. For example, if you know a message obviously cannot change *and* query data at the same time, and you separate those actions into commands and queries, and you recognize the inherent asynchronousness of the communication, you can begin to see that sending a message is not the same as making a method call. With a method call, you invoke code (presumably changing state) and get a response to that action, which could be the result of a query. You are performing a command *and* a query at the same time. The fact that, with messaging, there is not a "call" and there is not a "return," means that you simply cannot perform a command and a query at the same time. At best, you get a response to a command that could be a query, but that is the same thing as if it where two messages: one to invoke the command and another to request the state.

When we separate commands from queries, we begin to embrace the asynchronous nature of our distributed systems and we no longer think of message invocation being dependent upon return. We think more of starting background processes and being informed of completion or results. The two are *independent*.

It is vital for distributed systems to embrace the independent nature of the components. If you send a message to a message queue, that obviously queues the message for delivery at a later time/date, but blocks your application from continuing until a response or result is sent back, your application will not function property. At best case, it will look unresponsive and clunky. At worst case, it will time-out and corrupt its state, since will not know how to reconcile its current state from that of another subsystem.

Message bus

Once you accept that you are doing **message passing**, and you build up a coherent and distinct set of messages, and use a distinct message channel, you have built a **message bus**.

The message bus pattern enables subsystems to communicate independently of one another with a common/shared set of commands.

Context: When designing systems where subsystems need to communicate with one another through a message channel.

Practice: Consider implementing the message bus pattern.

The bus part of a message bus is a subsystem that transfers data between components within a system. While we could consider a message queue to be the bus, it is really just the channel. *What* is sent via the queue is just as important in making a bus work. The definition of the messages, along with the channel, is the message bus.

The channel of the message bus provides a way to abstract the details of communication away from the application. With a message bus, a component just "sends" messages or "receives" messages. It is not concerned about the implementation details of the channel and does not need to implement those details. TCP/IP, for example, is a perfectly good means of communicating from one component to another. However, both ends need to implement code that connects, listens, sends, and receives on a socket. Those two, and *only* those two, components are intrinsically coupled together via that implementation.

Service bus

There are times when it is not possible to have an entirely shared set of message structures. It is possible that systems can be built which bring together a disparate set of subsystems that may be produced by a disparate set of teams, or even bring together a disparate set of products. A typical example of this is building a system that works with several legacy systems/subsystems that already exist and already communicate with a fixed set of messages of fixed structure.

A **service bus** often occurs in enterprise situations where an enterprise is attempting to integrate disparate systems like this, but these systems cannot communicate with one another directly. Service buses introduce the ability to route messages, transform data, map data, and so on, in order for individual systems and subsystems to communicate with one another effectively.

Context: When considering an architecture that must integrate several disparate systems or subsystems.

Practice: Consider using a service bus to manage integration of subsystem communications.

Cloud

Much of how applications can be distributed is a type of offering by one or more cloud services. Companies such as Amazon and Microsoft offer services such as compute services to support elastic execution of your code remotely. If this code needs to interoperate with some else, that distributed communication needs to be performed in a way compatible with the cloud services you are using.

Products such as Azure offer abilities such as message queues and service buses to facilitate integrating subsystems in a distributed fashion.

To a certain extent, you can offload the creation and maintenance of parts of your system, such as message queues and services buses, to cloud services such as Azure. This lets you focus on the value that your system offers.

To support the cloud, and any of the services available in the cloud, a system must be designed in a distributed way. Much of this chapter discusses various practices that help deal with working with various cloud services. These services are simply remote components in a distributed system.

It is important to recognize this distributed nature in order to design an application that works effectively and efficiently with cloud services. Recognizing the asynchronous nature of communication with cloud services helps to build a responsive and robust system. Recognizing that communication is inherently a request/response, or a command/event and query/result, paradigm will help create robust communication methods as well as create a responsive user-interface.

There are many different types of cloud services. All of which are intended to reduce the burden of systems and infrastructures, from needing to deal with the day-to-day headaches of implementing and supporting such services within an organization. "Cloud" is such an overused word nowadays that it's hard to not think of some type of service that isn't "cloud" provided. Offloading e-mail services to an e-mail service provider is an example of using a "cloud" service.

A distributed system is a distinct system that offers specific functionality. It relies on certain infrastructural components for it to work, but for the most part, the type or location of those components does not matter. A system may depend on data storage for it to operate correctly, but where that data is stored and what type of subsystem it is stored on is often irrelevant. Often implementation and maintenance of distributed systems get caught up in the infrastructure of the system, and focus is taken away from the value or the purpose of the actual system.

When it comes to building a distributed system, the "cloud" options are very specific. There exist many types of services that can be leveraged for distributed systems. Of course, what a distributed system needs, and what it can use in terms of what service providers offer, is specific to each system. But we can look at some typical cloud offerings that are available.

Infrastructure as a Service

Infrastructure as a Service (**IaaS**) provides the physical and virtual infrastructure for a system to exist. This includes services such as physical or virtual machines, firewalls, load balancers, and so on. It's rare that this service is used on its own. It's more likely that Platform as a Service is used and the IaaS part just "exists" to provide Platform as a Service.

Platform as a Service

Platform as a Service (**PaaS**) is a cloud service that offers a stack of software and infrastructure. Compute services are often PaaS. They offer a particular operating system with network infrastructure and storage to execute specific code.

Software as a Service

Software as a Service (**SaaS**) is when a cloud service offers the execution of a particular category or type of software. Data services are sometimes SaaS. They offer an instance of a particular type of database.

The types of services that are useful when implementing a distributed system could consist of the following:

- Compute
- Storage/data
- Message queue
- Service bus

A compute service falls under PaaS. A specific platform (such as Windows or Linux) is required in order to execute a certain code. Often, a more granular execution is required in the form of virtual machines, in which case a more IaaS offering might be used. IaaS offerings that provide virtual machines are often still called "compute" services.

A storage service could simply be raw disk space, in which case it is more like IaaS. However, storage for many distributed systems, while necessary, is really just there to support data services. Data cloud SaaS services are generally more useful to distributed systems because that is how the storage will be used. To be fair, all cloud services use storage in some form. It is rare that a system needs only storage. For example, a **virtual machine** (**VM**) uses storage, but you only care about the VM service. Offloading to a cloud storage or data service means you gain elasticity. As your system uses more data, the service provider is happy to expand their infrastructure as a rule, automatically giving you more storage so they can charge you more. You have less to worry about in terms of physically upgrading storage.

As we have seen with message queues and service buses, buying off-the-shelf allows you to concentrate on the purpose of your system. Using cloud services for your message queue and service bus is just another way of buying this type of software. Cloud services, potentially make it easier or faster to get up and running with these types of components.

Context: When designing and implementing distributed components.

Practice: Consider making use of cloud-based services for data, compute, service bus, or message queue.

What are the benefits of offloading some of your components or infrastructure to the cloud? The easiest benefit to quantify is the maintenance benefit. Your organization is no longer maintaining that infrastructure. No one in the organization needs to perform software updates, they do not need to monitor infrastructure in order to replace failing components, no space is required to house them, and so on. With some organizations, this means the difference between a capital expenditure and a cost. This can often mean that systems can be built much more quickly with cloud services because the process for incurring a monthly cost is much less political work than incurring a new capital expenditure. During conception, no one needs to evaluate the hardware, procure the hardware, install the hardware, and so on.

TCP/UDP

A distributed system can involve components which effectively need to operate in a more tightly coupled way. Use of a message queue or a service bus may be overkill. Alternatively, some components may simply need to communicate with third-party services or products in a specific way, like via TCP/UDP.

Although the act of designing and creating a distributed system that communicates via TCP or UDP seems straightforward at a high level, some of the details can be a bit tedious. At a high level, it may simply seem like one side sends data and the other side listens and receives data. Nevertheless, these components are decoupled by way of independent computers and network (that may involve several connection points in between such as switches and routers). It is very easy for the communication between these components to become disconnected or redirected and delayed.

It is very important to have robust communications, even when implementing TCP or UDP. Care must be taken to detect and compensate, or report, error conditions. This is often quite a bit of work compared to using other channels such as a message queue.

Context: When deciding whether to implement low-level communications.

Practice: Only choose low-level communications when it is required and adds value.

There may be times when off-the-shelf components or legacy components communicate only via TCP or UDP. In these cases, it is necessary to implement low-level communications such as TCP or UDP. However, in these cases, that implementation can be abstracted into a **bridge**. The bridge would implement the communication with those external components, then integrate into the rest of the system. This allows how the bridge integrates into the rest of the system to evolve independently from those external components (that likely will not evolve, or at least not at the same rate).

Debugging

There comes a time in every application's life where it will need to be debugged. A non-distributed application is usually easy to debug since you can simply execute it in a debugger. Once in the debugger, you can perform various actions that the debugger provides, such as breakpoints or stepping through code.

When dealing with distributed systems, since some of the systems are remote from one another, debugging can be a bit more challenging. One option is to make use of remote debugging. This involves installing debugging components on computers so that the system can be debugged remotely. Once configured, remote debugging is generally the same as local debugging. Remote debugging is fine for sandboxed and test environments, but is generally frowned upon in production or acceptance environments. Installing components other than those that are required to run the system is often denied.

Even when you can debug remotely, there may be so many processes in play that you cannot debug them all in one remote debug session. So you cannot trace code and data that go from one process to another. When remote debugging is not an option, it's important to log information so that what is going on in the system as a whole can be observed.

Logging

Subsystems, and systems in a distributed system, have a high level of independence. A message sent by one subsystem occurs asynchronously. The *send* of a message does not occur at or near the *receipt* of that message on the other end. If the intended receiver of that message was unable to receive that message, it could be an astoundingly lengthy amount of time (as in seconds) before the loss of the message is detected. However, when you are looking at even 500 transactions per second throughput, a few seconds is a lot of data to wade through to figure out when the problem occurred and with what data.

Logging is vital to being able to track down problems in a distributed system.

There are logging frameworks and tools that do all sorts of different types of logging, and abstracts away the details of different types of logs. I recommend using some sort of logging framework to abstract where you want to log, from the fact that you are logging. For example, you may want to sometimes log *some* information to a file and log *some* information to the Windows Event Log. You do not want to need to change your code whenever you want to change that "configuration."

Context: When implementing logging.

Practice: Choose a logging framework to abstract logging configuration from your code.

That logging framework can simply be the .NET Framework. For example, you can use the `Trace` class to log information, shown as follows:

```
var sourceSwitch =
  new SourceSwitch(switchDisplayName,
           TraceLevel.Error.ToString());

if (sourceSwitch.Level == SourceLevels.Error)
  Trace.WriteLine("Something wicked this way comes.",
           "Error");
    }
  }
```

We create a `SourceSwitch` object with the name stored in `switchDisplayName`. The `SourceSwitch` object gives us information about what trace level we want to support. We then check `sourceSwitch.Level` to make sure the trace level of `Error` is on in the switch (by default, `Error` is on).

This will write the text **Error: Something wicked this way comes.** to the debug output by default. However, you can configure listeners to "redirect" that to other destinations. For example, if you also wanted to log to a file named `log.txt` in the current directory, then you could add the following section to your `app.config`:

```
<system.diagnostics>
  <trace autoflush="true">
    <listeners>
      <add name="logFileListener"
        type="System.Diagnostics.TextWriterTraceListener"
        initializeData="log.txt"
        traceOutputOptions="DateTime" />
    </listeners>
  </trace>
</system.diagnostics>
```

This will then write **Error: Something wicked this way comes.** to both the debug output and to the file `log.txt`.

In addition, if we wanted to configure what types of messages to log (error, debug, informational, and so on), then we could add the following to the `system.diagnostics` section in the `app.config` file:

```
<switches>
  <add name="sourceSwitch" value="Warning" />
</switches>
```

This would configure any `SourceSwitch` we created with the name `sourceSwitch` to have a `Level` of `Warning` instead of `Error`. In our example code, no message would be displayed because we are checking for `Error`. `SourceLevels` have the following hierarchy: `Critical`, `Error` `Warning`, `Information`, and `Verbose`. Therefore, you could also include `Error`, if the switch were configured as `Critical` by doing a bitwise comparison, shown as follows:

```
if ((sourceSwitch.Level | SourceLevels.Error) ==
  SourceLevels.Error)
{
  Trace.WriteLine("Something wicked this way comes.",
           "Error");
}
```

Of course, if you wanted to include other information, such as date/time, thread ID, process ID, or the call stack, then the code being logged would need to take on the responsibility of gathering all that information and include it in the invocation of `WriteLine`.

Fortunately, `System.Diagnostics` has some other tracing functionality that is a little more powerful with regard to how it can be configured. The `TraceSource` class offers us the ability to do much the same as `Trace.WriteLine`. We need to use it slightly differently than we used `Trace`:

```
TraceSource traceSource = new TraceSource("traceSource");
traceSource.TraceEvent(TraceEventType.Error,
  1000,
  "Something wicked this way comes.");
```

Here, we create a `TraceSource` object with the name `traceSource`. We then call the `TraceEvent` method to trace a particular application-specific event. We include a message with that event message, `"Something wicked this way comes."` Events always have an ID, but a message is optional. If you are using `TraceSource` to log to a text file, it is very useful to include a message. This particular event is a type of `Error`, so we also pass along `TraceEventType.Error`. The definition of `TraceSource` includes `SourceSwitch`. So, unlike using `Trace`, we do not need to manually create `TraceSwitch`.

This code operates differently, in that it does not assume any defaults like `Trace` did. If nothing were configured, the default action would be to log nothing. Therefore, to do any logging, we need to add some configuration. For example, if we wanted to log to the debug output *and* to the file, like in our `Trace` example, then we could have the following `system.diagnostics` section in our `app.config`:

```
    <trace autoflush="true"/>
    <switches>
      <add name="sourceSwitch" value="Error" />
```

```
    </switches>
    <sources>
      <source name="traceSource"
              switchName="sourceSwitch"
              switchType="System.Diagnostics.SourceSwitch" >
        <listeners>
          <add name="textwriterListener"
           type="System.Diagnostics.TextWriterTraceListener"
           initializeData="log.txt" />
        </listeners>
      </source>
    </sources>
```

This outputs text to both the debug output and our `log.txt` file in the following format:

traceSource Error: 1000 : Something wicked this way comes.

`TraceSource.TraceEvent` works slightly differently in that it does not output messages based upon the hierarchy of the `TraceEventType` types. However, the switch value is effectively a bit field so you can define how many types you want to support. For example, if you want to display both `Critical` and `Error` messages, you can create a switch in your `app.config`, shown as follows:

```
    <switches>
      <add name="sourceSwitch" value="Error,Critical" />
    </switches>
```

In our example, we only output the type (`Error`), ID (`1000`), and the message. We could include things such as a stack trace thread ID by modifying a trace listener. For example:

```
        <listeners>
          <add name="textwriterListener"
            type="System.Diagnostics.TextWriterTraceListener"
            initializeData="log.txt"
            traceOutputOptions="ThreadId, DateTime, Callstack"/>
        </listeners>
```

This would cause our trace listener to be created with `TraceOutputOptions` of `TraceOptions.ThreadId`, `TraceOptions.DateTime`, and `TraceOptions.Callstack`. What is output to `log.txt` would now look similar to the following:

```
traceSource Error: 1000 : Something wicked this way comes.
ThreadId=9
DateTime=2012-05-18T18:41:44.7358105Z
```

```
Callstack=   at System.Environment.GetStackTrace(Exception e, Boolean
needFileInfo)
at System.Environment.get_StackTrace()
at System.Diagnostics.TraceEventCache.get_Callstack()
at System.Diagnostics.TraceListener.WriteFooter(TraceEventCacheeventC
ache)
at System.Diagnostics.TraceListener.TraceEvent(TraceEventCacheeventCac
he, String source, TraceEventTypeeventType, Int32 id, String message)
at System.Diagnostics.TraceSource.TraceEvent(TraceEventTypeeventType,
Int32 id, String message)
at Test.Program.Method() in C:\src\Program.cs:line 11
at Test.Program.Main() in C:\src\Program.cs:line 23
at System.AppDomain._nExecuteAssembly(RuntimeAssembly assembly,
String[] args)
at System.AppDomain.ExecuteAssembly(String assemblyFile, Evidence
assemblySecurity, String[] args)
at Microsoft.VisualStudio.HostingProcess.HostProc.RunUsersAssembly()
at System.Threading.ThreadHelper.ThreadStart_Context(Object state)
at System.Threading.ExecutionContext.Run(ExecutionContextexecutionCont
ext, ContextCallback callback, Object state, Boolean ignoreSyncCtx)
at System.Threading.ExecutionContext.Run(ExecutionContextexecutionCont
ext, ContextCallback callback, Object state)
at System.Threading.ThreadHelper.ThreadStart()
```

Logging influences performance, so you need the ability to turn it off and on. Logging frameworks provide this ability through configuration nicely.

What to log

Now that we know *how* to log, it is useful to talk about *what* to log. After all, we're logging to be able to find problems easier. If what we're logging doesn't do that then it's not going to be much use.

Dealing with distributed systems, one of the most difficult problems to track down is when one component attempts to communicate with another, but the other doesn't get the communication. If we're dealing with an independent message channel, one component can successfully pass along the message to the channel, and another component may never get the message out of the channel. Everything is basically successful here, except our "protocol" is being violated.

One way of helping to diagnose this type of a problem is to log every transfer of control in or out of a component. For example, if Component A sent a message to Component B, we'd log that fact. I would generally classify that as an informational message and use an appropriate logging category. And when a message is received in Component B, we'd log the fact that a message was received. It is often useful to include a correlation ID when logging this information so the path of a particular message can be traced through multiple logs.

Context: When utilizing logging in distributed systems.

Practice: Log when control passes externally to or from one component to another.

Clearly, when problems occur within a subsystem, it is important to have that information in a log. This can be categorized as logging errors. Sometimes, it is pretty clear when to log errors, but sometimes it's not so clear. When it comes to exceptions, what not to log is confusing to some people. To be clear, we do not want to log every possible exception wherever they can be raised, and we do not want to "hide" exceptions by logging all of them as they occur.

Context: When utilizing logging in distributed systems.

Practice: Log all error conditions, including any context related to the cause of the error.

When you handle exceptions, you "handle" them. This means the application has not encountered an error, the application has compensated for it. Therefore, logging errors in exception handlers is generally not the right thing to do. You can consider some exceptions to be a "warning" and log it as a warning, but if you have caught an exception, the application should be able to continue in a known, correct state.

Context: When considering what to log within a system.

Practice: Do not try to log all exceptions.

There are some exceptions to the do-not-try-to-log-all-exceptions. Any unhandled exceptions are intended to terminate the application. This is the recommended practice, if you don't know what to do to compensate for the exception, then the application is in a corrupt state and cannot continue running reliably. However, just before exiting, we can log the exception so that it is tracked. Exception handlers that do this are considered **top-level exception handlers** or **last-chance exceptions handlers**. They occur where the application hands back the state to the system. The most common place for this is the exit from `Program.Main`. For example:

```
static void Main()
{
  ILog log = GetLog();
```

```
        try
        {
          // work is done here
        }
        catch (Exception ex)
        {
          log.Fatal("Unhandled exception", ex);
          throw;
        }
      }
```

Here, we have a `try/catch` block effectively around the body of the `Main` method. If any uncaught exceptions occur in the application, they will be caught in this exception handler and passed along to the logger to do whatever the logger was configured to do. The code re-throws the exception instead of returning from `Main`. While returning from `Main` would result in the same thing, we re-throw to make it clear that this is in no way "handling" the exception.

This is not the only place where an application passes back control to the system and never gets it back. Every application must do the `Program.Main` control transfer, but some applications also use multiple threads. Exceptions that occur in other threads are out-of-band exceptions. This means they occur off the main thread, and therefore nothing in the main thread is able to encompass the potential exception with a `try` block (except at a "top level"). Just as with `Program.Main`, we can log these exceptions with top-level or last-chance exception handlers. Following are some examples:

```
static void Main()
{
  var thread = new Thread(
    new ParameterizedThreadStart(MyThreadProc));
  thread.Start(myState);
}
// ...
private static void MyThreadProc(object state)
{
  MyState myState = (MyState)state;
  try
  {
    // do some work here
  }
  catch (Exception ex)
  {
    myState.logger.Error(
      "unhandled exception in MyThreadProc",
      ex);
```

```
        throw;
      }
    }
```

In this example, we simply create a `Thread` object and create a delegate to our `MyThreadProc`. Within `MyThreadProc`, we effectively wrap the body of the method in a `try/catch` block, and any unhandled exceptions are caught and logged before the control returns back to the system, never to return to your code.

```
static void Main()
{
  ILog logger = GetLogger();
  var thread = new Thread(() =>
   {
       try
       {
           // do work here
       }
       catch (Exception ex)
       {
           logger.Error(
            "Unhandled exception in background thread pi-rho",
          ex);
          throw;
       }
   });
  thread.Start();
}
```

This example is almost identical to the previous, but we are using an anonymous method in the form of a lambda. Here, we used the captured `logger` variable, so we can use the `Thread` constructor whose delegate does not take parameters.

```
static void Main()
{
  ILog logger = GetLogger();
  ThreadPool.QueueUserWorkItem(_=>
  {
    try
    {
      // do work here
    }
    catch (Exception ex)
    {
      logger.Error(
```

```
            "Unhandled exception "+
            "in background thread pi-rho",
            ex);
          throw;
        }
      });
    }
```

This example is almost identical to the previous, except we are using `ThreadPool.QueueUserWorkItem` and an anonymous method in the form of a lambda.

```
static void Main()
{
  ILog logger = GetLogger();
  var task1 = Task.Factory.StartNew(() =>
     {
          // code that could throw an exception
     })
    .ContinueWith(t =>
    {
      if (t.Exception == null) return;
      foreach (var exception
            in t.Exception.Flatten().
          InnerExceptions)
      {
          logger.Error(
          "Unhandled exception occured in" +
          "thread pi-alpha-rho",
           exception);
      }
      throw t.Exception;
    }, TaskContinuationOptions.OnlyOnFaulted);
}
```

This example uses the newer TPL and the `Task` class to invoke an asynchronous task. The "body" of the task is executed without wrapping it in a `try/catch` block. Any exceptions that occur will be caught by the system and passed along to the continuation (implemented with `ContinueWith`). We use the option `TaskContinuationOptions.OnlyOnFaulted` to tell the framework to only invoke this continuation, if the task invoked with `StartNew` threw an exception.

Focusing exception handling like this, and utilizing logging when catching these unhandled exceptions, is a fairly easy practice once you get the hang of it.

Context: When implementing logging of unhandled exceptions.

Practice: Log exceptions only in last-chance or top-level exception handlers.

Health monitoring

No matter what level of detail you have in logging, it does not do any good if no one knows to look in the log.

There are various tools to help monitor the computers and systems within an enterprise. Historically, this was done with Microsoft Operations Manager. Microsoft System Center now includes Operations Manager. These applications are designed to monitor computers, applications, and systems, and get current status and inform people of anomalous situations.

So, what has this got to do with the system you want to build? Well, Operations Manager is extensible and can be extended to do something specific to your application. Nevertheless, this development is time-consuming, and unless your system adds value to the system monitoring space, this might not be an efficient use of the development resources. Not to mention the ramp up and training time required for users of System Center to work with your system. Despite Operations Manager's extensibility, it supports the ability to provide alerts in response to monitoring various different aspects of a computer and its system/infrastructure. It can monitor that a computer is responding to requests, if services are running, the computer's event log, and so on. Nevertheless, it cannot monitor application or system-specific health information if it cannot know about it.

So, how can we "integrate" into applications such as this, so that they can monitor the health of our distributed system without extending Operations Manager?

Tips for communicating information to your System Center professional:

- Provide computer information for computers in the system
- Provide database information for databases used by the system
- Provide locations of any SharePoint instances
- Provide locations and names of any Windows services
- Provide the location and details of any Event Log entries
- Provide the location and details of any log files

What your distributed system uses, and what "failure" means, is very specific to your application. A complete list of what you should provide to someone configuring Operations Manager: you should analyze and document the components of the system, the integration points, and the various criteria for success, failure, and error conditions in the system. That information can be used to monitor your system specifically, and provide alerts when things are not working correctly.

You do not need to use Event Log as your sole means to provide system-specific monitorable information for Operations Manager. Operations Manager has various components that understand how to get data out of a database, for example. You just need to provide the information to whoever is configuring Operations Manager, so that they can use values in a specific table in a specific database as criteria for alerts.

My experience with what defines what it means to "fail" or to have an "error" in a system has shown that this information is often evolutionary. We may not know all of the ways a system may fail, and we tend to learn of new ways as they happen. That's fine, what does and doesn't get monitored for health can change over time.

Proactive monitoring

It is fairly easy to come up with, or at least discover, criteria for an error or a failure. These things are straightforward: service is no longer running, Event log has an event of ID 1000 for the `MyApplication` source in the application log, and so on. These are important things to monitor, but they are *reactive*, and they do not prevent errors or failures.

It can be a little harder to be reactive with monitoring. To some degree, being reactive is application-specific. What it means that Application A is "about to fail" is very specific. There are some general things that you can use to aid in reactive monitoring. Typical reactive-type monitor includes things such as storage usage, like disk space or database usage. Operations Manager can send an alert when storage usage has risen to a certain percent. This provides an ability to avoid errors and failures.

Application-specific criteria for reactive monitoring is usually something that needs to be created. It is rare that all of the data is available for most reactive criteria. For example, the rate at which messages are being communicated may be an indication of impending error or failure. A certain sequence of messages may be an indication of impending error as well. Having a way to detect these things, and make them monitorable, can aid in having reactive monitoring.

Summary

As you can see, a distributed system has certain attributes and needs. Recognizing the asynchronous nature of a distributed system can help ensure it is designed properly and operating in a way that is most efficient and effective. A system that's constantly compensating for, or fighting, its asynchronous nature is hard to maintain and usually hard to use.

Try to analyze your system to see if it actually is a distributed system. If you already know you have a distributed system, see if you are fully recognizing its asynchronous nature. If you are not already performing automated health monitoring, do yourself a favor and look into it. Look into how products such as Microsoft System Center Operations Manager, or WhatsUp Gold, will help detect errors and failures quickly. Also, look into how you can use these tools to prevent errors and failures.

In the next chapter, we will discuss web services. We'll get into practices with WCF services, ASMX services, implementing services, consuming services, and authentication and authorization.

10
Web Service Recommended Practices

When we think of developing modern applications on the Web, it's hard not to think of web services in some fashion.

Many websites today fall under the moniker of "Web 2.0". Web 2.0 means different things to different people, but one of the major features of Web 2.0 was the use of Asynchronous JavaScript and XML (AJAX). This basic design means that after a particular "page" was served up to a browser, portions of the page were requested and downloaded out-of-band with the rest of the page. This meant the browser would actually download content asynchronously, allowing the user to interact with the page while some of the content was being downloaded. This also means that interaction with a page did not require the entire page to be re-loaded when that interaction affected the look or content of the page.

While AJAX basically meant that snippets of JavaScript were downloaded and executed in the browser to update content or the look and feel of a page, these requests were served.

Web services, of course, do more than serve as a technology to facilitate AJAX. A web service is *a software system designed to support interoperable machine-to-machine interaction over a network*. With AJAX, this machine-to-machine interaction involves a browser on one machine facilitating the interaction with another, remote, machine over the network.

A web service is really just another process listening for requests at a specific URL. Hosting a website is also a process listening for requests at a specific URL, but web services generally provide machine-readable information that will be processed by another application. A website also provides machine-readable information, but that machine-readable information is generally in the form of hypertext markup (that is, HTML) whose sole purpose is to be visually displayed to a user.

For many, Web Services mean Service Oriented Architecture (SOA). SOA is based on Service Orientation, which is based on eight design principles:

- **Standardized Service Contract**: A contract-first approach of consistently applying design standards across a service inventory
- **Service Loose Coupling**: Ensures that a contract doesn't impose implementation-specific coupling on clients to the contract
- **Service Abstraction**: Builds on object-oriented abstraction in that only information applicable to invocation of the service is published through the contract
- **Service Reusability**: Involves designing a service that can be used independently
- **Service Autonomy**: Involves the degree to which the service controls its own resources and reliance on external resources
- **Service Statelessness**: Involves reducing or eliminating session-related state
- **Service Discoverability**: Involves the meta-information published about a service that details the functional context and capabilities of the service
- **Service Composability**: Suggests that systems should be easily composed of multiple services as well as services potentially composing other services

Tomes of information could, and has been, written about Service Orientation. This chapter doesn't attempt to get into practices specific to Service Orientation because of this; but, it's important to recognize it as a goal of any particular web service and that the web service should be designed to be consistent with that goal.

Context: When designing a web service where Service Orientation is a goal.

Practice: Consider Service Orientation design principles.

Typically, most web services are not Service Oriented—they're meant to be used by specific clients within specific platforms or programming languages. That's not to say that web services that are not Service Oriented are bad; they simply have different goals. Service Orientation is intended to be used to publish services to unknown types and quantities of clients. When designing a web service, certain Service Orientation design principles can be used. If all these design principles are used but there is not a specific goal of being Service Oriented, it might be a good idea to step back and review whether Service Orientation really does apply and apply it consistently.

Effectively, you need to know why you're implementing a web service and be able to choose a design or design practice that fulfills that requirement.

Any framework that provides the ability to listen for socket connections provides an ability to implement a "web service". This chapter doesn't involve web services at such a low level. This chapter concentrates on the built-in, or supported, mechanisms to build and create web services within Visual Studio. Specifically, this chapter covers web services with Windows Communications Foundation and *traditional*
web services also known as ASP.NET web services or ASMX web services.

Implementing WCF services

MSDN describes WCF as:

> *Windows Communication Foundation (WCF) is a framework for building service-oriented applications.*

While this is true, WCF offers many different ways for applications to communicate. It would seem that ASP.NET web services are largely deprecated for general process intra-process communications—including web services—so, we'll start with WCF.

Let's be realistic; WCF does a lot. It's meant to abstract the implementation details of inter-process communications away from a particular application. Due to this, it needs to provide the ability to configure these details independently from the application making use of WCF. So, configuration of WCF can be very, very complex.

Editing configuration

Most of the time, configuring WCF is a deployment detail. Making use of WCF is simply a matter of implementing (and possibly defining) a service contract. The details by which WCF brokers or translates the communication between your implementation and the client is all defined within configuration. Your implementation could end up being used through a web service endpoint (basic or WS-* HTTP), a named-pipe endpoint, MSMQ endpoint, and so on. How the endpoint is ultimately defined is a deployment detail, and is defined in the configuration of a particular deployment.

.NET 4 makes configuring WCF endpoints slightly easier. Endpoint configuration is now optional, and endpoint and binding details are inferred from the base address of the service. That is, the endpoint and binding can be defined by how you host your service. You can still use config; but it is no longer mandatory.

Conceptually, you can host a WCF service without ever having viewed or edited its configuration. However, if you need to configure it at all, you'll soon realize that configuration involves navigating a complex hierarchy of XML elements and attributes.

XML is designed to be human readable, and WCF XML configuration is as readable as any other series of English words. But that's about where the "readability" ends. Just as a sentence strewed together with a series of random words is 'readable" in that you can understand each word in the sentence, so too is WCF XML configuration. You need to understand the semantic and relationships of the various elements and attributes ("words") within the XML configuration. If all you want to do is host a web service with WCF, learning all that semantics probably offers very little value.

Fortunately, XML is also machine readable. Within the SDK, there exists an application that will read/write WCF XML configuration sections in your `app.config` (or `web.config`) and lets you configure your WCF services with a graphical user interface. It's easy to create a WCF service config section that will cause runtime errors or simply won't work. I highly recommend using the configuration editor whenever possible.

Context: When configuring a WCF service.

Practice: Prefer to use the Service Configuration Editor Tool.

Configuration of a WCF service seems almost infinitely configurable; so, we're only going to cover a subset of those configuration abilities, and concentrate on only some of the web service configuration.

Running the WCF Service Configuration Editor is as simple as selecting **Tools | WCF Service Configuration Editor** from the main menu. Once you load your `app.config` file, you'll be presented with an interface similar to the following screenshot:

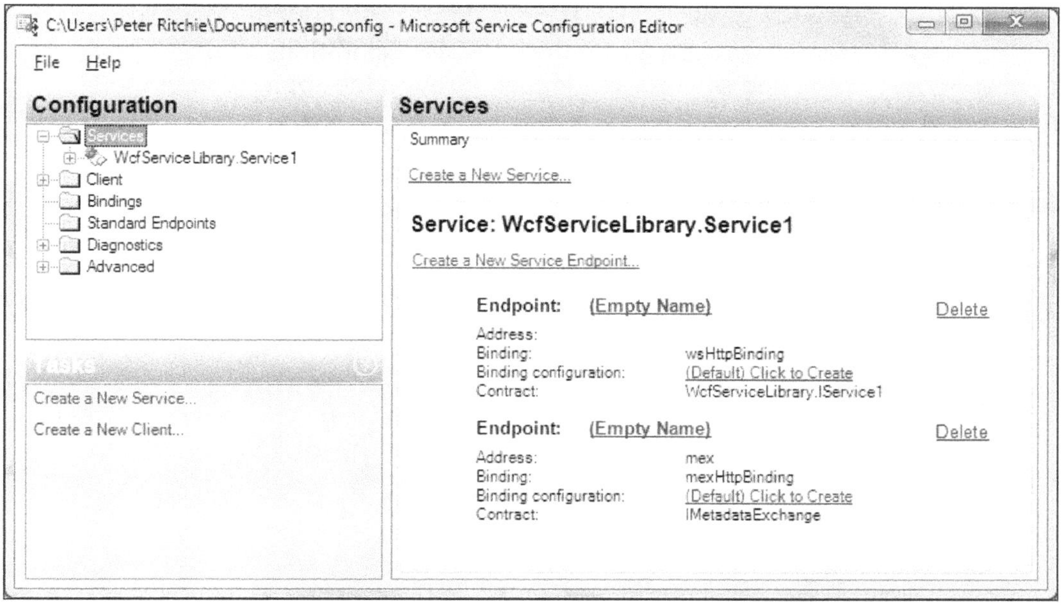

Why and how you'd configure a service depends partially on how the service is hosted. So, let's look at some hosting options.

Hosting a WCF service in any form requires the definition of a contract. This contract is defined in code via the definition of an interface with specific attributes applied to it and its members. Let's look at an example:

```
using System.ServiceModel;

namespace WcfServiceLibrary
{
  [ServiceContract]
  public interface ICalculator
  {
    [OperationContract]
    int Add(int a, int b);

    [OperationContract]
    int Subtract(int a, int b);

    [OperationContract]
    int Mulitply(int a, int b);

    [OperationContract]
    int Divide(int a, int b);
  }
}
```

This definition defines a service contract `ICalculator` through the application of the `ServiceContractAttribute` on the interface. Operations `Add`, `Subtract`, `Multiply`, and `Divide`, are defined through the application of the `OperationContractAttribute`.

Implementing the service contract is just a matter of providing an implementation of the interface, for example:

```
public class Calculator : ICalculator
{
  public int Add(int a, int b)
  {
    return a + b;
  }

  public int Subtract(int a, int b)
  {
    return a - b;
  }

  public int Mulitply(int a, int b)
  {
    return a*b;
  }

  public int Divide(int a, int b)
  {
    return a/b;
  }
}
```

The rest is really just deployment and configuration. "Deploying" means hosting the service somewhere, so let's look at some hosting options.

Hosting

It should be obvious from the code we've shown so far that restrictions on where, when, and how, to host are few and far between. The unfortunate side-effect of this decoupling is that the code isn't offering you any indication on hosting. Once you get beyond that, the power and flexibility becomes obvious.

Which hosting option should you pick? The decoupled nature of the contract and the contract implementation means there's potential for future options; but, we'll focus on the existing recommended options.

There are two types of hosting: hosting within your own host (self-hosting) and hosting with another host that supports WCF contracts. IIS is an example of something that supports hosting WCF contracts. You can basically host your service anywhere you want; but the most common is to host it within an application and host it within a Windows service that you've created. There are pros and cons to each hosting option.

IIS, of course, has its own specific responsibilities. IIS primarily hosts websites and web applications. A WCF service that isn't related to anything you might already be hosting in IIS might seem a bit out of place. IIS has some specific features that impacts anything deployed within it, for example, process recycling. IIS may decide to recycle a given process. A service shouldn't be retaining state in memory; but a WCF service must be prepared to be recycled at any point and time when hosted within IIS. If you're already deploying websites, simply deploying another component within it (the WCF service) is almost trivial. If you would like to use a transport other than HTTP, IIS hosting is out of the question—it only supports hosting HTTP services. IIS actually forwards messages to hosted services (hence the HTTP restriction). A side-effect to this is that IIS will activate your service if it's not already running before forwarding a message to it. This feature is called **message-based activation**.

Context: If you're hosting a WCF HTTP web service that interoperates or acts as an adjunct to an existing web application or site.

Practice: Consider hosting within IIS.

IIS doesn't do much good for you if you need to control the life span of your service, or if you want to support a transport other than HTTP. If you're not already hosting IIS, needing to install, configure, and maintain IIS simply to host a WCF service might seem a bit overkill. In these cases, it's likely best to self-host the service.

Context: If you want to support a transport other than HTTP, control the process life-span, or don't already have IIS hosting a site or application.

Practice: Consider self-hosting the WCF service.

Hosting WCF services in IIS

There are really two options for hosting in IIS. The first option is creating your service within an existing web project. You can simply add a WCF Service to your web project. For example, right-click on the project in the Solution Explorer and select **Add\New Item...**.Navigate to the **Web** category in the language category of your choice and select **WCF Service**:

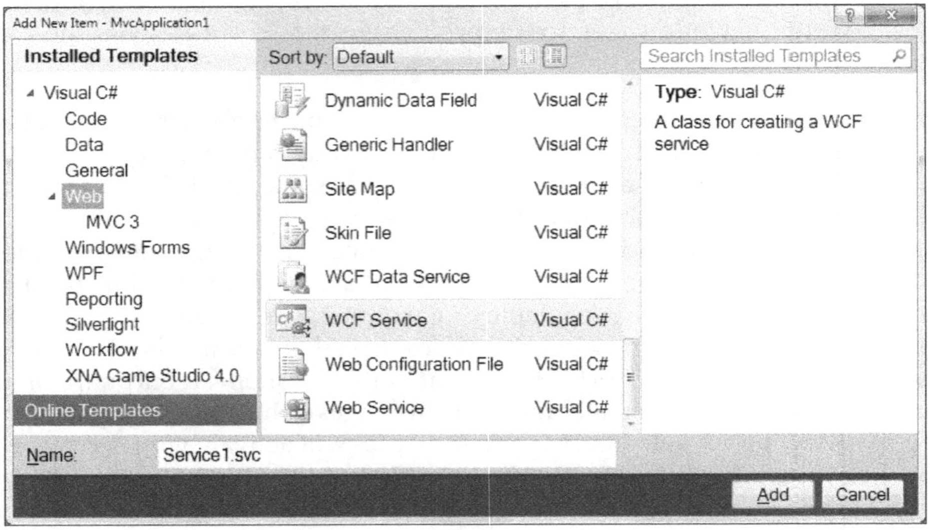

This creates a `.svc` file that contains the `ServiceHost` information and hooks up the contract implementation to a URL within the site. This `.svc` will look similar to the following:

```
<%@ ServiceHost Language="C#"
  Debug="true"
  Service="MvcApplication1.CalculatorService"
  CodeBehind="CalculatorService.svc.cs" %>
```

This file defines the language the code behind is implemented in, the name of the class that implements the service (in this case, `MvcApplication1.CalculatorService`), and where that service implementation is located (in this case `CalculatorService.svc.cs`). That *code behind* file will look like any other WCF service implementation, for example, the default looks like the following:

```
using System;
using System.Collections.Generic;
using System.Linq;
using System.Runtime.Serialization;
using System.ServiceModel;
```

```
using System.Text;

namespace MvcApplication1
{
  public class CalculatorService : ICalculatorService
  {
    public void DoWork()
    {
    }
  }
}
```

Based on the default generated contract:

```
using System;
using System.Collections.Generic;
using System.Linq;
using System.Runtime.Serialization;
using System.ServiceModel;
using System.Text;

namespace MvcApplication1
{
  [ServiceContract]
  public interface ICalculatorService
  {
    [OperationContract]
    void DoWork();
  }
}
```

This also creates a default contract interface and a default contract implementation. So, if you've already created your contract and implementation, you'll have to delete the generated one and hook-up your existing implementation manually (keep reading).

To manually add an existing WCF Service implementation to a site, you simply need to create the `.svc` file. Once you add the `.svc` file to the project (right-click on project in Solution Explorer, select **Add | New Item...**, select **General | Text File** and add a file with a `.svc` extension like `CalculatorService.svc`), add the `ServiceHost` information to the file with `Language`, `Debug`, and `Service` attributes. The `Service` attribute should contain the class name of the service implementation you would like to use. For example, if we wanted to use the service implementation we detailed in a previous section, our element would look similar to the following:

```
<%@ ServiceHost Language="C#"
  Debug="true"
  Service="WcfServiceLibrary.Calculator"%>
```

Windows service WCF self-hosting

So far we've seen that hosting a service has been fairly simple. Configuration of the transport hasn't come up. Hosting in IIS just adds the `.svc` file to a page on the site's URL—implying HTTP.

To add a Windows service project to host the WCF service, simply right-click on the solution in Solution Explorer, select **Add New Project...**, Select **Windows | Windows Service** in the language category of your choice, enter the name you would like for the project, and press **OK**.

Self-hosting in a Windows service requires that the service be manually bound. This is a simple process of creating a `ServiceHost` instance with the type of the service implementation and a base address. For example:

```
serviceHost =
  new ServiceHost(
    typeof(Calculator),
    new Uri("http://localhost:8080/hello"));
```

You may need to add a reference to `System.ServiceModel` if your project doesn't already have a reference to it (it doesn't by default).

Of course, simply instantiating the instance doesn't fully integrate with the service, you want to support stopping and starting this WCF service when your service starts and stops. To do this, you can make a call `ServiceHost.Open` in your service's `OnStart` override, and call `ServiceHost.Close` in the `OnStop` override. For example:

```
public partial class Service1 : ServiceBase
{
  private ServiceHost serviceHost;
  public Service1()
  {
    InitializeComponent();
    serviceHost =
      new ServiceHost(
        typeof(Calculator),
        new Uri("http://localhost:8080/hello"));
    CanShutdown = true;
    // Enable metadata publishing.
    ServiceMetadataBehavior smb =
      new ServiceMetadataBehavior
      {
        HttpGetEnabled = true,
        MetadataExporter =
```

```
            {PolicyVersion = PolicyVersion.Policy15}
        };
    }

    protected override void OnStart(string[] args)
    {
      serviceHost.Open();
    }

    protected override void OnStop()
    {
      serviceHost.Close();
    }

    protected override void OnShutdown()
    {
      using (serviceHost)
        serviceHost = null;
      base.OnShutdown();
    }
  }
```

In this example, we're also being good citizens and disposing our service host when shutdown occurs (making sure to set `CanShutdown` to true in order to be notified of shutdown).

WCF self-hosted

Self-host in other types of applications is very similar. For example, to do the same thing in a console application would look similar to the following code:

```
static void Main(string[] args)
{
  using (var host = new ServiceHost(typeof(Calculator),
    new Uri("http://localhost:8080/Calculator")))
  {
    // Enable metadata publishing.
    ServiceMetadataBehavior smb =
      new ServiceMetadataBehavior
      {
        HttpGetEnabled = true,
        MetadataExporter =
          {PolicyVersion = PolicyVersion.Policy15}
      };
```

```
        host.Description.Behaviors.Add(smb);
        host.Open();
        Console.ReadLine();
      }
    }
```

If you try to run this in a version of Windows that includes UAC (Vista or greater) you will likely get an `AddressAccessDeniedException` when you try to open the host. This is because Windows does not give permission to access URLs to users by default. You'll have to give yourself access to that URL with the `netsh` command. For example:

```
netsh http add urlaclurl=http://+:8080/Calculator user="Peter
Ritchie"
```

If you're deploying a WCF service to Windows Server 2008 or Vista (or later, presumably), you have the option of deploying to the **Windows Process Activation Service**. The process is the same as deploying to IIS once WAS is installed and configured, but you then have the flexibility of not needing IIS and being able to use TCP, Named Pipes, or MSMQ, in addition to HTTP.

Manual testing

All the testing of the classes used within your service should be tested thoroughly with unit tests. For example:

```
[TestMethod]
public void AddTest()
{
  Calculator target = new Calculator();
  int actual = target.Add(2, 3);
  Assert.AreEqual(5, actual);
}
```

However, testing that the service is hosted properly can be done with another tool called `WcfTestClient`. Once you run `WcfTestClient`, and add a service reference to your URL, you'll see a window like the following screenshot:

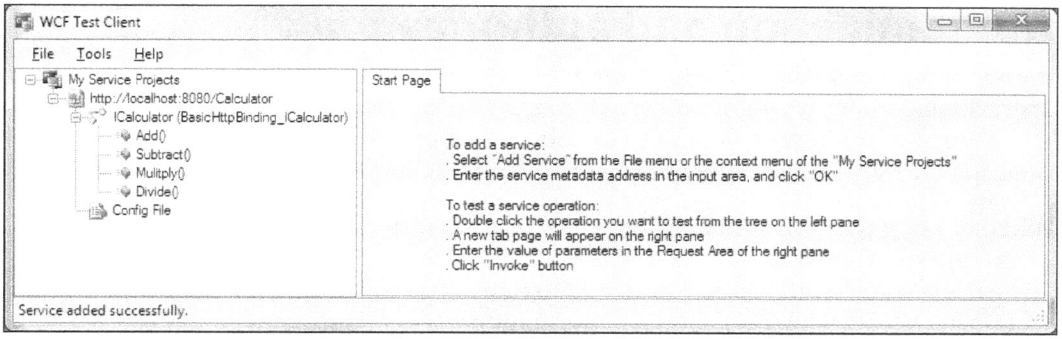

This lists all the services that are hosted at the URL, as well as all the operations that the service supports. Double-clicking on any of the operations will open a tab that lists all the parameters that the operation accepts. For example:

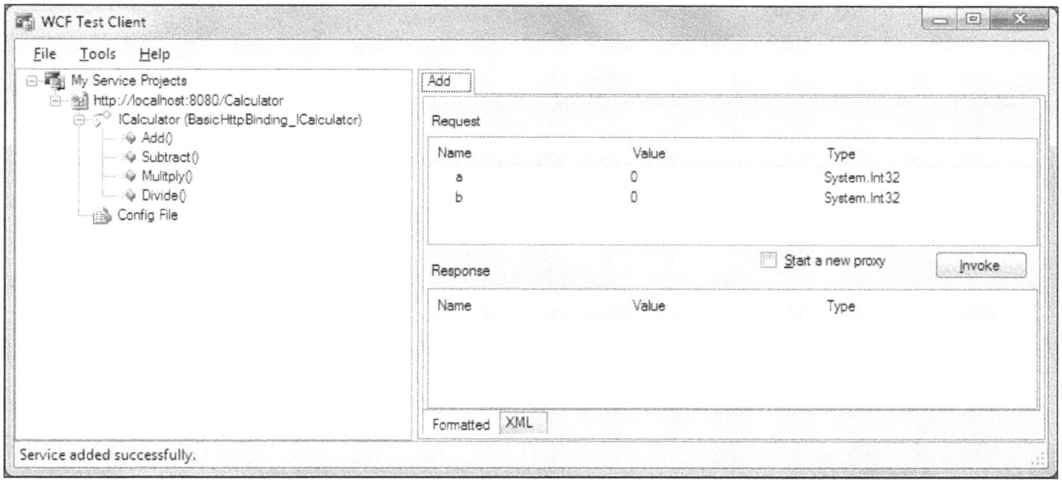

You can edit the values for each parameter in the **Value** column and press the **Invoke** button to invoke the operation. The result from the operation will be displayed in the **Response** section of the window.

Context: In order to quickly test a WCF service.

Practice: Consider using `WcfTestClient`.

Authentication and authorization

If your service is published within an organization, simply implementing the operations and deploying your service may be completely acceptable. However, if you want to publish or deploy your service to a publicly visible server, you may need to control who uses your service or even who has access to certain operations.

When dealing with a public ASP.NET website, your users won't be on the domain where the site is hosted; so you won't be able to use any integrated domain security. The easiest solution that I've found is to use custom validation and integrate your custom validator into whatever validation mechanism you want to use. To create a custom `UserName` validator, simply create a new class and derive it from `UserNamePasswordValidator`. Override the `Validate` method and do whatever validation of the username and password is necessary for your application. In our example, we'll just check canned values. For example:

```
using System.IdentityModel.Selectors;
using System.IdentityModel.Tokens;

namespace WcfServiceLibrary.Authentication
{
  public class Validator : UserNamePasswordValidator
  {
    public override
      void Validate(string userName, string password)
    {
      // TODO: lookup userName and password somewhere
      if (userName == "Peter" && password == "password")
        return;

      throw new SecurityTokenException(
        "Unknown Username or Password");
    }
  }
}
```

If you want to use ASP.NET Membership, you can simply pass along the username and password to the `ValidateUser` method. For example:

```
if (!System.Web.Security.Membership.ValidateUser(
  userName, password))
{
  throw new SecurityTokenException(
    "Unknown Username or Password");
}
```

To get your WCF service to use your validator, you'll have to do some configuration. This is done most reliably through the WCF Service Configuration Editor.

Once you run the editor and open the `web.config` for the project that has your `.svc` file in it, if you have the default `system.serviceModel` section, you'll have to create a `services/service` element in that section. Simply select **File | Add New Item... | Service** from the main menu. This will bring up the **New Service Element Wizard**. Click on the **Browse** button to select the assembly that contains the type that implements the contract you want to make available. (For example, in our examples that's `WcfServiceLibrary.dll`) Selecting the dll will now enumerate all the contract implementations in the assembly. Select the one you want (in our examples, it is `WcfServiceLibrary.Calculator`) and click on **Open**. The wizard shows the type you selected in the **Service Type** text box, click **Next**. The wizard will show the contract that this type implements in the **Contract** text box, to accept that one (in our examples, it's `WcfServiceLibrary.ICalculator`), click **Next**. The next screen allows you to select the communications mode. We want `wsHttpBinding`, so make sure **HTTP** is selected and click on **Next**. The next screen is the interoperability method screen. Again, we want `wsHttpBinding`, so change to **Advanced Web Services interoperability** and click **Next**. Delete all the text in the **Address** text box in the endpoint address screen and click **Next**. You will be prompted that an empty address will require you to define the address in code. This is fine because ASP. NET is defining our address, so click on **Yes**. The overview screen will outline the configuration including a **Binding** of **ws2007HttpBinding**. This is different than we want; but we'll fix that in a moment, so click **Finish**.

`ws2007HttpBinding` is more flexible; but it doesn't seem to work with a custom validator. To change that to `wsHttpBinding`, navigate to the **Services** node for the contract type that we just added (for example, `WcfServiceLibrary.Calcuator`) and select the first node in the **Endpoints** node (it should be **(Empty Name)**), in the right-hand detail window click on the **ws2007HttpBinding** beside the **Binding** entry, then click on the drop-down bottom to the right and select **wsHttpBinding**.

Next we want to create binding configuration, on the left-hand tree window, click on the **Bindings** top-level node, then click on the **New Binding Configuration** link on the left detail window. In the **Create a New Binding** list, select **wsHttpBinding** and click **OK**. We're creating a binding with a security mode that requires UserName information upon request, so click on the **Name** property on the right-hand details window and enter `RequestUserName`. Click on the **Security** tab on the right-hand window and change the **Mode** to **Message**. Make sure the **MessageClientCredentialType** is set to **UserName**.

Next, we want to add a service behavior that uses our custom validator, so navigate to the **Advanced** top-level node on the left-hand tree and expand it. Next, click on the **Servicebehaviors** node and on the right-hand window click on the **New Service BehaviorConfiguration** link. First, change the name to something more meaningful, like "`CalculatorServiceBehaviour`" (without the quotes). Next, we want to add several child elements, so click on the **Add** button and select **serviceMetadata**. Then add **serviceDebug** and **serviceCredentials**. This adds three nodes under the **CalculateServiceBehaviour** node in the **Service Behaviors** node on the left. Click **serviceMetadata**, then change the **HttpGetEnabled** property to **true**. Click on the **serviceDebug** node and change the **includeExceptionDetailsInFaults** to true. Then click on the **serviceCredentials** node and change the **UserNamePasswordValidationMode** to **Custom**. Then enter the full type name of the validator type (in our example, this is `WcfServiceLibrary.Authentication.Validator, WcfServiceLibrary`). Then click on the **serviceCertificate** node on the left tree window below **serviceCredentials** and enter the information for the certificate you would like to use. (In our example, **FindValue**: **PRI**, **StoreLocation**: **LocalMachine**, **StoreName**: **TrustedPeople**). Next, we want to enable ASP.NET compatibility mode, so select the **Hosting Environment** node in the **Advanced** node on the left tree and check **Enable ASP.NET compatibility**.

Now save the new configuration.

Now, to use any of the operations in our contract, correct client credentials will have to be included. Unfortunately, `WcfTestClient` doesn't support `ClientCredentials`, so in order to test you'll have to write your own code.

To test your service with credentials, simply add a service reference for your service type, then set the `ClientCredentials` property on your client object to whatever credentials are valid and invoke an operation. For example:

```
var client =
  new CalculatorServiceReference.CalculatorClient();
client.ClientCredentials.UserName.UserName =
  Settings.Default.Username;
client.ClientCredentials.UserName.Password =
  Settings.Default.Password;
Debug.Assert(5 == client.Add(2, 3));
```

In this example, we've stored our username and password in settings, and named our service referenced `CalculatorServiceReferenced` (in the **Add Service Reference** form).

As you may have noticed, we've created a custom validator and configured the hosted service behavior to use that custom validator; but our service contract implementation has not changed at all. All these other responsibilities have been kept out of our service code. This different behavior is also just a deployment detail. If we wanted to host a service that didn't require credentials, we'd just change the config file. So, we could simply keep testing as we had before adding client credentials and use `WcfTestClient`.

With Visual Studio, you can have different config files for different deployments. In your debug configuration, you could have no `UserName` behavior, but in the release configuration, it could have `UserName` behavior. This allows you to develop without security, but make sures security is there in a release deployment regardless of what you do while developing.

Context: When developing WCF services.

Practice: Consider different debug and release model configurations to ensure a specific release configuration is being deployed.

Different transport options

So far, we've seen the HTTP transport with WCF services. But there are other options like TCP and Named Pipes. HTTP transport is good when you want to support web service clients that aren't using WCF. HTTP is also mandatory in various IIS hosting scenarios.

Context: When need to support web service clients that aren't using WCF, or web service clients implemented in variety of other languages/platforms.

Practice: Consider using the HTTP transport.

TCP transport is currently the fastest network transport. It communicates data with binary encoding. TCP transport is optimized for when both ends of communication are using WCF.

Context: When both ends of a communication or the network are using WCF.

Practice: Consider TCP transport.

Named pipes can use shared memory as a means of communicating between two processes. Of course, anything that doesn't have to go over the wire to communicate is going to be much faster.

Context: When communicating via WCF between two processes on the same computer.

Practice: Consider named pipes transport.

ASP.NET Web Services

ASP.NET Web Services are officially considered "legacy technologies"; it's recommended that web services now be implemented with WCF.

Context: When developing web services.

Practice: Use WCF instead of ASP.NET Web Services.

Authentication and authorization

ASP.NET has a feature called membership. Membership allows Internet web applications and sites to utilize application-specific authentication and authorization. With pages, authorization is fairly simple. You simply define the access rules either in the Web Site Administration Tool or directly in the web.config files. Any user that is unknown will be redirected to a login page whenever they try to access a page that requires authorization.

With web services, ASP.NET membership gets more complex. There's nothing stopping you from configuring access rules to deny unauthorized users from accessing a web service URL (either WCF or ASP.NET web service). But those URLs are being accessed programmatically—not with a browser. If a site URL requires authorization within the ASP.NET authorization subsystem, it will be redirected to a human-readable login page that will cause the code attempting to access a web service much grief.

Context: When using ASP.NET membership and site authorization.

Practice: Always grant unauthorized user access to URLs containing ASP.NET Web Services.

There are a few ways that this can be handled. One common method is to use authorization tokens. Technologies like OAuth use this basic idea. OAuth is a means by which sites providing personal information allow users to grant access to that personal information to third-party applications or sites. Access to personal information (for example, personal information query services) is granted to the code by providing an access token. This token is effectively used like a username/password combination. The third-party code requests access to services by providing the access token.

The easiest way to support an access token of course, is to simply include it as a parameter in every web method, for example:

```
[WebService(Namespace = "http://tempuri.org/")]
[WebServiceBinding(ConformsTo = WsiProfiles.BasicProfile1_1)]
[System.ComponentModel.ToolboxItem(false)]
public class CalculatorWebService :
  System.Web.Services.WebService
{
  [WebMethod]
  public int Add(string accessToken, int a, int b)
  {
    if (Validator.IsTokenValid(accessToken))
      return a + b;
    throw new SoapException("Access denied",
                            SoapException.ClientFaultCode);
  }

  // ...
}
```

In our `Add` method, there is a string `accessToken` parameter that is passed along to our custom validation routine in our `Validator` class. If the token is not valid, we throw an access denied SOAP exception.

Building tokens into every method that we want to publish in our web service can be a bit tedious. ASP.NET web services build on SOAP (Simple Object Access Protocol), which includes things like headers. Rather than having method signatures with parameters to deal with authentication, we can push that up a level into the SOAP headers. This involves writing a bit of code to define the structure of our SOAP header. If we are dealing with just an access token, that header may be simple:

```
public class CalculatorAuthentication
  : System.Web.Services.Protocols.SoapHeader
{
  public string AccessToken;
}
```

Anything that wanted to use the token, would then add a public field of that type to the class. That field would then be populated by the ASP.NET web service framework, and we could use it to authenticate the caller, for example:

```
[WebService(Namespace = "http://tempuri.org/")]
[WebServiceBinding(ConformsTo = WsiProfiles.BasicProfile1_1)]
[System.ComponentModel.ToolboxItem(false)]
public class CalculatorWebService
  : System.Web.Services.WebService
{
  public CalculatorAuthentication AuthenticationHeader;

  [WebMethod]
  [SoapHeader("AuthenticationHeader")]
  public int Add(string accessToken, int a, int b)
  {
    if (Validator.IsTokenValid(
      AuthenticationHeader.AccessToken))
    {
      return a + b;
    }
    throw new SoapException("Access denied",
      SoapException.ClientFaultCode);
  }
  // ...
}
```

This pulls out the token from the parameter list; but doesn't remove the caller authentication from our calculator code—`Add` is still authenticating the caller and taking on too much responsibility.

Fortunately, the SOAP header is available in the HTTP stream, so we can peek into that stream from outside of our web service and pre-authenticate tokens before any of our methods are called. This can be done by writing an `IHttpModule`. For example:

```
public sealed class WebServiceAuthenticationModule
  : IHttpModule
{
  public void Dispose() {
  }

  public void Init(HttpApplication app)  {
    app.AuthenticateRequest += OnEnter;
  }
```

```
private static void OnEnter(
  object source, EventArgs eventArgs)
{
  HttpApplication app = (HttpApplication)source;
  HttpContext context = app.Context;

  // If the request contains an HTTP_SOAPACTION
  // header, look at this message.
  if (context.Request.ServerVariables["HTTP_SOAPACTION"]
    == null)
  {
    return;
  }

  Stream httpStream = context.Request.InputStream;

  // Save the current position of stream.
  long posStream = httpStream.Position;

  // Load the body of the HTTP message
  // into an XML document.
  XmlDocument dom = new XmlDocument();
  string accessToken;

  try
  {
    dom.Load(httpStream);

    var xmlNode = dom.
      GetElementsByTagName("AccessToken").Item(0);
    accessToken = xmlNode != null ?
      xmlNode.InnerText : "";
  }
  catch (Exception e) {
    XmlQualifiedName name = new
      XmlQualifiedName("Load");
    SoapException soapException = new SoapException(
      "Unable to read SOAP request", name, e);
    throw soapException;
  }
  finally{
    // Reset the stream position.
    httpStream.Position = posStream;
  }
```

```
        if(Validator.IsTokenValid(accessToken))
        {
          context.User =
            new GenericPrincipal(
              new GenericIdentity(accessToken),
              new string[0]);
        }
      }
    }
```

In this module, we subscribe to the `AuthenticateRequest` event on the application upon initialization. When the application would like authentication, it raises this event. During the handling of this event (`OnEnter`), we check that there is a `SOAP_ACTION` variable, and if so, we peek ahead into the stream looking for the `AccessToken` XML tag. If the tag exists, we validate it with our `Validator.IsTokenValue` method and create a `GenericIdentity` instance within a `GenericPrinciple` constructor and assign it to the context's `User` property to pass along the authenticated token.

Within our methods, if we wanted to check to see if the "current user" is authorized to execute the method, we could simply check the identity's `IsAuthenticated` property. For example:

```
[WebMethod]
[SoapHeader("AuthenticationHeader")]
public int Add(int a, int b)
{
  if(User.Identity.IsAuthenticated)
    return a + b;
  throw new SoapException("Access denied",
    SoapException.ClientFaultCode);
}
```

Or, if we supported roles:

```
[WebMethod]
[SoapHeader("AuthenticationHeader")]
public int Add(int a, int b)
{
  if(User.IsInRole("CanAdd"))
    return a + b;
  throw new SoapException("Access denied",
    SoapException.ClientFaultCode);
}
```

Of course, this pushes extra responsibility into our service methods.Of course, this won't work unless you register the `IHttpModule` in the `web.config`:

```
<system.web>
  <httpModules>
    <add name="WebServiceAuthenticationModule"
          type="MvcApplication1.WebServiceAuthenticationModule,
            MvcApplication1"/>
  </httpModules>
    <!-- ... -->
```

How you validate the sender of the token would be up to you; you may want the token to be signed in some way.

Summary

Web services can seem very easy to develop, until you start trying to harden them. It's when authentication and authorization come into play that complexity increases dramatically.

Hopefully, this chapter has offered some good practices that you can use or evolve to suit your specific needs.

Index

Symbols

A

B

C

D

E

L

M

N

O

P

Q

R

S

T

U

V

W

Y

About Packt Publishing

Packt, pronounced 'packed', published its first book "Mastering phpMyAdmin for Effective MySQL Management" in April 2004 and subsequently continued to specialize in publishing highly focused books on specific technologies and solutions.

Our books and publications share the experiences of your fellow IT professionals in adapting and customizing today's systems, applications, and frameworks. Our solution based books give you the knowledge and power to customize the software and technologies you're using to get the job done. Packt books are more specific and less general than the IT books you have seen in the past. Our unique business model allows us to bring you more focused information, giving you more of what you need to know, and less of what you don't.

Packt is a modern, yet unique publishing company, which focuses on producing quality, cutting-edge books for communities of developers, administrators, and newbies alike. For more information, please visit our website: `www.packtpub.com`.

About Packt Enterprise

In 2010, Packt launched two new brands, Packt Enterprise and Packt Open Source, in order to continue its focus on specialization. This book is part of the Packt Enterprise brand, home to books published on enterprise software – software created by major vendors, including (but not limited to) IBM, Microsoft and Oracle, often for use in other corporations. Its titles will offer information relevant to a range of users of this software, including administrators, developers, architects, and end users.

Writing for Packt

We welcome all inquiries from people who are interested in authoring. Book proposals should be sent to `author@packtpub.com`. If your book idea is still at an early stage and you would like to discuss it first before writing a formal book proposal, contact us; one of our commissioning editors will get in touch with you.

We're not just looking for published authors; if you have strong technical skills but no writing experience, our experienced editors can help you develop a writing career, or simply get some additional reward for your expertise.

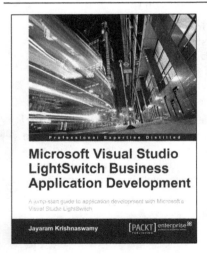

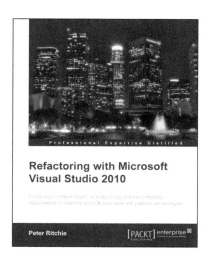

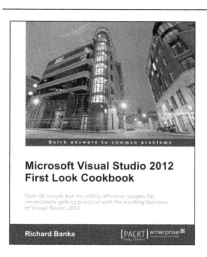

www.ingramcontent.com/pod-product-compliance
Lightning Source LLC
Chambersburg PA
CBHW060527060326
40690CB00017B/3411
* 9 7 8 1 8 4 9 6 8 7 1 6 4 *